Reflecting Critically on the Political Psyche

With passion and originality, within this new book, Samuels presents powerful material on culture and politics (including a critical take on political violence) and a compassionate account of the role of an individual when it comes to progressive politics.

Initial chapters include his commentary on Edward Albee's shocking play *The Goat* and a provocative and critical view on liberal idealisation of 'the Other'. Then, there is more of Samuels' celebrated work bringing therapy thinking to bear on politics, and as far as the practice and organisation of therapy is concerned, readers will find new work on how to organise a good training (you must use pluralism) and a robust account of what a critical psychotherapy might look like. A section on Jungian matters includes Samuels' work on Jung and 'Africans', whose importance has long been recognised, and a scintillating 'balance sheet' for Jungian analysis, setting its strengths and weaknesses alongside each other. In a clinical section, Samuels shows us what he means by the dynamic idea of the 'activist client'.

With each chapter being preceded by a special 'retrospective introduction', as well as including experiential exercises to ground the ideas, this unique collection of papers will be of interest to psychotherapists, Jungian analysts, psychoanalysts, and counsellors, as well as academics working in those fields.

Andrew Samuels has made notable contributions to psychotherapy, Jungian analysis and studies, and psychoanalysis for over 50 years. He has had the honour of receiving two *Festschrifts at* the ages of 60 and 70. He is a relational Jungian psychoanalyst, professor, activist, and political consultant (including to Britain's National Health Service). He founded or co-founded many organisations within the 'psy' field, including Psychotherapists and Counsellors for Social Responsibility (PCSR), Psychotherapy and Counselling Union, Analysis and Activism, International Association for Jungian Studies, and the Confederation for Analytical Psychology. He was the elected chair of the UK Council for Psychotherapy from 2009 to 2012 and has worked as the consultant for Routledge's Jung List since 1984. His many books have been translated into up to 21 languages. These include *Jung and the Post-Jungians* (1985), *The Father* (1985), *A Critical Dictionary of Jungian Analysis* (1986), *The Plural Psyche* (1989), Psychopathology (1989) *The Political Psyche* (1993), *Politics on the Couch* (2001), *Persons, Passions, Psychotherapy, Politics* (2015), *A New Therapy for Politics* (2018). A selection of video lectures and 'rants' is available on www.andrewsamuels.com

Reflecting Critically on the Political Psyche

Therapy, Testament and Trouble in Psychoanalysis and Jungian Analysis

Andrew Samuels

Routledge
Taylor & Francis Group

LONDON AND NEW YORK

Designed cover image: Pablo Picasso (1951), Massacre en Corée.
In Musée National Picasso-Paris. © Succession Picasso/DACS,
London 2024.

First published 2025
by Routledge
4 Park Square, Milton Park, Abingdon, Oxon OX14 4RN

and by Routledge
605 Third Avenue, New York, NY 10158

Routledge is an imprint of the Taylor & Francis Group, an informa business

British Library Cataloguing-in-Publication Data
A catalogue record for this book is available from the British Library

ISBN: 978-1-032-98502-2 (hbk)
ISBN: 978-1-032-98500-8 (pbk)
ISBN: 978-1-003-59898-5 (ebk)

DOI: 10.4324/9781003598985

Typeset in Times New Roman
by Apex CoVantage, LLC

'Samuels has nailed it again! Compelling reading for his signature insights on culture, politics, therapy and Jungian psychology – and for his personal confessions. His explorations of therapeutic thinking in relation to politics, and his commitment to pluralism, so influential for post-Jungians and neo-Jungians of my generation, will endure. His impact is also apparent in psychoanalysis generally – and in psychosocial studies, where he has played a pioneering role. Samuels is not only one of the most important thinkers of his era, but he has also been an outstanding teacher and talent scout, enabling new generations to gain their own recognition.'

—**Stefano Carpani**, *Author and Curator of Jungianeum*

'Samuels has his finger on the pulse of our current global moment, bringing out of the shadows the inevitable reductionism cloaked in the heroism of psychotherapy that goes, itself, unanalysed. By turning stale theoretical notions on their head, he holds out an image of a living and breathing psychology that is radically self-reflective and therefore remains vitally relevant. Here is a must read not only for those of us who analyse and train the next generation of psychoanalysts, but for anyone interested in a deeper understanding of our current epoch as it offers a fresh model of psycho-political engagement centred not on chronology of sanitized theories but on engaging the polemics and disputes inherent in them.'

—**Tiffany Houck**, *Director of Training, Jungian Psychoanalytic Association, New York*

'For over fifty years, Samuels has been pushing the boundaries of psychoanalytic thought, redefining what it means to 'do' psychotherapy and conduct research. This new volume sees him at the height of his intellectual powers, unafraid of turning over stones and asking the difficult questions that others dare not pose. Indeed, no stone is left unturned, as Samuels weighs in on the most important topics and controversies of our day – from political violence to the green agenda, from race to ethical therapeutic practice (and the moments we have fallen woefully short). Nothing escapes his critical eye, unrelenting interrogation and playfully insightful analysis. The book is a reminder to all in the fields of Jungian analysis, psychoanalysis and psychosocial studies how much we owe to Andrew, whether in eager resonance or passionate disagreement. It is a testament to the leadership and vision he has brought to the field: a commitment to challenging his audience and colleagues to have courage, think more deeply, and feel more critically – while never losing sight of an obligation to conduct our 'core business' with care and compassion. This is Andrew at his best, most controversial, and most scintillating.'

—**Kevin Lu**, *Professor of Applied Psychoanalysis, Royal Central School of Speech and Drama, University of London*

'This book crowns the work one of the most brilliant, sincerely intersubjective, and plural thinkers in the Jungian and relational psychoanalytic worlds. Each chapter is a gemstone, elaborating freshly, authentically and thought-provokingly on a variety of themes in the political psyche that Samuels has explored over a lifetime: Pluralism, the 'Other', political violence, Jung and 'Africans', social justice, and activism (to name some). Multiple parts of himself and his reflections for different readers, for the first time introduced to each other and collected together in a delicate equilibrium that resists synthesis. Samuels' creative contributions will definitely endure – and I very much doubt this will be the last we will hear from him.'

—**Monica Luci**, *Author and Lecturer, Department of Psychosocial Studies, University of Essex*

To absent friends – some people are
never forgotten

Contents

Acknowledgements

First, I want to say something about my long relationship with Routledge and not just to thank my current editor, Katie Randall.

Back in 1984, I was invited to a lunch at Bertorelli's on Charlotte Street in Fitzrovia in London, where three directors of the company then called Routledge and Kegan Paul invited me to create a contemporary Jungian list. This was weird because at that time I had not published a single book with them. So I became their consultant for what is still called the Jung List. That was over 40 years ago, and I have worked with eight editors since then.

This work for Routledge has been one of the things in my career of which I am the most proud. I think there have been nearly 200 books. It has kept me in touch with developments in a marvellous way. I have been so pleased that a project to help people turn their PhDs into books also got off the ground – the Monographs in Analytical Psychology series. And also a series called Jung/Culture/Politics. I edit both of these.

Another big thank you – long, long overdue in public – is to the editors and contributors of the two *Festschrifts* with which I have been gifted, one at age 60 and one at age 70. The best way to express this sense of profound gratitude for the recognition is simply to give the bibliographic details of these two volumes here:

Heuer, Gottfried (2010) Ed. *Sacral Revolutions: Reflecting on the Work of Andrew Samuels – Cutting Edges in Psychoanalysis and Jungian Analysis*. London and New York: Routledge
Carpani, Stefano (2021) Ed. *The Plural Turn in Jungian and Post-Jungian Studies: The Work of Andrew Samuels*. London and New York: Routledge.

Finally, in these Acknowledgements, I would like to thank the four colleagues who kindly responded to my request that they endorse this book: Stefano Carpani, Tiffany Houck, Monica Luci, and Kevin Lu. (This is how endorsements are often done – the author takes care of finding the endorsers!)

Those even more in the know will see immediately that these endorsers are not my contemporaries, the usual suspects who endorse my books – as I endorse and promote theirs. These four are, for sure, already established, well-known, and important contributors to the field. But I wanted this book in particular to speak to the future, and so there was a definite agenda in asking people not of my generation to endorse the book.

The Collected Works of C. G. Jung

References to *The Collected Works of C. G. Jung* are by *CW* volume number followed by either paragraph or page number. Edited by Read, H., Fordham, M., Adler, G, and McGuire, W. Published London: Routledge and Kegan Paul; Princeton, NJ: Princeton University Press. Translated mainly by Hull, R. Permission to quote is, as usual, gratefully acknowledged.

Permissions

Chapter 2 was first published as 'Global politics, American hegemony and vulnerability, and Jungian-psychosocial studies: why there are no winners in the battle between Trickster Pedro Urdemales and the Gringos.' *International Journal of Jungian Studies*, 7 (3). pp. 227–241 (2015). Permission to publish from Brill Academic Publishers is gratefully acknowledged. Published with revisions.

Chapter 6 was first published as 'The role of the individual in progressive politics – possibilities and impossibilities of "making a difference"'. *Psychotherapy and Politics International* 12(2), pp. 99–110 (2014). Permission to publish from *Psychotherapy and Politics International* is gratefully acknowledged. Published with revisions. Permission to use Jason Francisco's translation of the untitled poem by Jerzy Ficowski from *Odczytanie Popiołów* (1979) (with assistance from Piotr Słomian) is gratefully acknowledged. See jasonfrancisco.net/poems-of-ficowski

Chapter 7 was first published as 'Taking the green agenda out of the margins – psychological strategies'. Chapter 4 in *Depth Psychology and Climate Change: The Green Book*. Ed. Dale Mathers (2020). Permission to publish from Taylor & Francis is gratefully acknowledged.

Chapter 8 was first published as 'Pluralism and psychotherapy – what is a good training?'. In *Implausible Professions: Arguments for Pluralism and Autonomy in Psychotherapy and Counselling*. Eds Richard House and Nick Totton (1997/2011). Permission to publish from PCCS Books is gratefully acknowledged.

Chapter 9 was first published as 'Everything you always wanted to know about therapy (but were afraid to ask): Social, political, economic and clinical fragments of a critical psychotherapy'. In *European Journal of Psychotherapy and Counselling*, 16:4, pp. 315–330 (2014). Permission to publish from Taylor and Francis Journals is gratefully acknowledged.

Chapter 10 was first published as 'Political and clinical developments in analytical psychology since 1972: Subjectivity, equality and diversity – inside and outside the consulting room'. In *Journal of Analytical Psychology*, 59:5, pp. 641–660 (2014). Copyright The Society of Analytical Psychology. Permission to publish from John Wiley & Sons is gratefully acknowledged. Published with revisions.

Chapter 11 was first published as 'The future of Jungian analysis: strengths, weaknesses, opportunities, threats ('SWOT')'. In *Journal of Analytical Psychology*,

62:5, pp. 636–649 (2017). Copyright The Society of Analytical *Psychology*. Permission to publish from John Wiley & Sons is gratefully acknowledged.

Chapter 12 was first published as 'Jung and "Africans": A critical and contemporary review of some of the issues'. In *International Journal of Jungian Studies*, 11:2, pp. 23–34. Permission to publish from Brill Academic Publishers is gratefully acknowledged. Published with revisions and additions.

Chapter 13 was first published as 'Sinking like a stone: Activism, analysis and the role of the academy'. Introduction to *Spectre of the Other in Jungian Psychoanalysis: Political, Psychological, and Sociological Perspectives.* Carter, M. & Farah, S. (eds), pp. 1–8 (2023). Permission to publish from Taylor and Francis is gratefully acknowledged.

Chapter 14 was first published as 'From sexual misconduct to social justice' In *Psychoanalytic Dialogues*, 3:3, pp. 295–321 (1996). Permission to publish from Taylor & Francis Journals is gratefully acknowledged.

Chapter 15 was first published as 'The "Activist Client": Social Responsibility, the Political Self, and Clinical Practice in Psychotherapy and Psychoanalysis'. Published with revisions. In *Psychoanalytic Dialogues*, 27:6, pp. 678–693 (2017). Permission to publish from Taylor & Francis Journals is gratefully acknowledged. Published with revisions.

Chapter 16 was first published as 'The transcendent function and politics: *No!*'. In *Journal of Analytical Psychology*, 55:5, pp. 241–253 (2010). Copyright The Society of Analytical Psychology. Permission to publish from John Wiley & Sons is gratefully acknowledged.

A note on permissions

The author wishes to congratulate those publishers of books and journals that allow an author to make free use of their own material in subsequent publications (provided due acknowledgement of prior publication is given). This practice should be taken up more widely or even universally. Otherwise, one waits for ages and goes through unnecessary hurdles to get permission! So, here I commend: Brill Publishers, John Wiley & Sons, and *Psychotherapy and Politics International*.

Introduction

I found myself wondering if this would be my last book. That gave it a special piquancy and maybe even importance (at least to me!). So, what's it all about?

I refer to myself as promiscuous, meaning that I work in a large number of related areas, writing for different journals and speaking at diverse conferences and seminars that are often quite distinct from one another. So people who might see me in a Jungian journal are unlikely to see me in a political journal or a psychoanalytic journal. And the same is true going the other way. In a way, the book – for the first time in my writing career – introduces the various parts of myself to each other.

Not all the chapters have been published, and a couple of them have remained private because I have been nervous about their reception, wondering if I had gone too far. Well, at this stage of my career and life, it really doesn't matter all that much if I have gone too far.

I have divided the book into five parts: Culture, Politics, Therapy, Jungian, and Clinic. Mostly these subdivisions hold up, but sometimes the reader will perhaps wonder why some material is in this chapter or section rather than in another. The reason of course is that I have written in Hermetic vein, linking that which has not often been linked. So there are linkages and probably some muddles. Also, the stuff was written over a period of time.

In writing this brief Introduction, I turned to the Introductions of all of my previous books. In *The Plural Psyche* (1989), I wrote this, which I just could not improve on for this book:

> I hope I've published this book at the right moment. At the moment when the ideas and intuitions are sufficiently coherent to warrant expression but not so integrated and systematised that ossification results. Like any psychological work, the book teeters between developing its own language and the need to us a common language. However, even a common language is a changing language – it must be, to remain alive – and I have tried to explain why certain new words get used.

Here are a few notes intended to make reading this book easier.

DOI: 10.4324/9781003598985-1

Each chapter begins with a 'Retrospective Introduction', giving my feeling responses to what I have written plus explanations about the material that seemed necessary. Each chapter also has a note at the top called 'Talking Points' which does what it says on the tin. Previously published work is judiciously updated. The connections between the chapters are carefully signposted. I allowed a very few repetitions where I really wanted readers to know what the fuss was about. References are given at the end of each chapter because I don't like the fiction that this is a book produced all at the same time. It isn't. The earliest chapter comes from 1996, the bulk of the rest from 2015 onwards.

As is the case in many of my books, the reader is invited to do specially created experiential exercises. These are designed to ground what is being read in lived experience and facilitate a personal response to the material.

Here are a few thoughts with which to conclude this Introduction.

We have seen a 'political turn' in all the psychotherapies in the past 20 years. In a way, this is a recovery and a recreation of their original radical nature. This turn has been accompanied by an ever-growing literature, which is often cited in the chapters that follow.

I think it is fair to say that I have been in the forefront of this international phenomenon in my work with, for example, the Jungian Analysis and Activism movement, Psychotherapists and Counsellors for Social Responsibility (PCSR), and the UK-Palestine Mental Health Network.

So, I am probably a pioneer – and an enthusiast for the linking of what I call 'therapy thinking' with contemporary politics and culture. But I have also become sceptical and concerned that, in our excitement for the political turn in our field, we analysts and therapists are missing the point about how little we really have with which to contribute. The potential is there, but where are the tangible results? Maybe we don't want to engage with this embarrassing theme.

I discovered the limitations of the contributions of depth psychology when working as a political consultant with leading politicians, political parties, and activist groups in the UK, the United States, and elsewhere. I will describe experiences of this work at Presidential and Prime Ministerial levels and also in connection with working in the UK National Health Service context at the King's Fund (https://www.kingsfund.org.uk/).

I am wondering how to make the desire of therapists to contribute to society turn into a reality. To do this, we certainly have to cross some borders and be promiscuous! Surely we can go beyond our narcissistic investment in proving our theories right? Surely we can reach out to other groupings beyond the 'psy' field, maybe those deploying quite different epistemologies to ours, so as to work collaboratively and in an interdisciplinary vein?

In this book, there is some reflection and self-reflection, including some stringent and revealing self-criticism. But maybe the doubts and scepticism may not come through because of the nature of writing with a professional and academic audience in mind. One aim of this book is to construct a space in which people can work out where they really stand in relation to psychotherapy and society.

To return to the thought that this could be my last book, I hope that it isn't. There is another one in the works which will include a few of the interviews people have done with me. And I want to signal what else will be in the yet-to-be-written book that is not in this one: Work on male therapists, exploring their motivation to take up this work. Then there will be more self-reflective critique of the use of therapy thinking in political writing. One chapter will be on 'economic sadism', posing the question of why it is so hard to achieve economic equality and justice.

Anyway, I hope you enjoy *this* book, and I really welcome dialogue, so e-mail me if you want at andrew@andrewsamuels.net

Further Reading

A creative and interesting summary of some of the themes in my work generally that also references material in this book may be found here:

Carpani, S., (2024). *Absolute freedom: Individuation an individualization in second-late-modern societies.* London and New York: Routledge, 25–29.

Part I

Culture

Chapter 1

Oh no! Not another chapter on 'the Other'

Retrospective Introduction: I wrote this because I found myself asking: Why are there so many psychotherapy and psychoanalysis conferences, panels, and papers (Jungian and non-Jungian) on 'the Other' these days? Is it a much-needed reparation for Western, white, male, heteronormative oppression of anyone and anything different? Or just a liberal fad that salves the conscience but leaves unjust imbalances of political and economic power intact? Or both?

Talking Points: It's time to challenge the liberal fascination with and idealisation of the Other. Our contemporary Western world will not be saved by Indigenous cultures. And how far can we go in accepting otherness? In Edward Albee's play The Goat, the hero falls in love with a goat. Her name is Sylvia. Are you OK with that?

The overall title of the International Association for Analytical Psychology (IAAP) Congress in Vienna in 2019 was 'Encountering the Other'? And a recent conference of the International Association for Jungian Studies (IAJS) bore the title 'The Spectre of the Other'? I could list dozens of other conferences in the fields of psychotherapy and analysis that use the same language. What is going on?

The chapter falls into four sections: (1) Reparation or liberal hypocrisy or both? (2) how Otherness is done, (3) limits of tolerance, and (4) Islam and the Other.

Reparation or liberal hypocrisy or both?

I meant no offence when I trailed the idea in my Introduction, that there are two sides to this coin. The first is that we are definitely engaged in overdue reparation for colonial, heteronormative, and neoliberal oppression. This includes the role of the psychological professions in both perpetration and repair (or its absence).

The second is that just at the very moment we enter or encounter the world of the Other, we often use the moment to conceal a failure to challenge the power relations, barbarism, and inequality of our own Western world.

Recognising that we project a lot (negative or positive) onto other people doesn't amount to much if political and personal behaviour remains much the same. That's why it is so important for therapists of all schools to twin their analysis of the

DOI: 10.4324/9781003598985-3

social and political world with activism in relation to its problems. This is why writers like the psychoanalyst Castoriadis (1997) and the social theorist Spivak (1999) refer to 'radical alterity'. This introduces ideas of justice to the discourse. And maybe we should remember what they chose to put on Marx's tombstone in Highgate Cemetery: 'The philosophers have only *interpreted* the world, in various ways. The point, however, is to *change* it.'

I am expressing a concern that what we do in relation to the Other and Otherness is too easily positioned as an internal moral and emotional challenge for an individual that smooths away the disruptive and traumatic nature of his or her own times, in his or her own spaces, and within his or her personal and intimate relationships.

I will conclude this first section by recalling that, at the age of 16, the French poet Arthur Rimbaud wrote in a letter 'Je est un Autre'. The line has become famous. There are many possible translations but, for me, 'I is an Another' will do. At the heart of these few words lies paradox piled upon paradox. If 'I is another', then what is the fate of Otherness and the Other? Doesn't the binary of subject (or self, or I) and Other just collapse under the weight of its own contradictions? Does Rimbaud mean there is no 'I' and no 'another'?

I hope to have cleared some ground, set the scene, and raised a number of questions about why I want to discuss this theme.

How Otherness is done

I have an elephant's child question in mind, meaning something naïve yet difficult. Do these Others really want us to enter, explore, or encounter their world? What do they get out of it? The problem I am raising here is often called 'Orientalism' after the book by the Palestinian academic Said (1978).

Said felt that buried within modern admiration for the culture of the Other was something not only deeply patronising but also palpably hostile and controlling.

For many years, as shown in the next chapter, I have been protesting at the claim that knowledge of and even adherence to the practices of Indigenous cultures, such as the numerous Native American and Australian Aboriginal and African cultures, may save the West. The political and spiritual practices and beliefs of these Others, if attended to and learned from, would go a long way to ameliorate some of the ills from which Western culture suffers. Native American sweat lodges for white American alcoholics are a good form of therapy. Or so it is claimed. *The Other will heal us.*

Well, the Other won't heal us. Yet I feel I should complexify my refusal of Orientalising idealisation of the Other. The situation is complicated by the way in which this may also be 'a good thing'. After all, isn't it positive that we correct collective attitudes in which Africans and other persons of colour and Indigenous people are regarded as unworthy of serious and respectful attention due to their hopeless inferiority? Isn't it positive that we challenge xenophobia, racial hierarchy, and fantasies of immigration policies by praising and protecting the Other?

Up to a point is my insecure answer. But I really do not know.

Nevertheless, despite such caution, I truly believe it is not provocative to say, as I am doing today, that idealisation of the Other often enables those of us in the West to avoid the social problematics of our own time, the degradation of our own dwelling places, and patterns of abusive and dysfunctional relationships from which our own people suffer.

I am proposing that passionate involvement by Westerners with things Indigenous can be a chimera, an illusion. It is often claimed by Jungian scholars that Indigenous peoples have a better relation to 'nature' and to the 'cosmos' than 'we' do. When I read such accounts, I get uneasy, as you will see in the next chapter. Going back to salvation and healing, the fact that the West has got divorced from nature, and seems to want to murder the Earth, is a problem the West will have to solve for itself. I don't think it is a head trip but reasonable scepticism to query *whether salvation for the West lies outside the West*. The turn to Indigenous peoples and their ideas and ways is little more than a band aid for our wounds.

But saying that does not rule out cultural dialogue. I have explicitly said on many occasions that I actively seek to learn from or to be involved in the lives of Indigenous peoples and to become acquainted with their philosophies. I have lived in Southern Africa (in Swaziland, and I recommend Adam Kuper's writings on that nation; also see Chapter 14). Much has also been learned from Barbara Fletchman Smith (2011) and Isla McKenzie-Mavinga (2009) and others about how to utilise in therapy practice ideas about emotional distress in relation to offending ancestral spirits. In fact, I think that a lot of what such analysts and therapists are concrete examples of what is now commonly called the decolonisation of analysis and therapy.

Regarding therapy, in a paper titled 'The hidden politics of healing: foreign dimensions of domestic practice' (Samuels 2002), I agreed that psychotherapy can learn from the methods and approaches of Indigenous healers from many different traditions. But I also said that we in the advanced, old therapy centres in Europe and North America can learn a lot from what our young colleagues (allegedly our students) think and do in the frontier areas where therapy has just arrived – a bit like Christianity arrived in what became the colonies!

In the therapy world, I have been involved for decades with what is called the 'diversity and equalities' agenda. Access to therapy and access to training for therapy and analysis is restricted by ethnic and financial factors. These exclusions of the Other impoverish our profession.

So I hope I have conveyed that I do not have any problem with speaking TO the Other. Nor OF the Other. But I am doubtful about speaking FOR the Other. Perhaps the only Other I want speak FOR is the dead Other.

Said felt that buried within modern admiration for the culture of the Other was something not only deeply patronising but also palpably hostile and controlling. He was, of course, a pioneer in the study of 'Othering' – what is described in *Orientalism* as 'disregarding, essentialising, denuding the humanity of another culture, people or geographical region'. And once the Other has been firmly established, the ground is softened for any transgression: violent expulsion, land theft, occupation, invasion, and sexual exploitation. However, the whole point of Othering is that the Other doesn't have the same rights and the same humanity, as those making the distinction.

Drawing the camera lens back a bit, I am initially going to illustrate this by reference to the place of the Other in nineteenth- and twentieth-century European painting. An interesting example of Orientalism in practice is Gauguin's attractive, seductive – yet rather controlling – Tahitian scenes of 1896.

Another example is a little more disturbing. There was an exhibition at the Royal Academy in 2017 titled 'Matisse in the studio'. Matisse was among the first to import African and Arabic-Islamic art and craft to Europe, even before Picasso. There was quite a vogue for everything 'Other' and supposedly academic journals sprang up that looked into African and Arabic cultures. Except that was not really what they were for. They were, in fact, a form of soft porn for the educated.

In the December 1906 issue of *Le humanitee femine*, with the subtitle of 'Femmes d'Afrique', kept by Matisse in his studio, he came across a photograph of a 'Jewish woman from Algeria'.

Matisse did a series of paintings and, above all, bronzes based on the Jewish woman from Algeria. But she is never mentioned or referenced. She has gone, absorbed into the canon of Western art.

You can still enjoy and be moved by the art, but today let's also think about the politics at work here, the use, even the exploitation of the 'Other'. The creativity and beauty can often mask the more disturbing dimensions. Central to the understanding of the Other is the definition of the Other *in sexual terms*. The photograph was a nude, viewed from the rear.

No factor in nineteenth-century self-definition was more powerful than the sense of alleged sexual pathology. The Other's pathology is revealed in her anatomy, and the Jewish woman and the prostitute are both bearers of the stigmata of sexual difference and thus pathology.

Limits of tolerance

In this third section, I want to discuss some of the limits on alterity and on loving respect for the Other. I will do so via a turn to literature.

Edward Albee's play *The Goat – Or Who Is Sylvia?* has been successfully revived in London (Albee 2000). Many readers will know this play and may have been to it. But for those who don't, this is the *succès de scandale* in which the protagonist falls in love with a goat that he names Sylvia. He can't give her up. He loves the goat and he says that the goat loves him.

His wife finds out, their family breaks apart, and in the end, the wife kills the goat. The play is a tragicomedy that challenges liberal values and assumptions – and complacencies – around Otherness. One Otherness is the Otherness of a respectable professional person who falls in love with a goat and consummates it. And there is also the way in which a goat is Other to the human.

The play addresses transgression of sexual norms, and in that sense, it is indeed an entrance into the world of the Other on many levels. It pushes its twists and turns to an extreme where, as the psychoanalyst Muriel Dimen put it in her seminal writings on perversion (2005), there are limits to moral relativism in relation to perversion. No matter how sophisticated, we cannot avoid what she called the EEW factor. We cannot avoid EEW whatever our progressive and tolerant ideals might tell us.

The play *The Goat* is a kind of Greek tragedy, in that fate drives the hero just as surely as it drives Oedipus. In the published version of the play, Albee adds a subtitle 'Notes toward a Definition of Tragedy'. In ancient Greek, the word is *tragoidia* which means 'goat song'. No one knows why tragedy is goat song, but Albee is going back to the source here.

I think the play not only looks at the Otherness of Animal in the experienced lives of most Westerners. There is a wider relevance. The love affair begins when the hero, an architect whose work involves metal, concrete, and glass, is in rural America looking for a second home in the bucolic countryside. He is in flight from the city, and this leads him into the encounter with the goat.

You can see images of zoophilia on the walls of prehistoric caves. When I searched on the net, I found most had been defaced.

But by the time of the Greeks, things in Europe had radically changed and narratives of the animal–human sexual connection always lead to disaster. Think Minotaur. Or the disastrous sequel to Leda's rape by the swan. Or Virgil mocking the Greeks for sleeping with animals. And don't some English people call people from Wales 'sheep shaggers' as a mark of contempt? This is Otherness with horn and furry hairy coat.

I am bringing this material here not to argue that we should give up on alterity or on mobilising the positive aspects of our concern for Otherness. Rather, I want to utilise Albee's challenge to your and my limits. Although *The Goat* features the mother of all *coniunctios*, the transcendence of the man-goat opposites, it ends with one of the most shattering images I've seen in the theatre when the wife enters dragging the carcass of the goat that she has slain.

I would like us to focus on the response of the wife. What follows is a little confused but I think you will get it OK. Stevie, the wife, says:

> That you can do these two things . . . and not understand how it. . . . How it cannot be dealt with – how stop and forgiveness have nothing to do with it? and how I am destroyed? How you are? How I cannot admit it though I know it!? How I cannot deny it because I cannot admit it!? Cannot admit it, because it is outside of denying!? Knowing it – knowing it's true is one thing, but believing what you know . . . well, there's the tough part.

In the third section, just finished, I have explored the limits of tolerance when Otherness is in the air.

Islam and the Other

Islam is usually discussed in terms of its being the Other, whether this is fair and well informed or not. I was interested to see what Islam might have to offer us as we gradually work out our ideas and feelings about Otherness. In this spirit, in the final section of the chapter, I turn to today's Islamic social philosophy to see what it might teach us about how to negotiate Otherness.

I have learned a lot at depth from Imams about Otherness. They have referred me to the central and important Islamic idea of *Ta'Aruf* found in Surah 49 Ayat 13 of the *Qur'an*:

> Oh Humanity, we have created you male and female, and have made you peoples and tribes, that you might come to know one another.

I find this *Ta'Aruf* a brilliantly inspiring take on difference that does not gloss over the violent conflict that encounters with the Other inevitably bring. In this reading of things, a point or purpose *(telos)* is given to difference and even to the violence that difference can bring. If we want to know the Other in any meaningful way, then that Other has to be radically different from ourselves. But we don't automatically love the other do we? Admitting that instantly brings questions of aggressive conflict and violence to the foreground.

There is more to this than simply getting to know the Other, important though that is. Analysts and therapists know how full engagement and dialogue with an 'other' benefits the self. I can only whisper the next thought, which is that this might be true even when the dialogue is tinged and irradiated by political violence.

We can see a fascinating congruence between Islamic social thought and depth psychological ideas about the interconnectedness of hate and love and how aggressive and even violent acts may also reflect desires for contact, touch recognition, and mutual recognition.

Personal coda

Unfortunately, I can't end the chapter and this section on *Ta'Aruf* and what we can learn from Islam without the following anecdote about how I became an Other.

I first started to write about *Ta'Aruf* in the mid to late 1990s. I wrote about how, in certain respects, Islamic commentators were functioning as the 'therapists of the west', critiquing the banality and materialism of our cultural practices and ways of living. I quoted one Muslim critic as saying that in the West we live 'in a brothel'. In general I found many of their observations about the spiritual voids in our existence to be spot on. Well, it was an idea, you don't have to agree with it, just try to realise what I was getting at, in order to appreciate what happened next.

Anyway, many blogs and comments, including from fellow therapists and analysts, began to discuss what I had written. They started to state that 'Samuels is saying that *terrorists are the therapists of the West*'. I got hate mail, things thrown at my house, excrement put through the letter box, the whole treatment. Maybe I was asking for it, but the experience brought me closer to the roots of Islamophobia and of being an Other which is why I am ending the chapter on such a note.

References

Albee, E., (2000). *The goat or who is Sylvia? Notes toward a definition of tragedy*. London: Methuen.

Castoriadis, C., (1997). *The imaginary institution of society*. London and New York: Routledge.

Dimen, M., (2005). Sexuality and suffering, or the eew! Factor. *Studies in Gender and Sexuality*, 6, 1–18.

Fletchman Smith, B., (2011). *Transcending the legacies of slavery: A psychoanalytic view*. London and New York: Routledge.

McKenzie-Mavinga, I., (2009). *Black issues in the therapeutic process*. London: Palgrave Macmillan.

Said, E., (1978). *Orientalism*. New York: Pantheon.

Samuels, A., (2002). The hidden politics of healing: Foreign dimensions of domestic practice. *American Imago: Studies in Psychoanalysis and Culture*, 59 (4, Winter), 459–482.

Spivak, G., (1999). *A critique of postcolonial reason: Toward a history of the vanishing present*. Cambridge, MA: Harvard University Press.

Chapter 2

Global politics, American hegemony, and vulnerability

Why there are no winners in the battle between Trickster Pedro Urdemales and the Gringos

Retrospective Introduction: The original paper was published in 2015. Back then, as now, the role of the United States in global politics received intense scrutiny. In addition, again as nowadays, the problematic of Indigenous peoples and cultures was of great interest within depth psychological circles. The chapter retains the polemical and intensely concerned spirit of the original as well as my conclusion that there are no winners when it comes to the battle between an Indigenous Trickster and the Gringos.

Talking Points: Pedro Urdemales is a Latin American Trickster who fools a rich American Gringo. Or does he? Surely naked American military and economic power will win out in the end? There are no easy conclusions regarding the battle between the neoliberal and capitalist West, and the global south: 'Everybody has won and all must have prizes' (the Dodo Bird verdict from Alice in Wonderland).

Introduction to the cultural politics of the chapter

The background to the chapter is constituted by intense interest within psychoanalysis and Jungian analysis and studies in selected features of Indigenous cultures, such as the numerous Native American and Australian Aboriginal cultures. These, as mentioned in the previous chapter, are held to hold seeds of political and spiritual tendencies which, if attended to and learned from, would go a long way to ameliorate some of the ills from which Western culture suffers. To what extent this is a search for 'salvation' for the West by means of a turn to Indigenous cultures – which are thereby idealised – is a controversial and tendentious matter which, by its very nature, will not be settled herein.

The situation is complicated by the way in which any such idealisation – an attitude strenuously denied by students of Indigenous peoples – may be rather a niche problem in that for many, if not in academia but in the general population, Native Americans (or African and other Blacks, or Aboriginal Australians) are generally regarded by the white Western majority as not worthy of serious and respectful attention due to their ineluctable inferiority. This is shown by their poverty, alcoholism, and prevalence of mental illness – all things that are claimed

DOI: 10.4324/9781003598985-4

to be their fault. So the danger is that I am disputing something that is not in fact generally accepted.

Nevertheless, it is not provocative to caution that idealisation of the Other, were this accepted as existing, would enable those of us in the West to avoid the problematics of our own time, our own place, our own people. Passionate involvement by Westerners with things Indigenous can obscure politics – not only the politics of the treatment by the United States of its Native American citizens but also politics itself. It is a recognisable pattern by now – the 'exotic other' (in Renos Papadopoulos's phrase 2002) takes the space needed by the ordinary other.

There is a concern in my mind that my text will be regarded as Panglossian with regard to the problems besetting the West – even if the monoliths of 'the West' and 'Indigenous culture' are noted to be unsatisfactory because simplistic. Most concerning would be that I am heard as some sort of white supremacist, with a deprecatory attitude towards Indigenous peoples and cultures. This is far from the truth. My concern is over the positioning of the Indigenous as what I will continue to call the 'salvation' for Western culture in general and for Western politics in particular. Anyway, I feel I should note at this point that I have no illusions whatsoever about the supposed superiority of Western culture, art, technology, economy, and philosophy.

There is a possibility, when one is evaluating the idea of salvation in this context, that there will be an elision of the difference between salvation in the sense of personal growth, development, and epiphany, on the one hand, and political transformation, on the other hand. It is beyond the scope of this chapter to explore what people are after psychologically, and what they want for themselves from at depth engagement with Indigeneity. But the question concerning the political outcomes of such engagement remains to be answered. In terms of personal gain, I myself found the sweat lodge a mind-blowing experience, tobacco smoking to be revelatory, and the various Native American rituals I have participated in were strong experiences despite (or because of?) the fact that the tribal Elder was a native New Yorker. But this isn't quite what I mean by 'politics'.

It is often claimed by Jungian scholars that Indigenous peoples have a better relation to 'nature' and to the 'cosmos' (e.g. Tacey 2009). But these concepts are not fixed and may even be mutable within an Aboriginal worldview. This would be worth studying. Do Indigenous traditions evolve over historical time? I suspect that they do but that it is difficult to access the process.

Finally in this introduction to the politics of the paper, here is a last thought. Why don't we cut out the middleman? The middleman here being Jung. Why not develop a broadly based liberation psychology, using whatever tools and sources come to mind? Jung, too, of course. But in terms of bridging the Western-Indigenous binary, hasn't Jung had his chance already? He will always be there in intercultural discourse but as a much-diluted spectral presence not a (or the) guide.

Navajo and Western cultures, Navajo and Western psyches: critique of a contemporary Jungian account

I begin with a detailed discussion of an important recent paper (Bernstein 2014) in the area of the interface of Jungian psychology and Native (i.e. Indigenous cultures) and then move on to discuss other roles for the Jungian community in relation to serious political, economic, and ecological concerns.

As Bernstein says, the paper is a position paper concerning the relations between Navajo and Western cultures (and, as Bernstein adds more controversially, between Navajo and Western 'psyches'). In what follows, I pay close attention to the text.

Agreement

Where Bernstein and I are in agreement – and this is a big area of agreement – is that there is a real and present planetary danger due to the politics and psychology of climate change denial. Hence, I am with him when he writes, 'It is my contention that the Western psyche, the Western ego construct, is being thrust into reconnection with nature' (p. 20). I am not sure of the basis of the rest of the sentence where he adds, 'This is the result of evolutionary processes'.

Cultural evolution

I am not at all sure I can agree with what Bernstein writes in the general area of what could be called 'cultural evolution', specifically as follows:

> What I've come to realize and have written and lectured about for ten years is this: It was Western humanity, the precursor to Western civilization that got thrown out of the Garden of Eden. From that point on it was split off from nature and the spirit world associated with it.
>
> (p. xx)

I found this a rather problematic generalisation. Isn't it a bit risky to claim that only Westerners exist in a post-lapsarian state? Doesn't that make them incorrigible sinners? There is a problematic excess of moral authority in this remark which damns the West for all time. What is of interest is that my term 'salvation' for what is sought by some Jungians who engage with Indigenous cultures is spot on when, according to Bernstein's account, salvation for Westerners is denied them by their having been thrown out of the Garden of Eden.

Bernstein writes (p. 21):

> In exploring the Navajo approach to illness and healing, it is important to remember that theirs is a psyche that has never been split off from nature. Here I am talking about the psyche itself, not any one individual's ego. Theirs more resembles the psyche from which the Euro-American psyche emerged as a result of evolutionary process than ours does.

I think many, not only me, would find this positioning of Navajo and Western psyches to be tendentious. Bernstein is arguing that the Navajo psyche came first and that the Western psyche grew ('evolved') out of it. Of course, I realise that Jung's psychology permits such claims to be made but from anthropological and political standpoints this is pretty difficult to substantiate.

He adds: 'My formulation is that Genesis gave the Western psyche an evolutionary mandate for "dominion" over life' (p. 21).

Jewish scholars, well schooled in Torah and Talmud, would protest, on textual grounds, this reading of Genesis. There have been several articles in *Tikkun* magazine on a Jewish approach to ecology, equally claimed to derive from Genesis.

Bernstein writes:

One can almost feel the circularity and timelessness of this Navajo cosmology as compared with the linearity of the Eurocentric psyche. I would say that Freud's psychology became the logos psychology of Western culture and that Jung's psychology had one foot (at least) still stuck in the tar of the indigenous psyche from which our Eurocentric psyche has emerged.

(p. 27)

I am no expert on comparative cosmology, but surely there are numerous Western examples of circularity and timelessness, and, it could be argued, radical approaches to temporality these days are markedly Western (e.g. Yiassimedes 2014). With regard to Freud, surely his work on the drives and on the phylogeny of the core complexes represents as close an interest in 'the primitive psyche' as anything Jung wrote. Isn't there an element of special pleading for Jung here?!

Alignments of Indigenous healing with Jungian analysis and therapy

I think it is very difficult to align Indigenous methods of healing with a Western system like Jungian analysis. One ends up noting how well (or poorly) the Indigenous system *aligns* with the Western one. It could be argued that is a form of colonialism, in which the Indigenous approach is valued in proportion to its alignment with the Western system

This criticism was also made of Vera Buhrmann's articles in the *Journal of Analytical Psychology* comparing Xhosa healing approaches in South African with contemporary clinical analytical practice. As Fred Plaut once said to me in 1995: 'Funny how the Xhosa healers seem to have had Jungian analytical training!'

Bernstein writes on p. 26:

The Navajo are ever conscious of holding the tension of the opposites . . . in balance, if possible. In Navajo cosmology energies that become chronically out of balance constitute the definition of illness for the individual and . . . the community, and a healing ceremony is sought. As we know, Jung stressed the importance of holding the tension of the opposites – a very rich and creative concept, most particularly when applied on behalf of individuals and collective 'individuation.'

With the greatest respect, this reads as if the Navajo have already, intuitively and/or inherently, attained the clinical potency of Jungian analysts. Is it to be accepted that Navajo healers 'hold the tension of opposites' when this maxim stems from an utterly different time and place? I can see that it makes the Jungian clinician more aware of the deep similarities between all modes of healing but that is a non-controversial point.

Then Bernstein adds (p. 27): 'The Navajo view of psyche is very compatible with the Jungian concept of the Self.'

For me, this begs the question – through what prism is the Navajo view of psyche being viewed if not the pre-existing Jungian one? How this is different from colonial or neo-colonial takes on cultures stated to have been 'discovered' the West, attitudes which we are all somewhat ashamed of these days.

Animism in clinic and society

Bernstein writes (p. 24) as if things like this cannot be found in Western society and in the contemporary clinic:

> One can't hear rocks speak or receive the blessings of eagles that have come for that purpose if one is not open to noticing what is not familiar or what one's family, friends, colleagues, and peers consider nonordinary or worse yet, weird or crazy.

In my practice, and, I dare say, in the practices of many therapist attuned to social, ecological, and cultural dimensions of life, what we find is precisely as described by Bernstein: Social phenomena, material entities, and the earth and animals, all speak to me and to my client.

More widely, Charles S. Pierce is a Western philosopher who considered what effects things possess in and of themselves; they are not dead. Of course, our consumerist addictions may well be an undesirable example of this kind of Western animism.

Clinical issues

On p. 23, we read of a patient: 'She began to tell me about an encounter she'd had with a horse and some trees. She spoke of the messages she got from them – the horse, in particular, was insistent on his message to her.'

Again, this kind of clinical report has a long history in classical Jungian analysis of Western individuals.

Bernstein comments: 'I came to understand this ceremony as what we, as Jungians, are endeavoring to do when we do dream analysis: apply the archetypal energy brought by the dream symbols to the psyche and soul of the patient' (p. 23).

I do not know exactly what the Navajo ceremony is 'endeavouring to do'. Nor is what Bernstein writes the only thing that one could say about dream interpretation in Jungian analysis. But what interests me is the goal of spotting the parallel. Is Bernstein saying merely that this is an interesting parallel? Or that Jungian analysts are on the right track and this is confirmed by reference to Navajo approaches? Or the opposite, that the Navajo must be doing something right because what they do resembles what we Jungian analysts are endeavouring to do?

Bernstein states on p. 21, 'Although for our purposes, here I will emphasize what Western medicine and psychology can learn from Navajo clinical approaches, I do not intend to set up any kind of dichotomy by saying that one is better than the other.'

I understand what Bernstein is saying about his intention and I support that. But when we look at his depiction of the two paradigms of 'dominion' and 'reciprocity', his preferences are pretty clear.

Complementarities

I have written at length elsewhere about the use and abuse of Jung's 'complementary' approach (1993, pp. 144–146). Bernstein is squarely in this tradition. What Jung did was to assemble two lists of qualities or essences. One list might be for those of a man and the other for those of a woman. Or one list might be about a German and the other about a Jew. I think this methodology is terribly suspect because of the dynamical relationship between the two lists. Put them together, and there is a perfect wholeness. Divide them along complementary lines and one can see how each list constructs the other list. If the socially dominant list is presented first, as in most analysis, then it is not at all hard to predict the contents of the second list.

One thing that is interesting about Bernstein's two lists is how closely they resemble lists that Jungians have assembled with regard to men and women and to fathers and mothers.

There is an irony wherein an approach to these issues that seeks to overcome Western dualistic, binary, and hierarchical ways of thinking uses precisely these features to make its case. Huskinson (2014, p. 75) developed an analogous critique of 'green' discourses. She writes: 'I can't forgo the perception that the so-called "green discourses" are themselves guilty of sustaining dualistic thinking in the face of their very efforts to undermine it.'

Without further comment, I will cite the two lists so that my remarks about their construction and manipulation can be illustrated.

Psychic Paradigm of Dominion	Psychic Paradigm of Reciprocity
Patriarchal monotheism.	Right-brain predominance balanced with
Dominance of left-brain consciousness.	left-brain consciousness.
Cartesian duality.	Principle of balance, harmony, and
Splitting, without consciously holding	repair – not 'fixing' or 'curing'.
the tension of the opposites,	Duality as balance and harmony, not as
and therefore prone to missing	splitting.
the potential for emergence of a	A balance of masculine and feminine
'transcendent function'.	energy at all times, in all things.
Power-oriented towards supremacy of	Experiences shadow dynamics
the ego due to absence of the	as normative but in need of
mediating influence of a living	management.
relationship with nature – that is, an	Healing based on restoration and repair
archetypal deficit in the capacity for	without guilt. (There is no need for
humility.	guilt when the presumption is the
Shadow dynamics typically are seen as	need and possibility for restoration.
pathology.	The Native languages I am familiar
Dominion denies and is threatened by	with have no word for guilt.)
the idea of an archetypal dimension	
of reality capable of overriding ego	
control; as a result it carries a phobic	
need to deny engaging the possibility	
of transrational experience.	
Beholden to a human-centred concept	
of psyche – that is, that psyche	
exclusively resides in, and emanates	
from, the minds of humans. Nature,	
thus, exists outside of psyche.	

I move on from this attempt to understand Jerome Bernstein's viewpoints to get more into the heart of the chapter.

Pedro Urdemales – Latin American Trickster Extraordinaire

There are important Latin American Trickster tales involving a character called Pedro Urdemales. 'Urdemales' means 'weaver of evil' in Spanish. Yes, Tricksters are not in fact nice guys, saints, messiahs, rescuers, oracles, artists, and creatives – or even politicians. Pedro does not use magic to fool the Gringo in the story of 'The Magic Burro' (Sherman 1996). In this sense, he resembles Tyl Eulenspiegel or the Jewish Trickster Hershele. He uses his wits.

One day Pedro was in a bit of a hurry. But he had no horse, not even a burro, and trudging along on foot wasn't too appealing on this hot, dusty afternoon.

What should he do? Maybe an ordinary man would have shrugged and walked wearily on. But Pedro was no ordinary man. He sat down and began carving the figure of a burro out of a piece of wood.

Soon a man from north of the Mexican border, the arrogant sort called a gringo, came riding along on a fine horse. Pedro quickly got up and pretend ed to be about to mount his wooden burro.

"What are you doing?" the gringo asked. "That's nothing but a piece of wood!"

"Hush!" Pedro cried. "You don't want to insult her. This may look like a piece of wood, but it's actually a magical burro."

"Is it, now? Well, it's a pretty carving. I'll buy it from you."

"Oh no, I couldn't sell her!" Pedro cried. "She's the only one of her kind, and I'd never be able to find another."

"What does she do, this magical burro?"

"Well now, once you get on her back, she turns into flesh and blood. And when you ask her to run, why, not even the wind can catch her. I couldn't possibly insult her by selling her."

"No? Then will you trade with me instead?"

Pedro pretended to think it over very carefully. "I don't know . . . she is the only one of her kind . . ."

"Come, trade with me! I will give you my horse for that burro."

"Your horse? Ah well, if I must trade, I must. But I'd better change clothes with you as well; my burro might be frightened by your foreign garb."

So the gringo dismounted and changed clothes with Pedro. Pedro leaped into the saddle. "One warning," he called. "The magic will only work if you wait till I am out of sight before you try mounting."

The gringo agreed, and waited till Pedro had ridden out of sight. The gringo mounted the wooden burro. "Come on," he said. "Come on! Come to life! Run! Do something!"

The wooden burro did something. It remained a piece of carved wood.

And Pedro, riding in his new clothes on his new horse, got to where he was going with no trouble at all.

Pedro certainly does seem to fool the Gringo, preying on his greed and naiveté. But does he really? A mixture of psychological and political thinking will now be used to explore whether there is indeed a clear-cut winner in Trickster tales like Pedro's.

Pedro is in the well-known line of Tricksters who crazily destabilise political systems, undermining and sometimes overthrowing the powerful. The academic literature (e.g. Pelton 1980) suggests that this version of the political Trickster is quite widespread, but the same literature cautions that much further Trickster material is not as programmatic as this. In the chapter, I seek to re-position the Trickster in a political sense, not as a personification, nor a presence, nor an energy field or inspiration – *not in fact as anything at all*. Hence, I have to apologise for the fact that, in terms of Trickster studies, this chapter follows a *via negativa*, a negative path, as in apophatic theology.

Summary of the arguments that follow

(1) It is a big mistake to read the Trickster as a positive phenomenon either in politics or in any other way. It is just as erroneous to read him negatively. These categories are not relevant.

(2) Do not trust that the female Trickster can protect women and girls. If women and girls get too excited about 'discovering' her, it may lead to them dropping their guard as if their struggle was over.

(3) Tricksters cannot defeat capitalism and its military machines. (By the way, nor can psychology, which is why I titled my paper [2010] in the *Journal of Analytical Psychology*: 'The transcendent function in politics – NO!'. It appears in this book as Chapter 16.)

(4) Nevertheless, thinking about Tricksters may produce useful ideas about contemporary global politics. But such ideas will be *our* ideas not Trickster's ideas. I'll give examples in due course.

(5) 'Jungians' – analysts and academics alike – have to consider who they are as citizens, where they stand in the political spectrum, and what they might take responsibility for.

Diverse readings of the political Trickster

Tricksters and other manifestations of Indigenous cultures have bamboozled Western/Northern scholars, and not only Jungian analysts, into thinking that exotic 'other' cultures are richer/deeper/better/closer to nature than their own. I certainly see this idealisation as warranted protest – but not really a desire to re-establish contact or reconnect, so, as indicated, I am not in agreement with Jerome Bernstein on this though I respect the integrity of his work on these matters. Perhaps this unstoppable yearning for some other place or time or culture than our own is not in fact a rather intriguing cultural complex.

In connection with the possibility that Western engagement with indigeneity may show signs of a cultural complex, Thomas Singer posted as follows on the discussion list of the IAJS on July 13, 2014:

What I called 'The Burden of Modernity' (unpublished lecture, 2014) resulted in many of the early Jungians turning to other cultures, often to indigenous or ancient [myths], in hopes of finding psychological and spiritual rebirth. By the mid twentieth century, the Existentialists turned in another direction in response to the same horrifying stimuli – they concluded that the cosmos was absurd and did not look elsewhere for some sort of renewal. Again, the Jungians 'pivoted' to the hope that the psyche (both individual and collective) might find else-where, in other cultures and in other times, something other than the horror and absurdity that surrounded them. This is certainly a common and not exclusively Jungian response to the burden of modernity and we could think of it as a cul-tural complex.

What we are seeing in what might be termed the 'Navajo turn' is evidence of the depressing and shame-inducing effects of living in exploitative, colonial, and het-eronormative societies. It is impossible to feel proud of belonging to such societies, and this is a serious collective wound. But it cannot be healed by looking elsewhere, outside our world, which is the only world we can be in. The past is not a solution to the problems of the present, nor a signpost to the future. We do not really know what to do about our present politics. Can we trust that there are 'solutions'? What-ever the answer, we can certainly continue to question and speculate about what a solution might look like or why we need one-line or single narrative solutions to political conundrums. So, with some proffered 'Jungian' 'solutions' in mind, it may not be advisable to put our faith in a return of the feminine principle, or some kind of re-balancing of inner and outer, or, in fact, in any kind of triumphalist psycho-solution.

The turn to other cultures, or to principles (such as the 'masculine principle') felt to be other to the dominant tendencies in our own societies such as 'the mascu-line principle', reminds me of the genre of adventure literature that uses the catch-phrase 'with one mighty bound he was free'. Our hero, faced with an impossible situation, in a deep pit with dozens of violent Natives dancing around brandishing spears, somehow gets out. The phrase comes from a situation where a newspaper serial writer had written his hero into a corner and had puzzled all night for a way to get him out, until finally a colleague suggested the writer simply type 'and with one mighty bound Jack was free'. There may be quite a lot of this in the current engagements of psychotherapy and psychology with politics. When a turn to the Navajo or any other Indigenous culture is presented as a solution to the political and other ills of the West it is as if all Westerners have to do is to enter the sweat lodge, visit Ladakh, and do Yoga. From the psychoanalytic side, Kleinian calls for the establishment of the depressive position as a cure all for the excesses of the financial system are just as problematic (e.g. Tuckett 2011).

I am sorry to sound so negative but despair may be the only place to start from if one wants to make something happen politically. Despair and disgust are organic to political struggle. It happens in the present moment; it is very dangerous to those who struggle, and political endeavours always fly under the flag of failure.

Continuing to discuss idealisations of the Trickster and other 'Native' features, many of these overlook his utter lack of moral sense, political programme, or anything sensible at all. When he edited my book *The Political Psyche* (Samuels 1993), John Beebe taught me that to ask moral questions of the Trickster completely misses the point. And in his seminal paper 'The Trickster in the arts' (Beebe 1981), Beebe focused not on artists who might be hailed as Tricksters but on what you could call 'Trickster pop-ups' in artistic production. That is very different. Beebe and I agree with Jung that just occasionally Tricksters are quite 'sensible' – which is of course a further trick. *It is an accident, though.* 'You can't sew a million seeds without getting one potato', as my grandfather from the Polish Shtetl used to say,

So when we applaud the fact that, as anthropologists tell us, Tricksters undermine the structures of power, let's not give them one iota of credit for it – for it is simply what they do, not because they think it is the right thing to do. It is action not reflection. Impulsive, unconscious, immature, often violent, definitely not relational! In Helena Bassil-Morozow's words in a personal communication (2014):

> Tricksters will disturb even well-built and useful systems because they do not discriminate between good and bad, they just target anything remotely 'structural' in its nature. The trickster's aim is not to bring happiness and positivity to the world – it is to challenge structural rigidity. Sometimes this involves a challenge to civilization itself because it is based on ordered existence. It is a task devoid of any moral goals or aims.

The Western/Northern romantic version of the Trickster shows up our admiring yet deeply patronising Orientalism. It is pathetic that we still do this. It is equally pathetic that we try to update the myths and archetypal patterns so that Perseus becomes Percy whose sword is his ballpoint pen and whose shield is his watch – and so on and so forth. Worst of all, we look for examples of 'contemporary Tricksters' in society, literature, and the arts, or in dreams, quite forgetting that these entities called Tricksters have their own social and historical contexts. There is less about them that is ahistorical, essential, and universal than we care to perceive.

I have been guilty of this kind of idealisation myself, specifically in relation to Machiavelli in 1993 in *The Political Psyche* in the chapter titled 'The lion and the fox: morality, Trickster and political transformation' (pp. 78–102). I loved the idea of the foxy politician, but perhaps this was an error. So this is somewhat of a recantation – though to be fair to myself I did try in that book to stick to the idea that Machiavelli's politically successful fox needed balancing out with his altogether less appealing image of the warlike lion.

Similarly, when praising the mutability and relativity of moral imagination in a chapter in *The Plural Psyche* (1989) titled 'Moral imagination in a depressed culture', I did try to balance it out with an emphasis in moral process on original morality (innate moral sensibility and integrity). But, again, my preference for the fluid and mutable won out. I'm glad to have revisited these things even though it's been painful.

In general, as I hope is clear by now, I want to protest against the simplistic equation of Trickster and imagination or creativity. People who make art or have ingenious solutions to problems are not Tricksters, even if they occasionally draw on Tricksterism.

Tricksters are not people. People are not Tricksters.

The rise and fall of the female Trickster

I think I coined the phrase 'the female Trickster' at a conference in Chicago in 1984 and developed it throughout the 1990s. It was a good idea politically to initiate a search for her despite Tricksters having no coherent body schema. That is something else that we like to forget – not remembering, for example, how the Winnebago Trickster sends his detached penis off to punish a chipmunk with disastrous dismembering results? There is no actual body at all.

In the research I have done, female tricksters cover a huge spectrum. There were the Mothers of the Plaza de Mayo in Buenos Aires who used the hyper-feminine activity of sewing their scarves of mourning as cover for their organised standing up to the Junta in the hope of finding out about the fate of their 'disappeared' children (an example of Rosie Parker's 'subversive stitch').

Then there was the rash of energetic and tough/tender private detectives created by writers such as Sara Paretsky that both Tannen (2007) and I explored. Paretsky's creation, V.I. Warshawski, prefers you not to know her name is Victoria. She knows every bar and cheap eatery in Chicago's Loop district, and she can wisecrack herself out of the tightest corner. She works for individual clients, up against the system, the establishment, the powerful. And she certainly uses tricks (in the sense of smart stratagems) to get results.

But today I want to add to my ongoing enthusiasm for V.I. a serious question about whether what she does is in fact any use to anyone other than the individual client. All over the world, women are mutilated, raped, and exploited. Femicide is ubiquitous. Even in the allegedly liberal and democratic West, they earn less than men for the same work, don't get equal shares of political or business power, and are more likely to be murdered by their male partners than the other way round. There is no protection for women to be found in the female trickster. She is not a safe, good mother or a social worker, you know. And V.I. says explicitly that she doesn't want kids.

It is the absence of any suggestion of safety or even survival that explains why I still find what Margaret Atwood wrote in *Surfacing* in 1972 so moving and educational. It is not a portrayal of a feminist hero or a womb to which one could retreat when threatened:

> The forest leaps upward, enormous, the way it was before the Americans cut it, columns of sunlight frozen; the boulders float, melt, everything is made of water, even the rocks. In one of the languages there are no nouns, only verbs held for a longer moment.
>
> The animals have no need for speech, why talk when you are a word.
>
> I lean against a tree, I am a tree leaning.
>
> I am not an animal or a tree, I am the thing in which the trees and animals move and grow. I am a place.

In the two sections thus far, I've protested against idealisation of the Trickster and specifically of the female Trickster, and now for the third section.

Why there are no winners in the battle between Pedro and the Gringos

Pedro Urdemales hasn't really seen off the Gringos. That is just a feel-good thing. They do have him in chains, whether these are intellectual, political or physical. Tricksters may seem cool but they cannot really survive crude, brute financial and military power.

If we really love Tricksters, then we regard should them as a sort of endangered species and use all our energy for a political project that will create an environment in which to protect them. But would there be any point in doing that? Pedro doesn't give a shit about what we Western/Northern liberal folks say and do!

But in the context of the story in which he fools the gringo, Pedro seems to have got the upper hand. This will make most Jungians cheer. While I do not think we can ignore the narrative thrust of the story, there is this other story, that I just mentioned, of Tricksters crumbling as the drones fly and the tanks rumble. (As I write in August 2024) the genocide in Gaza continues. That is why I say there are no clear-cut winners here and this could be the basis for dialogue between people like me who disdain Orientalism and our opponents in debate.

Tricksters in the context of global politics

In this section, I want to show how, in spite of those melancholic caveats and doubts, this material is still highly relevant to some of the most pressing political issues of our time. I will look in turn at inequality of wealth, the problem of the United States, the importance of getting out of the Western box, and the rewriting of political psychology.

Inequality of wealth within and between nations is getting worse and worse, and any idea that wealth will trickle down is delusive (Picketty 2014). But attaining equality will be a long struggle, and one aspect is that there is a seemingly ineluctable psychology of inherited wealth at work. Inherited wealth is a form of economic sadism with its own specific dynamics (see Samuels 2014).

Anyway, Tricksters, *by accident as well as design*, are quite good at undermining the wealthy. For example, the West African Trickster Ananse tricks the rich merchant Akwasi so that Akwasi ends up ordering Ananse to make love to his wife Aso. Again, I need to stress that we will not see greater economic equality *because* we line up behind a Trickster. Occupy was never a Trickster movement. But what Tricksters do in their own automatic and mindless way suggests things that we ourselves might do – bot, for us, as acts of political consciousness and organisation. It will not be Tricksters in the streets; it will be you and me in the streets. Or signing letters and petitions on-line.

With inequality – and hence power – in mind, it may still be the case that today's Tricksters could inspire people to challenge the *hegemonic, imperial power of the United States*. This hegemony is the single most destructive distortion in global politics today. The American pattern of distribution of wealth and income has become the world's pattern. However, I want to say explicitly that the 1%–99%

divide *is not the fault* of the Gringos. It is what huge empires do. There is little point in being anti-American in pursuit of global social justice. And many Americans know very well that something wrong is happening.

Nevertheless, there is an American dimension to some of these economic phenomena that cannot be ignored (we might remember Margaret Atwood's casual reference, back in 1972, to 'the Americans'?). Every year the American historian William Blum publishes his 'updated summary of the record of US foreign policy'. This shows that, since 1945, the United States has tried to overthrow more than 50 governments, many of them democratically elected; grossly interfered in elections in 30 countries; bombed the civilian populations of 30 countries; used chemical and biological weapons; and attempted to assassinate foreign leaders.

In many cases, Britain has been a collaborator. The degree of human suffering, let alone criminality, is little acknowledged in the west, despite the presence of the world's most advanced communications and nominally most free journalism. That the most numerous victims of terrorism – 'our' own terrorism – are Muslims is unsayable. That extreme jihadism, which led to 9/11, was nurtured as a weapon of Anglo-American policy (Operation Cyclone in Afghanistan) is suppressed.

Many have asked why and how this has been happening, why and how we tolerate it, we who are either Americans or closely connected to and allied with Americans?

Enter the Trickster in a way you don't want to see him perform. What we are seeing is not (repeat not) a war between Pedro Urdemales and the Gringos but a tragic and malevolent Grand Alliance between them. Pedro the Trickster has pulled off his most terrible trick. He has permitted us to allow ourselves to become indoctrinated, to allow lies that justify the risks of war. As Harold Pinter once wrote, 'the scale of our indoctrination is a brilliant, even witty, highly successful act of hypnosis, as if the truth never happened even while it was happening'. It is the wit of Trickster Pedro, so easy to applaud when things fit into our moral schemas, that is perpetuating the sick global politics of war and inequality that is the real foundation of our severance from nature and its beauties.

I referred earlier to American power as a 'distortion'. One way to manage this distortion is via political organisation and alliance – alliances of nations and regions, and alliances of the oppressed, as liberation theologians call for. This highlights the need for non-Western nations to get out of 'the Western box', as I call it. I was so happy when President Lula of Brazil blamed the banking crisis of 2008 on the West or the North:

> The crisis was caused by no black man or woman or by no indigenous person or by no poor person. This crisis was fostered and boosted by irrational behaviour of some people that are white, blue-eyed. Before the crisis they looked like they knew everything about economics, and they have demonstrated they know nothing about economics.

Challenged about his claims, Lula responded: 'I only record what I see in the press. I am not acquainted with a single black banker.'

In contemporary Western politics, if one wants to do something about economic inequality, environmental despoliation, species depletion, climate change denial, and the refusal of sustainable economics, there is a need to get out of the Western box. Be that as it may, my argument is that it is fruitless to get into an Eastern Box or a Southern Box. Or a Native American Box. Or a Box called 'the Feminine'. Perhaps the political message is that we should try to stay away from boxes, for they are all way too 'little' (apologies to Pete Seeger!). There are no cheap and easy solutions.

Before reaching the last section of the talk, on the responsibility of Jungian analysts and academics, let me summarise the paper thus far. Following an introduction to the cultural politics of the paper and a discussion of Jungian engagement with indigeneity, I made the following points: (1) It is a big mistake to read the Trickster as a positive phenomenon. (2) The female Trickster cannot protect women and girls. (3) Tricksters cannot defeat capitalism and its military machines. (4) Nevertheless, thinking about Tricksters inspires useful ideas about contemporary global politics. I gave the following examples: what to do about economic inequality, challenging the power of the United States, and getting out of the Western box.

The social responsibility of Jungian analysts and academics

These are just a few brief reflections on what it means to be a Jungian or post-Jungian academic or analyst in today's world. It is a *credo*, I suppose.

I suggest that the Jungian person who stalks contemporary culture, and who is these days trying to engage with its politics, has always been marginal and decentred, not at all integrated but rather an actor performing many roles in many scripts, characterised by lack, somewhat faded as well as jaded, jerky, marginalised, alienated, split, guilty, empty, nomadic. Not a Trickster, as I said, but on occasion Trickster-powered, if you like. A minority figure, anyway. I think there is something we can do with this vision of a marvellously rebellious Jungian: the misfit, the rebel, the troublemaker, and the round peg in a square hole.

To embrace this vision of ourselves, we have to firmly reject Jung's aristocratic, elitist, and supercilious political ideas, including his Orientalism, his patronising admiration (which was, of course, genuine admiration) for non-Western cultures.

Here's a by-no-means unusual quote from the 'Definition' of individuation in Psychological Types (1926): 'It is obvious that a social group consisting of stunted individuals cannot be a viable and healthy institution' (emphasis added). Or this, from the 1916 paper 'Adaptation, individuation, collectivity': 'Whoever is not creative enough [to individuate] must re-establish collective conformity with a group of his own choice, otherwise he remains an empty waster and a windbag'.

So, as Jung sees it, we have stunted individuals here, wasters and windbags over there, and truly individuated people in the first-class cabin. There is simply no marriage of equality and individuation, whether devotees of individuation can accept it or not. No wonder Shamdasani (2003, p. 307) summarises Jung as saying 'individuation was for the few'. But there are a lot of people in the world, not just 'the chosen few', not just the Jungian 1% or, more accurately, the Jungian 0.1%.

Don't Jungian analysts and academics, along with others in the liberal professions, have to question whether or not we really want to live in gated communities, sending our children to elite schools and colleges, staying in fine hotels, employing servants – and, in general feeling, ourselves to be other than average human beings? Better, say I, to be 'stunted', remembering that in alchemical process, the *lapis* can't be reached without the assembly of ordinary, base elements found everywhere and every day. Or, as George Orwell wrote in *1984*, 'if there is hope, it lies in the proles' (i.e. the proletariat). Or, in the words of Leonardo Boff, who was accepted by acclamation as an Honorary Member of the IAAP in 2013, 'God is in the poor who cry out. And God is the one who listens to the cry and liberates, so that the poor no longer need to cry out'.

Tricksterish coda

In the coda that follows, I will now turn my text on its head. Ideally, I would say instantly that this is not the act of a Trickster but the act of someone trying, with all his limitations, to be honest. Would readers believe that? Surely it is the act of a Trickster, to turn the talk completely on its head. Or is it the act of a late middle-aged academic who wants to have his cake and eat it, to swing both ways?

Whatever, I found that I could not leave my text here, devoid of hope, unremittingly negative, rude to the hospitable Americans, a dun-coloured political tract, especially if heard in a mean-spirited way. Why shouldn't we wrong-headed and anti-intellectual Jungians have our fun, our place in the sun? What's so wrong with being wrong? Isn't being Orientalist an alienable right of any free Westerner?!

What I am saying is that, in spite of all the foregoing that attests to the contrary, I do still see Tricksters, especially but not only female tricksters, as doughty and inspiring 'leaders' in the battle against the political ills of our world. The fox lives! Not to say this would be an act of betrayal leaving Trickster out on the road, lonely and so cold.

Tricksters suggest that, if the bodily zones can be muddled and confused, then no established order is safe. Anything can be muddled. The personal can be political, the fixity of gender roles probed, and tyranny challenged (if not always overthrown). Trickster's grandiosity may be central to political creativity. What is condemned by the well-analysed and reasonable folk as immature fantasies of global solutions can be reframed as a backdrop to effective politics.

When I first wrote about the Trickster in politics, I cited the Romanian revolution of December 1989 as demonstrating, via the foolhardy bravery and struggle of the unarmed workers and students who refused to leave the square and the street. I wrote this chapter originally in 2014 with recent memories of the Arab Spring and of the changes back then in Ukraine in mind. The changes that infuriated and terrified Russia. The point is that grandiosity of aim can be the ground of realisable ambition. Trickster's denial of mortality is a political statement for it is fear of death that plays a part in maintaining the political *status quo*.

Because of this contrariness, which comes from deep inside me, and because I agree with William Empson about the key value of ambiguity, I am still prepared to look for the transformation of politics Trickster could lead.

References

Atwood, M., (1972). *Surfacing*. London: Virago.

Beebe, J., (1981). The Trickster in the arts. *San Francisco Jung Institute Library Journal*, 2 (2).

Bernstein, J., (2014). Nonshamanic native healing. *Psychological Perspectives*, 57 (2), 129–146.

Huskinson, L., (2014). Psychodynamics of the sublime, the numinous and the uncanny: A dialogue between architecture and ego-psychology. *In:* L. Huskinson and M. Stein, eds. *Analytical psychology in a changing world: The search for self, identity and community*. London and New York: Routledge, 72–87.

Jung, C. G., (1916). Adaptation, individuation, collectivity. *CW18*.

Jung, C. G., (1926). Definitions. In Psychological types. *CW6*.

Papadopoulos, R., (2002). The other other: When the exotic other subjugates the familiar other. *Journal of Analytical Psychology*, 47, pp. 163–188.

Pelton, R., (1980). *The Trickster in West Africa: A study of mythic irony and sacred delight*. Berkeley, CA and Los Angeles, CA: University of California Press.

Piketty, T., (2014). *Capital in the twenty-first century*. Cambridge, MA: Belknap Press.

Samuels, A., (1993). *The political psyche*. London and New York: Routledge.

Samuels, A., (2010). The transcendent function in politics – No! *Journal of Analytical Psychology*, 55 (2), 241–253.

Samuels, A., (2014). Economics, psychotherapy and politics. *International Review of Sociology*, 24, 77–90.

Shamdasani, S., (2003). *Jung and the making of modern psychology: The dream of a science*. Cambridge: Cambridge University Press.

Sherman, J., (1996). *Trickster tales: Forty folk stories from around the world*. Atlanta, GA: August House.

Tacey, D., (2009). *Edge of the sacred: Transformation in Australia*. Einsiedeln: Daimon Verlag.

Tannen, R., (2007). *The female trickster: The mask that reveals*. London and New York: Routledge.

Tuckett, D., (2011). *Minding the markets: An emotional finance View of financial instability*. London: Palgrave Macmillan.

Yiassemides, A., (2014). *Time and timelessness: Temporality in the theory of Carl Jung*. London and New York: Routledge.

Chapter 3

Age is just a number

The delusion of maturity and the fiction of individuation

Retrospective Introduction: This was written and delivered at a conference in Sao Paulo in 2022. I was and remain concerned about the division of the population into categories (like 'millennials'). I was also concerned to dispute Jing's 'first half of life/ second half of life' division. I wanted to write something about age that did not get into 'wisdom' or frailty and death.

Talking Points: A chapter on age that does not focus on either wisdom or infirmity! Rather, the very notion of 'the generations' is seen through and Jung's division into first half and second half of life is debunked. Core concepts and attitudes within the therapy field are challenged, including individuation and maturity. 'Age is just a number' is presented as a wholly new philosophy of life.

As Theodor Adorno said, 'in psychoanalysis nothing is true except the exaggerations'. So, in exaggerated vein, in this chapter, I praise what many may regard as immaturity. As Oscar Wilde said, 'Experience is just the name we give to our mistakes' (*The Picture of Dorian Gray* (1891/2000).

I am here to dispute the idealisation of aging and of old age. But you will see that I do not do this on the grounds that old age is horrible, painful, and often humiliating. Or that we die. It is a much more subtle matter than that.

I am here to say that *'age is just a number'*. This may sound superficial, and maybe it is, but it is time to explore the matter.

I am here to question the divide of one's life into the first and second halves of life. It means a deconstruction of the popular and Jung-inspired notion of the 'midlife crisis'.

I will suggest that eternal youths – the *puer aeternus* (eternal boy) and the *puella aeterna* (eternal girl) – are key relational psychoanalytic components in any radical approach to a full life, *regardless of the age of the actors*. They are not pathologies unless we make them so. I am not even sure they are 'archetypes'!

Why am I doing all of this? Well, most discourses on aging focus either on (1) death or on (2) wisdom and maturity. You find both, but especially the latter (maturity) in both Jung and, as it happens, in Confucius. I will discuss them in turn in a moment.

DOI: 10.4324/9781003598985-5

Turning now to *eternal* youth, I think that such an image is marvellously useful. But to realise that utility means one must de-literalise developmental psychology, using the insights of attachment theory and object relations, and the notion of development itself, for strange, poetic, metaphorical, new, incorporeal purposes. Hence, we can see the *puer* and the *puella* in an old person. And we can see wisdom in a baby or child. So we can have a foolish old man or woman – and, conversely, a mature and considerate baby.

Please note that I am not saying 'don't grow up'. Rather, I am saying that (1) eternal youth *is already* grown up, (2) we do not have to fight against the idea of growing up which just plays into the hands of the grown-ups, and (3) everyone is at all times possessed of eternal youth.

Please also note that I am not saluting 'young people', positioning them as saviours. *I am saying that, in a way, we are all young people.* Nor am I proposing a politics of 1968 nostalgia, something that Western people of my age – 75 at the time of writing – are prone to do. How amazing were the 1960s blahblahblah!

Making the moves I have indicated, means *wilfully and judiciously ignoring the division between youth and age.* Maybe it sounds better to say transcending that division. This is particularly difficult for psychoanalysts and especially Jungians to do. We are wedded to oppositional thinking. If you think of a youngster, you cannot avoid thinking of a geriatric. But what happens if we suspend disbelief, throw out our traditions, and say 'age is just a number'. This phrase – age is just a number – is something said by people defending relationships when there is a large age gap. But, here I am proposing it as a more general *Weltanschauung* or perspective.

So, youth: Youth is the Other to almost everything, including to youth itself. The British rock group The Who famously sang in their 1965 song 'Taking About My Generation' that they hoped to die before they got old.

Now to first half and second half of life. In Jungian psychology, much is made of the distinction between the first half of life and the second half of life.

Conventionally, the divide is the age of 40. In the first half of life, you are supposed to get established in a career, have a family, and indulge yourself as you wish. In the second half of life, you are supposed to become deep, reflective, and introspective. An introverted withdrawal from the world. You must start to approve being over doing.

I am sure you get the idea. It is widespread, way beyond the Jungian world. Think of the midlife crisis. The divide is often found in Indigenous cultures. But does it really hold up? I know that we like to make these separations, but I think they can lead to stasis and lack of vitality. For there is simply life! If you really want to sub-divide life, then the subdivisions are innumerable. For life is plural. I wrote a book called *The Plural Psyche* in 1989 and, even back then, I didn't care for developmental bifurcations. I coined the phrase 'personally eternal'. As Picasso protested: 'I don't develop; I am'.

Confucius, as it seems to me, may be regarded as a precursor of Jung's when it comes to the matter of the generations. In the *Analects*, one finds the famous passage, translated for me by a Chinese colleague:

At 30, I had established myself, at 40 I was no longer confused, at 50 I understood my fate in life, and at 60, I could take it in smoothly. At 70 I could follow my desires, because they no longer went against what is fitting.

I want to raise the Confucian question of respect for parents as well as respect for other older people. Why do we have to do this? Surely the experience of psychotherapy, in which accounts of parental abuse and lack of empathy proliferate, make us question this insistence that we value parents? Why must we 'honour' or father and mother? What is going on here? Let's look at 'the generations'.

We are obsessed with generational generalisations: silent generation, baby boomer, generation X, millennial, and generation Z. Please can we stop this awful algebra? It may be helpful if you are marketing and trying to sell a product. But I see it as profoundly anti-humane and anti-relational. Life is not organised in stages, phases, generations. And, to be honest, I think this whole stratified model is fundamentally Eurocentric, colonial, and white. I am uncomfortable with it.

Let's get back to eternal youth. It can be made into a pathology, including parthenogenetic fantasies of self-creation, hyper-spirituality, narcissistic self-centredness, and the object of homophobic vitriol.

But it also means being in a perpetually evolving state, redeemed by innocence and fuelled by vision of ceaseless new beginnings. When I think of examples of eternal youth, the list is endless. It is not a surprise that males are more prominent. They include Oscar Wilde's Dorian Gray, whose portrait painting aged, while the actual person remained the same and did not age at all.

Or King David is known for his slaying of Goliath, but less celebrated for his other penchants, such as stealing other men's wives and for 'warming' himself with young women.

Readers might like to look online for images of Donatello's sculpture, made in 1430–1440 and sometimes referred to as 'the homosexual David'.

And even the great Don Quixote himself is a *puer*, the one who invents both his own name *and* that of his beloved Dulcinea. The contemporary theme of self-invention is closely allied to that of eternal youth. It is part of what Zygmunt Bauman calls 'liquid modernity'.

You must dig a lot deeper to find the *puella aeterna*, and this is a patriarchal ploy, isn't it? As the Jungian analyst Susan Schwartz writes:

Puella is an aspect of the psyche that has been virtually ignored in the Jungian literature. She appears in the Western attitudes to be ever younger and thinner, devalued and stuck in the shadow of the patriarchy.

(2020, p. 89)

What has been written is generally horribly hostile. As if eternal youth in a woman is just not possible because of real-life bodily changes that depart from the female ideal appearance. Nevertheless, when Raquel Welch died, images appeared to catch a glimpse of the bodily *puella*.

Psychoanalysis has a huge problem with youth. The average age of the world's psychoanalysts is – well, I am not sure what it really is, though it is said to be very high. It seems that way, to be sure. Perhaps this is because young psychoanalysts so often present as older than they actually are. Not so many tattoos or piercings, if you see what I mean.

It is not easy to be a young analyst. Or even a young candidate. It is a taboo topic. This is carried over into practice where it is more usual to find the dyad being constituted as older analyst/younger patient. I think this is changing, but even though everyone remains interested in the psychological aspects of the trans-ference, the pattern persists. So analysts are not typically said to have paternal or maternal transferences to their younger male or female patients. Or, if they do, we just don't talk about it very much.

Being autobiographical for a moment, I was for some years the youngest Jun-gian analyst in the world. Although I was accepted for training first time and in my early twenties, leaks from the committee informed me that the question of my youth came up in the context of the limitations it would impose on the composition of my practice.

Similarly, in a controversial unpublished paper from 2018, titled 'The millen-nial female psychotherapist', Sissy Lykou recounted the prejudice and abuse she received from her older female colleagues. And when she gave the paper in public, her passionate celebration of the political achievements of her generation – for example, it was millennials who started Black Lives Matter – she was subjected to a degree of 'correction' by the exact same group of 'mother figures' that she was writing about.

Lykou surveyed the big national umbrella therapy organisations in Britain and, unsurprisingly, found that dramatically few of their members were under 40.

I guess Lykou would appreciate another line from The Who's 'Talking About My Generation' in which they asked people older than themselves why they didn't just fade away.

Following these professional aspects of my theme, I want to delve more deeply into what I see as a core conflict between eternal youth and 'maturity'. I call this 'the problematic of seeing both sides'. It is an approach to political conflict that radiates maturity – especially the maturity of the psychoanalyst – and its concomi-tant negotiatory approach to life. It is, if you like, taking the middle road in politics. Seeing all points of view. Being careful not to rush to judgement. Moderation. The golden mean. It is bullshit.

Psychoanalysts and all therapists tend to do that, for whatever reasons. The risk is, in Hamlet's words, that 'resolution is sicklied o'er with the pale cast of thought and we lose the name of action'.

You see, the problem is that middle of the road becomes middlebrow, meaning an absence of critical thinking. Or, worse still, what if middle of the road becomes middle aged? Sclerotic. Stuck. Constipated.

Are younger people doing any better? I would like to think so, but the honest answer is 'not really'. The facts are not very friendly for those like me who warm to younger people and what I hope to be their politics – progressive, radical, and relational.

For young people can definitely also be fascist, racist, climate change deniers, neoliberals, consumeristic and greedy, and sadistic. I struggled with this reality for some years before reaching the conclusion that it really cannot be helped that young people are disappointing and unreliable. You have to take the rough with the smooth. Or, so to speak, take the rough with the rough.

Where does psychoanalysis come in to all of these. I believe it remains so important that all the schools of therapy, not just psychoanalysis, twin their *analyses* of the social and political world with *activism* in relation to its problems. Analysis and activism.

Marx wanted to change the world not just understand it. In a sense, this as an attitude full of hope. Let's now do a brief detour into the idea of 'hope'. When I do workshops and talks, 'hope' is what lots of people want to talk about.

In our times, for people who regard themselves as progressive, as radical, as compassionate and egalitarian, as on the side of diversity and equity, even as leftist, *having hope is really difficult.*

Where is *our* hope going to come from, considering the state we are in, here and now, and outside in our fractured and suffering world? Climate crisis, pandemic, genocide, war, inequality, prejudice, and discrimination – and signs of fascism in many places.

Well, here, just for discussion, is an example of how eternal youth can express its interest and commitment in hope. I am thinking of Jan Palach, the young Czech student who self-immolated in protest of the Soviet invasion of his country in 1968.

I do not think it far-fetched to say that Palach and other self-immolators are expressing for us all a kind of *puer* hope that is, paradoxically, mature, grounded, and solid, despite its many contradictions. What people like Palach do *looks* despairing, pessimistic, and abnormal, but is it only that? Or is it not also an extreme example of what a normal individual possessed of eternal youth can contribute? Why do people do such things, if not in part motivated by eternal passion and hope? It is a denial of 'reality'. And it is an example of martyrdom as a form of heroic leadership. In Albert Camus' words: 'I rebel, therefore we exist'.

The hope-state I am identifying flirts with failure all the time. But as the great Sufi poet Rumi wrote in a translation provided by an Iranian colleague: 'Failure is the key to the door of the kingdom of heaven'.

What I will do now is to add risk to hope. *Risk.* Hope in politics involves *risk* to an incredible degree. The Latinate etymology of the English word risk is 'to run into danger'. Run, not walk.

This is the apparently 'immature' coupling I want to focus on: hope and risk. How taking risks carries and expresses hope. These are not opposites or counterpoints of each other; they are often indissoluble and that is where the challenge lies. Sometimes, the risk through which an individual puts themselves involves crossing a red line into the mysteries of self-sacrifice.

Do people – the *puers* and *puellas* – who take political risks on the authoritarian streets and squares of the world do so to link 'the spirit of the times' with 'the spirit of the depths' (to use Jung's words)?

Here are some further examples. I do not offer these snapshots in any way as an incitement or encouragement to political action. Political action flows, almost naturally and organically, from the actual existing state of affairs.

In 2021, a young Muslim British woman in her early twenties, Saffiyah Khan, reached out to a member of the English Defence League, our own White supremacist organisation (now defunct). She calmed the racist down because otherwise the police would arrest him. The photograph captured the popular imagination in Britain.

Then I think of the image of 21-year-old Palestinian paramedic, Razan Ashraf al-Najar, in Gaza just before she was shot. This was in 2018 not 2023–2025. She was running towards an injured person to give emergency first-aid.

Another image that comes to mind is that of the prison van taking Nelson Mandela and his colleagues from the courtroom to Robben Island in 1964. The prisoners give the clenched fist salute through the ventilation apertures. The trial was for planning violent revolution and committing sabotage. In his address to the court Mandela said this:

It [is] unrealistic and wrong for African leaders to continue preaching peace and non-violence at a time when the Government met our peaceful demands with force.

In Chapter 5, I explore the rationality of political violence.

As I come to the end of the chapter, and in support of my arguments herein, I just want to add that I think the present state of rock and roll music is fascinating. You can't get tickets for the Rolling Stones, or Bruce Springsteen, or Elton John, or Madonna, or Paul McCartney. Yes, this is nostalgia. Yes, this is delusive. But it is also a sign that the denial and refusal of aging is worth considering as something of value, not just as something stupid. When you attend a concert of one of these performers, your whole life flashes before your eyes. You have ONE life. It is the same life. It is to be considered holistically not as a series of stages or phases of development.

And no-one should go gently into the good night. Everyone can rave as their days come to a close.

I will conclude with anticipations of the problems this chapter raises.

It is a superficial text. But, as we are learning, depth is often hidden on the surface. If performativity means anything, it means that.

It is overly personal. Yes, it is. I know the material is a defence against fears of death. That is one of many angles I intend to pursue going forward.

Isn't the chapter a bit confused? In response, I turn to Lao Tzu who wrote – surely with tongue in cheek? – 'All are clear; I alone am clouded'

There is a lack of respect for the past and for ancestors in the chapter. True enough, but, to reverse the usual proposition, ancestors can become phantoms, and then they get in the way. Sure, the denial of the formative nature of our early years indicates a mother complex. But who here has no complexes? Jung said that 'every psychology is a personal confession'.

I will end with another very funny quote from Oscar Wilde's *The Picture of Dorian Gray*. It is sort of my own assessment and evaluation of my little piece:

> You must have a cigarette. A cigarette is the perfect type of a perfect pleasure. It is exquisite, and it leaves one unsatisfied. What more can one want?

I guess nowadays it would be a vape . . . .

References

Schwartz, S., (2020). *The absent father effect on daughters: Father desire, father wounds.* London and New York: Routledge.

Wilde, O., (1891/2000). *The picture of Dorian Gray*. Harmondsworth: Penguin Classics.

Chapter 4

Politically engaged art as inspiration in clinic and in culture – plus a reflection on the dangers of such a thing

Retrospective Introduction: This chapter was originally delivered as a lecture in 2022 in the same series of conferences in Brazil as the previous chapter. I wanted to find solid backup for the 'political turn' in the psychotherapies for which I had been a prominent advocate. As always in my work, I then found myself wanting to include a somewhat scathing critique of the idealisation of artists by therapists. It is a problem for my readers that I tend to embrace the destruction of my own work like this – but there it is.

Talking Points: People who want to broaden the scope of therapy to take in the social and political aspects of experience lack models to enable them to do it and to counteract the criticism they still encounter. In this chapter, political art is presented, providing such a model. But the dangers of idealising artists are also shown, including the awful matter of the famous Jungian analyst Joseph Henderson's sale of his patient Jackson Pollock's paintings and drawings brought to the analysis.

Introduction

The ideas in this chapter stem from the long-standing international project, spearheaded by Jungian analysts and therapists as it happens, to bring about a 'political turn' in the psychotherapies.

We know now that a political or social or cultural focus does not remove clinical work from the psychological field. To the contrary, it can inspire our healing work with individuals and small groups.

But I am, and want to be, more inflated than that! I want us to contribute, from our work and perspectives as therapists, to a revitalisation of our democracies: more liveliness, energy spirit, dynamism. More passion, fire, vigour, elan, vivacity, exuberance, bounce, verve, vim, pep. More brio and fizz. Vitality!

The main purpose of the chapter is to show how our ordinary clinical work can be inspired and challenged by some practices of politically and socially engaged art. The inspiration and challenge can be both direct and, as important perhaps, indirect: suggestive, heuristic, and a nudge. The art in question I have characterised, entirely pragmatically, and without academic rigour, under the snappy tag of 'agitprop'.

DOI: 10.4324/9781003598985-6

In headline form, the talk is about what 'we' – the analysts – can learn and adapt from 'them' – the artists – in connection with a few selected aspects of our work. Let's not forget that, after all, art can be a kind of therapy for society.

Despite these laudable examples, I am conscious of the danger of idealising art and artists or of forgetting that not all artists or art movements are progressive or leftist in their politics. Creation and destruction are twins. In this connection, Italian Futurism and its uncritical stance towards industrialisation and to fascism comes to mind.

On a personal level, writing this talk put me more in touch with what I lost and what I gained when making the move from running an experimental, progressive theatre group to becoming a therapist 50 years ago.

So I begin by saying that psychoanalysis and psychotherapy generally are projects that are discovering (or maybe rediscovering) that they are by nature political. In and out of session, we are often dealing with what I call 'the inner politician' (Samuels 1993, 2001, 2015).

Yet I believe we struggle to find ways of working *directly* as opposed to making symbolic interpretations of political, social, and cultural material as it arises in the clinical encounter. We seek to fully meet such material, in a responsible and relational manner (Samuels 1993, 2006). But we don't really know what to do when the dialogue gets political. Here, 'the artists' might help us.

For the fact is that we clinicians still experience the dead hand, the penumbra of criticism that this *Weltanschauung* or perspective is non-analytical and that the analyst will simply foist or impose his or her political views on the patient. When we psychoanalysts add a 'political turn' to our 'relational turn', aren't we acting *ultra vires*, beyond our authority or responsibility as analysts?

We know the answers to these criticisms, of course, but today there is not the time or context – or the need, perhaps – to rehearse them. Today is the moment to evolve ideas about how to do this psycho-political work in our offices as well as we can., work that links the spirit of the times with the spirit of the depths, in Jung's impressive words.

But let's recognise that psychoanalysis is not alone in making a discovery or rediscovery of a latent political mission. For example, Latin American liberation theology sets out to engage with societies experienced as unjust and destructive despite opposition from the Church establishment. And, germane to our theme today, so, too, have practitioners and theorists in the arts, despite criticisms from critics who regard the results as 'boring' and a betrayal, castigated as 'social realism', nothing to do with 'true' art.

Following these opening remarks, I'll move on to give a summary of what follows:

(1) I begin by looking at what can be learned at depth from a psychoanalytical adaptation of the theories of theatre practice developed by Bertolt Brecht.
(2) After that, I look at how feminist conceptual art theory and practice might add to our understanding of the analytical process.

(3) Then I work up an argument about what I call 'democratic art' (as found in the Ice Age) and how phenomena of this kind transform the range of clinical possibilities.

(4) The last section suggests what analysis might learn from the practice of dance theatre (*Tanztheater*) developed by Pina Bausch in Germany. Plus a delicious surprise!

Beyond empathy

You can call it the 'alienation effect, 'distanciation', or 'estrangement' – in German, *Verfremdungseffekt*. Brecht's much-studied attempts *to avoid empathic identification by the audience with the characters in a drama* seem at first sight to be utterly foreign to the values and practices of psychoanalysis. Empathy is our stock in trade, isn't it? Can you imagine relationality without empathy and a degree of identification with your patient? Surely 'analytical distanciation' would just be a return to the bad old days of neutrality and abstinence? Let's discuss these points for a while.

Brecht did not invent the idea of drama with a social conscience, but he developed the theatre as a space for social and political debate (Willett 1959/1964). The goal was to change the status and role of the audience leading to the creation of an 'active spectator', participating in an argument rather than identifying with a heroic character.

Now, there is talk of the 'active client', and even in my words the 'activist client'. It is a similar path to that of Brecht's.

In the old theatre, the centrality of the individual human being was taken for granted. But, for Brecht, the characters in a play are not heroic, but ordinary persons in a social context, engaged in an episodic narrative, often expressed – paradoxically – in lyrical language.

Brecht developed a raft of techniques to carry out the distanciation, including the use of placards on stage during the performance.

What does all this mean for clinical work?

I am proposing that Brecht's theories of theatre practice – alienation and distanciation in particular – are challenging and inspiring when the going in analysis gets political. If patient and analyst think together and argue together (whether they agree or not), then it still stays in the affective realm, still contributes to vitality. *Connection and distanciation function as two poles of the therapy project.* We connect and we also distance. The literature valorises connection and regards distance just as a professional task. Not, so, according to this Brechtian fancy of mine

The suggestion I am making is that patients, and their relationally involved analysts, start to practise 'ex-volvement', a neologism that implies standing outside the play of images, affects, and bodily processes that constitute the therapeutic (or any other) relationship. So the analysing couple might, in some circumstances (not all the time) reverse what they ordinarily do, *and distance themselves from emotion*. It is pretty extreme, actually, this suggestion of a deprivileging and radical reframing of the personal level. Affect, emotion, even intimacy itself – all become things to interrogate.

Here is a very brief clinical vignette of ex-volvement in the clinic. Yasmine is, let's say, Egyptian and a TV reporter on politics. I've disguised her identity. She came to analysis hoping that something might be done about her virginity at the age of almost 40. She chose a Jewish male analyst on purpose. On medical examination, it turned out that there was a physical problem as well as some psychological and cultural issues of great profundity and delicacy.

I do not think we could have worked through the emotional densities and cultural complexes within both of us, which you can quite easily imagine I should think, if, without naming it as such, if we had not been able to step back from affect and empathy. Instead, we entered actively into a kind of argument about fertility, femininity, and sexuality, mixed in with Arab-Jewish dynamics. We didn't name this two-way didactic flow in any way. We certainly didn't call it ex-volvement, nor was this the way we worked all the time. Maybe neither of us used placards, but we came very close to it.

The question I am introducing concerns the potential deceptiveness of the personal dimension. The personal can be misleading and deceptive. The personal often hides and leads to a wider issue. And that wider issue has the deepest of impacts on the personal. Here, I do not mean the collective unconscious. I mean, not to beat about the bush, the political world and the society wherein the analysis takes place.

Brecht's ideas are useful for providing a backup for the temporary avoidance of the personal and the highlighting of the political. He says to the clinician 'Follow the story, follow the argument – don't only get caught up in the human drama'.

Now, I move onto the next section of the talk, where I look at some feminist art practices that might also inspire and challenge the analyst.

I just want to add that what I said about Brecht-influenced analysis also works pretty well in connection with supervision.

Brides against the bomb

I will turn now to a reflection on feminist conceptual art practices, which, especially between 1970 and 1985, performed an alchemical *opus* or work on images and experiences of the everyday and familiar. There was a focus on the ordinary events and processes of the female body, such as menstruation or giving birth, showing how their everyday, quotidian nature was also something both special, and especially conflictual, and at both the individual and cultural levels (Parker and Pollock 1987). Isn't this what analysts want to do – work with the ordinary sacred, the sacred ordinary?

One particular piece of feminist performance art from 1983 comes to mind – Brides Against the Bomb. It was staged at a Campaign for Nuclear Disarmament festival at Glastonbury in England. Many issues are 'got' in this performance such as women's relation to the public sphere, international relations and 'defence'.

(In passing, I ask if the word 'defence' isn't the most mendacious in the political vocabulary. Think of the IDF, the Israel Defence Force . . .)

Anyway, the piece satirises marriage as the 'happiest day' of a woman's life, and everyone gets excited at the making of a 'good marriage' to 'a man from the Ministry of Defence', as the catalogue essay for the performance stated.

In the performance, a woman is then married to a missile. 'Missiles are not a necessity but there as part of a bad marriage'.

It's been my experience that many patients, not only women, find themselves saying things like 'I am married to a missile'. You don't have to stimulate or foment such metaphoric imagery, though sometimes people dream it, but it can be hard to know what to do with it.

A note on men

For example, when working with many men, I find much the same is happening. The male patient becomes aware of the wider and deeper significances of his ordinary body. This may concern everything to do with fathering and fatherhood, including when the patient – straight, gay, bi, trans, and non-binary – is in a pre-father phase, contemplating paternity. Equally, a number of male patients want to explore their feelings and ideas about choosing *not* to father, or of not being able to father, where this is desired. Men and women choosing not to have children may be one of the most interesting queer developments in Western societies.

Men in Western societies are assaulted by a battery of images and narratives about the malign nature of the male body, in contexts of domestic or child sexual abuse. It is hard to find images that show off 'man' in a more positive, or at least more nuanced manner. Hence, it remains problematic to find images of benign paternal erotics that don't degenerate into delusive idealisation or even caricature.

Perhaps this is one reason why, worldwide, according to my research, so many more women than men go to therapy. Masculinity and what is perceived as vulnerability are strange bedfellows. That was why a campaign to get men to go to 'talking therapy' used a suggestive image of a chap with to footballs in his hands and the caption 'I had the balls to go to counselling'.

By the way, I am also interested in and have written about why so few men become analysts and therapists, and it is important to ask those who have why they chose these professions. That is, sadly, for another time.

From this contemporary excursion into 'men in/and therapy', via a consideration of feminist art practices, I now turn my attention to the long ago.

Democratic art, democratic analysis

In this section of the chapter, I review what I am calling 'democratic art' with the idea of a more 'democratic psychoanalysis' in mind. The aim remains that of the whole talk: to review some engaged art practices whether of direct utility or of heuristic and suggestive interest to the clinician.

I am interested in the ways in which psychoanalysis and the psychotherapies have, perhaps unwittingly, excluded a sort of clinical lumpenproletariat, including those 'hard-to-reach' patients. Many of these patients are men, as I was saying just now.

So it is with democratic art. In the Ice Age, 40,000 years ago, something recognisable as art gradually appeared in Europe. It was sophisticated and intentional, involving highly developed cognition and applied imagination. Curators of exhibitions (Cook 2013) of such art asked: why do people make art at all? Why do they shape figures to look like women and men? Why do they record their ordinary daily lives? Why do they make symbol-laden art that is not based on 'reality', like the famous figurine of the Lion Man?

Humans have needed to make art, just as they have needed to make religion or politics. My suggestion is that patient and analyst alike can be inspired by the democratic realisation that imagination and creativity are not reserved for the Special Ones whose culture makes it easier for them to 'do' analysis. There should be no psychoanalytical equivalent of the 1% in the economic sphere!

This means that there are some significant challenges herein to how many of us envision the work. We value the therapeutic alliance, but could it not be said that there is a secret elitism in this core concept? Even something esoteric? Something that reflects the micro-politics of power and hierarchy within the analytical encounter? Who is deemed – and by whom – to have entered the Lodge of the therapeutic alliance, where the analyst (supposedly) is already waiting and ready?

Of course, as we know from studies of 'failures' in therapy and analysis, often the clinician is not actually there, occupying their part of the therapeutic alliance, stretching out their hand in love and acceptance. This is where the blocks and problems of the clinician come into play, and it is not talked about enough.

The parallel I want to draw is with the professionalisation of art, so to speak, since the Ice Age. Back then, maybe it was ritual, part of religion. Similarly, despite its roots in ubiquitous healing practices, analysis and therapy are now professionalised, administered by the membership of the secret society of the therapeutic alliance. The story of art inspires us to question ever more deeply our Masonic exclusivity – our *déformation professionnelle*. Time does not permit the full exploration of the damage done to healing therapy by excessive professionalisation, regulation, and bureaucracy. It is maddening, actually. It is too damn hard to train, and too damn hard to get therapy, unless you are rich. Someone once wrote of the role of the rich husband in the populating of therapy trainings. Yes, a generalisation. And, yes, a good point.

The moving relationship

Enter the body. I'd like to share what I've learned as a therapist from the dance theatre work of Pina Bausch and the Wuppertal Tanztheater. Bausch was a great artistic transmogrifier and another alchemist of the psychology and psychopathology of the everyday life we have all experienced in the flesh and in the soul: the longing for love, the incurable sadism, the crazy unpredictability and unfairness of life's relational mix of intimacy and isolation, and the *jolie laide* (beautiful ugly) nature of the world. Alchemists have always smelled out the gold in the shit and the shit in the gold.

In this clip from Pina Bausch's piece Cafe Muller – for which I will give the link in a moment, that you can type into your browser – we see something of the ritual and repetitive circumambulation of the agony and the ecstasy of relationship, of any relationship. We see a kinaesthetic practice, grounded in the entire body, the entire being, of the dancers on stage. Isn't it also an emblem of what happens to the two people in analysis, we could even say to the two artists doing their analysis together.

I hope you will watch with your bodies as well as your eyes.

https://www.youtube.com/watch?v=VCQ29EUwvrI

And here is the promised delicious surprise. Maria Pages is the consummate political Flamenco artist. Just look at the gender politics of this artistic performance. Again, I give the link:

https://www.youtube.com/watch?v=uGoRIvjJeWo

The dangers of therapists idealising artists

Let me begin with the story of Dr Joseph Henderson and Jackson Pollock. Henderson was a notable first-generation Jungian analyst who introduced the idea of the cultural unconscious which later morphed into the theory of cultural complexes.

In 1930–1940, Henderson treated the abstract expressionist pioneer Pollock in the Veteran's Hospital in New York. Henderson noted that Pollock was mure, psychotic, and alcoholic. Pollock brought to the analysis 83 drawings and paintings. He had Jungian interests and knew that Jungian analysts like to work with visual material. He works were not done explicitly for the analysis.

After Joseph Henderson left for San Francisco, Pollock went to another Jungian analyst, Violet de Laszlo.

In 1970, Henderson sold these works. There was a court case in 1971 in which it was alleged Henderson had no right to sell the works because they were confidential clinical material. The judge found him not guilty but heavily criticised him. The works were resold in the 1980s.

Throughout, Henderson used these pictures to illustrate lectures in which he discussed Pollock's mother and also schizophrenia in Pollock. In this respect, he more or less stays in role as a professional psychiatrist/analyst. (Pollock was not famous at the time of the analysis, by the way.)

Then Henderson made a startling admission. He said that he had a 'countertransference to the symbols'. Not clear when he developed this or what his countertransference was to the patient. But he was clear it interfered with his judgement over the drawings. This interests me. Was it an idealising countertransference? If it was, then it leads to many interesting reflections about the relationship of analysts/

therapists and artists. Have therapists generally idealised artists? If so, then, as idealisation and envy can go together, is there an envy of the artist generally in the therapy field? Maybe we envy the Bohemianism of the artist, who are like we therapists used to be?

Anyway, artists seem to very special from the therapy perspective? I played a trick on an audience when I was first developing these ideas. I said that I had been invited by a banker patient to visit the trading floor. I said how interesting it had been to see him in action. Consternation on the part of the audience at these egregious boundary violation.

Then I asked who in the room had been to an exhibition of their patient's paintings? Or a poetry reading? Or read a book by the patient? Lots and lots of hands went up. This showed to me that the idealisation I am writing about was alive and kicking.

I'd like to ask the analysts and therapists reading this to think about how they have responded to the patient or client who is an artist. Has it affected how you work?

References

Cook, J., (2013). *Ice age art: Arrival of the modern mind.* London: British Museum Publications.

Parker, R. and Pollock, G., (1987). *Framing feminism: Art and the Women's Movement 1970–1985.* London and New York: Pandora.

Samuels, A., (1993). *The political psyche.* London and New York: Routledge.

Samuels, A., (2001). *Politics on the couch: Citizenship and the internal life.* London and New York: Karnac.

Samuels, A., (2006). Working directly with political, social and cultural material in the therapy session. *In:* L. Layton, N. Hollander and S. Gutwill, eds. *Psychoanalysis, class and politics: Encounters in the clinical setting.* London and New York: Routledge.

Samuels, A., (2015). *A new therapy for politics?* London and New York: Karnac.

Willett, J., (1959/1964). *The theatre of Bertolt Brecht.* London: Shenval Press.

Part II

Politics

Chapter 5

The rationality of political violence

Retrospective Introduction: I have given this chapter on political violence as a lecture or experiential workshop many times since first starting work on it in 2015. It usually produces a strong reaction, and I discuss my anxiety about writing like this in the chapter. I am preparing it for publication in August 2024 when the death toll in Gaza is over 40,000 and Israeli society is in a state of collapse. For me, the strong part of the material is that it continuously doubles back on itself as I am confronted with the enormity of what I find myself believing.

Talking Points: Most psychological writing on political violence has the secret aim of bringing it to an end. Rarely, do we find support and praise for political violence. With great care and sensitivity, such support and praise are mustered in this chapter.

It may seem offensive and unnecessarily provocative to offer a chapter that asks questions on the potential value of political violence.

I am going to talk about the present-day *fascination* of the idea and image of political violence for people – like us – who do not carry out political violence, though may well have experienced it. Political violence takes place on the right and on the left. Political violence is an outcrop of a desire to end oppression. Political violence is an attempt to impose a *Weltanschauung* or specific perspective on everyone. Political violence fills our dreams and even our fantasies.

I am therefore talking about why I, and I suppose many people here are fascinated by fundamentalism when it turns to violence. In fact, I would say political violence, as an image, as an image, as an idea, as a Gestalt, is a powerful current *fascinans*, in Rudolph Otto's theological language. Otto compares being in the grip of the *fascinans* to being in a Dionysian state of mind. No wonder we are drawn in.

I have had a life-long fascination with one of the most celebrated acts of political violence: the assassination of Gaius Julius Caesar in 44 BCE. We'll return to Caesar later.

There is also a range of clinical motivations. One of my very first clients in 1972 was a member of the Angry Brigade. He is dead now so I can speak relatively freely. Britain's Angry Brigade was equivalent of the Baader–Meinhof Group or the Red Brigades, or the Tupamaros or the Weathermen. Although it became British lefty-chic to call them the 'slightly cross brigade', it was an important experience

DOI: 10.4324/9781003598985-8

to dialogue in therapy with someone who was talking about setting off bombs. My then supervisor – and hence I – was influenced by Thomas Szasz's ethics of psychoanalysis in which the business of an analyst is solely to analyse. This made it impossible for me to contemplate doing anything about it.

Anyway, Phil left therapy after a while and, to this day, remains one of only two clients in 44 years of practice who have gone off owing me money. In his case, the huge sum of £15. (The other one was an Israeli who chose me because I was Jewish and then discovered I was one of the founders of Jews for Justice for Palestinians. No prizes for guessing what happened then.)

So, over the years, I have worked with other clients whose attitudes to political violence do not resemble those of most liberal citizens. These clients chose me because of my writings, allegiances, and engagements. It was rarely an accident. This business of therapist selection continues to be important in all contexts – we don't discuss it enough, I think.

Whatever I have heard much in sessions about why 9/11 served the Americans right, about the role of Western foreign and military policies in the rise of ISIS/Daesh, about the biases of the Western media – for example, in relation to the bombing of Belgrade or the genocide in Gaza. I am not saying I am the only therapist who has worked with such clients, nor, at this point, whether I disagreed or agreed with what I was hearing. Such a simplistic report would not represent the relational and responsible approach to working with politics in the clinical setting that I have evolved over the years.

Exercise 1: Anyone reading this have experience with this kind of client? How did it go? Have you had or do you have clients and patients active in, or sympathetic to acts of political violence? How did it make you feel? OR, if no client referred to political violence, where there times when you considered they were engaged with the topic secretly or unconsciously?

I was very anxious about my choice of topic. In one way, this is surprising, because I have previously written a lot (Samuels 1989, 2001, 2015) about the integration of personal aggression in the developmental contexts of masculinity and the father and also as a gendered path of individuation for women. But this is less about violence in the family, or about men and their violent domination of society, or about women's engagement with violence, as victims and as actors (real or imaginary). It is about *collective political violence*. To be honest, I have found it emotionally difficult to imagine speaking with any kind of authority on this topic despite some small direct and personal experience of it. I am being pushed by my research outside of my therapist's comfort zone to take up an issue that regularly presents itself to other disciplines as an ethical dilemma.

The paper now falls into two sections: (1) a general exploration of political violence and (2) a discussion of how to turn the tap of political violence off once it has been turned on, including a suggestion for a politically active imagination involving violence.

A general exploration of political violence

The world is frighteningly coloured by the naked is-ness of political violence. It is hard to pick one's way through its embodied omnipresence, even if we are sometimes told – counterintuitively – that human violence is actually decreasing. Tell that the refugees and enforced migrants. Just recently, we can consider: Israel/Palestine, Egypt, Ukraine, Congo, Nigeria, Turkey, Tunisia, Syria, Iraq, the American southern states, and Paris, Berlin, Brussels, London, and Manchester. Truly, all over the United States at this very moment. U.S. Presidential Elections are shot through with violence.

My worry is that, by raising the problem of political violence, I might be perceived as making an inflated claim, either on my own behalf or on behalf of my profession, of offering to solve, or to salve, our terrifying situation. Yes, this possibility has worried me deeply.

What I am trying to do, and I know it is a little ambitious, is to probe the psychological limits of political violence. Political violence may be seen as the ultimate expression of passion in politics and, whether we like it or not, of an 'ethics of conviction' (to use Weber's term). But, on the other hand, political violence has the effect of halting whatever conversations might be going on and hence may be judged as an abject failure of politics. Be that as it may it is almost impossible to divorce politics and political violence. Exploring this matter has been a preoccupation of mine, a personal journey, for what seems like forever.

My questions about political violence are not at all new ones, particularly not when asked in overtly political settings. What definitions of political violence are of the most use to us? The chapter is intended as a sort of ongoing definition. When, if ever, is violent political behaviour justified in politics? If such violence is sometimes justified, then in what circumstances and carried out by which agents? Is political violence an unexceptional response to direct and indirect colonialism, as Fanon (1961) wrote in *The Wretched of the Earth*? Is an inevitable rebuttal of class prejudice, economic inequality, oppression, and frustration, in our era, a condemnation of austerity and neoliberal conceptions of the market and of capitalism? Is political violence justified as 'the last resort'? Or is it always a bad thing? How does political violence compare to war, especially wars claimed to be defensive?

All of these are important and complicated questions that have been much worked on in academic, activist, and faith circles. But I am a depth psychologist, and not a political theorist, so my take will be more specifically psychological.

My anxiety also stems from what happened to a far more important figure than I am, when he was accused of participating in and promoting political violence. This was one of my own heroes, the Palestinian academic and advocate for peace and dialogue in Israel/Palestine: Edward Said. Said was photographed participating in a ritual stone throwing at a far-off Israeli watch-tower on the Lebanon border. Responding to the furore that ensued, Said later stated that in one moment, understandably exploited by his enemies, 35 years of work for justice and peace had been thrown away. They even withdrew his invitation to give the 2001 Sigmund Freud Memorial Lecture in Vienna.

Analysts and therapists are used to digging out root causes and hidden meanings. How could they possibly be so crude as to take sides in a violent social or political dispute, let alone join in? But what if the crudity here lies in rising peacefully above the fray? Engaging with political violence raises serious problems for liberal individualists whose commitment is to keeping the peace and remaining balanced and even-handed. Moreover, in the world of analysis and therapy, the majority of us seem to have assumed that non-violence is the desirable default position in politics. Gradually, over around 40 years of being an analyst, I have come to see that even-handedness and non-violence may be rather elitist and Olympian perspectives to take up. They may carry a narcissistic shadow that claims maturity and a seasoned attitude to the real world. Such claims may simply not be valid. So I worry about the so-called balanced view that some colleagues take towards political situations in which there is no such balance to be found. Isn't this our very own 'analytic violence'?

These problems for analysts and therapists have been addressed incisively by Renos Papadopoulos (1998):

> Whenever we address violence, as mental health professionals, we are bound to locate it in the context of the pathology-health polarity. Violence . . . will invariably end up being pathologized; that is, violence will not be associated with health.
>
> (p. 45)

I can illustrate some aspects of our problem that Papadopoulos identified by recounting what happened when I asked the members of four separate online discussion lists in the analysis and therapy areas for assistance in finding literature that engaged the question of political violence with an open mind as to its usefulness and value. What I got back was around 20 references to *non-violence*, passive resistance, and Ghandi.

However, over many years reading and re-reading, I have not found the literature in favour of absolute non-violence in politics to be particularly convincing, though I respect it (can even love it) and can identify with what is being expressed. In part, any kind of Jungian background actually undermines one's confidence in absolute non-violence. Here I have been massively influenced by the psychological realism of James Hillman's book on war (2004) and Luigi Zoja's book on violence (2009). Without resorting to biologism or evolutionary theory, Hillman and Zoja's imaginative and scholarly treatments of the topic have made the unwavering adoption of non-violence as the only possible psychological stance very difficult. So, I don't find theories of absolute non-violence helpful.

But neither do I find romantic, artistic, and anarchist (or nihilist) glorifications of violence to be of assistance when bringing therapy thinking into an engagement with political violence. I certainly understand what Bakunin meant when he said 'The urge to destroy is a creative urge'. But I don't think this perspective or this language works well for us today. It feels a bit obvious.

Similarly, important ideas, such as those promoted by Zizek (2009) concerning the deep and universal presence of state violence, and the internalisations we all make of that, don't help us much when confronted as individuals with the problem of political violence.

I'll conclude the first part of the chapter with a brief discussion of what I call the 'Mandela-Ghandi hybrid'. I find this political fantasy to be a troubling sign of a massive psycho-political problem.

In a nutshell, I have often found that people with average to little knowledge of the South African situation regard Nelson Mandela as having followed the path of non-violence. Yet, in 1964, at his trial for planning violent revolution and committing sabotage, he stated:

It [is] unrealistic and wrong for African leaders to continue preaching peace and non-violence at a time when the Government met our peaceful demands with force.

Many people who today celebrate South Africa's liberal constitution find it difficult to accept that the carefully and tightly controlled and targeted tactics of the African National Congress's military wing – *Umkhonto we Sizwe* (Spear of the Nation, known as MK) played a significant part in bringing down the Apartheid regime and Mandela to power. And they forget the key role of Fidel's soldiers.

Let me give a little summary of where we have got to so far:

I started by reviewing my anxieties over this material. I imagine you can see now what I feared: that I would be badly misunderstood as advocating violence, and of departing from the balanced, even-handed and reflective position that an analyst should take: one that holds the tension of the opposites. I have also mentioned approaches that I respect but do not think will help us get past the ghettoization of violence that so often results from them: I referred to both the stances of non-violence and anarchism, and also to the theory of state violence.

Turning the tap on and off

In the second section, I want to make the ambivalence and agitation I feel about this crucial topic more conscious and move on to a discussion of what I call 'turning the tap on and off', meaning the tap of political violence.

So, how do we turn off the tap of political violence after it has been on for a time? Can we in fact do this? We certainly can't control the flow of things when violence enters the political picture. Hannah Arendt put it like this, in an article in the *New York Review of Books* in 1969:

If the goals of political violence are not achieved rapidly, the result will not merely be defeat but the introduction of the practice of violence into the whole body politic. Action is irreversible.

Yet even Hannah Arendt noted:

Violence, contrary to what its prophets try to tell us, is a much more effective weapon of reformers than of revolutionists.

And she quotes Conor Cruise O'Brien with approval: 'Violence is sometimes needed for the voice of moderation to be heard'.

Indeed, despite her worries over the widespread political violence in the United States and Europe in the 1960s, Arendt is ever careful to state and restate that political violence may be conceived of as 'rational'. I believe she would agree that sometimes, for anything to really matter, for example, for full attention to be paid to the situation of African Americans or Black Britons. *Sometimes it takes a riot.*

If we look around, we see that examples of rational political violence abound and have always done so. I find mages of the uprising in the Warsaw Ghetto in 1943 unbearably moving, as well as those of national liberation struggle, including that of Palestine today.

In the British Museum, there is a striking image of a damaged head of Julius Caesar in and now is the time to re-introduce Julius Caesar who was assassinated well over 2,000 years ago. Caesar, as you will recall, had already been Dictator since 49 BCE and Dictator for Life since the month before the assassination in 44 BCE. Though he had declined to be crowned as a king, the suspicion was that this was only a temporary holding back. As the celebrated British classical historian Mary Beard writes:

> The assassination was partly motivated by self-interest and disgruntlement. But the assassins were also defending the importance of Roman republican traditions going back to the expulsion of the Tarquin monarchs. The message would be that the Roman people had been liberated.

> (2015, p. 396)

In the play *Julius Caesar,* Shakespeare illumines both the individual and the civic dynamics of this epic moment. Brutus and the other conspirators claim that the justification for Caesar's assassination was that Caesar was politically ambitious:

> *Brutus:* As Caesar loved me, I weep for him;
> as he was fortunate, I rejoice at it;
> as he was valiant, I honour him:
> but, as he was ambitious I slew him.

And even arch-rhetorician Mark Anthony seems to agree that, *if* Caesar was ambitious (and Anthony will prove he was not), then it was a very bad thing:

> *Anthony:* The noble Brutus
> Hath told you Caesar was ambitious;
> If it were so, it was a grievous fault,
> And grievously hath Caesar answer'd it.
> *(All quotes are from Act 3, Scene 2)*

Let's play with this a little, in the spirit of active imagination, as if we are in a political clinic. Let's take a relational self-state perspective on this major act of political violence. Could it be possible that each citizen, each of us, can be both Brutus *and* Julius Caesar? Tyrant and liberator, liberator and tyrant? As in perpetrator and victim, victim and perpetrator.

Now, I would not seriously suggest that active imagination could be a mainstream tool for the achievement of political harmony. Yet, after the events in cities and countries over the last 25 years, many have commented on how hard it was to identify with the suffering of others at the hands of IS or Daesh. These Others were further away from the Western heartlands – in Beirut, Turkey, or Syria, for instance. My little active imagination is directly aimed at widening the possible scope of our *political* identifications.

Could we possibly try to construct some kind of very modest programme or set of thought experiments that would enable people in the West and North to develop a less absolute and critical and a more empathic and mirroring stance towards the political violence that 'they' (the Islamists, the Russians) do towards 'us', the peace-loving Western democrats that 'we' are supposed to be, even now?

What if we did try to identify with the wishes, hopes, and concerns of those living in the suburbs/banlieues of Paris or in Molenbeek in Brussels? These people are seething with resentments. I am asking: what is the political desire of these communities? What would they put on their very own list of political action points?

I don't know for sure, of course, but I want us to imagine what their list of political desires might be like.

I truly mean *their own desires*, not the list of desires of liberal and humane politicians and journalists, or the list of policies and actions of national Governments. Not what 'we' would like people with many seething resentments to do, but what 'they' might do or consider doing. Not even what they want 'us' to do, but what they want to do themselves, for themselves.

Some items of political desire would involve the mobilisation of the mainstream and official representative agencies speaking for those who are seething. The Muslim Establishment, if you like. Some would involve the full range of non-violent direct action such as demonstrations, even strikes or similar acts in the general area of labour and employment.

But, whether one likes it or not, and I damn well don't like it, this list would, if it is honestly and realistically compiled, have to include political violence. This is why the people we call 'terrorists' have such extensive support in their communities. There is in Nietzsche's words, 'a whole tremulous realm of subterranean revenge, inexhaustible and insatiable in outbursts'.

Political violence will more than likely be there, on this Indigenous, home-grown list. Because this list is 'their' list, not 'our' liberal and humane list. And their list is the key list, the most articulate of the real situation, the least heard, the most painful and uncomfortable to hear, the list we most need to hear and to bear. Don't preach about violence or about non-violence without taking time to imagine what this list of political desires from the *banlieues*, ghettos, and slums might be saying to you.

Exercise 2: You are a young Jihadist planning a bombing. Why?

Concluding thoughts

There is, of course, much more I could have said. I could have talked about the sexualised aspects of political violence, its tendencies towards sadomasochism, and its gendered and ethnic variations. But there hasn't been space.

I felt it to be important to dissect the monolith of political violence in an attempt to get beyond a blanket 'liberal' condemnation of them that is designed to avoid confronting what political violence tells us. Often, this condemnation is just a part of self-soothing political ritual for those in the West who are exposed to political violence, mostly on television. That was why a key strand of the talk consisted of a frank discussion of the utility of political violence, coupled with an exploration of the possibilities and limitations of non-violent political action.

Whatever, I hope you will agree, it matters a lot what our attitude to political violence is, it matters a lot how we relate to the idea of political violence, it matters a lot that analysts and therapists join in discussions about political violence. It matters because political violence in all its many forms is perhaps the key collective issue of our times. That is why I decided to speak on this matter.

Exercise 3: Please discover or develop your own fantasies of committing political violence in support of a cause that is important to you. If you have had such experiences, please reflect on them.

References

Arendt, H., (1969). Reflections on violence. *New York Review of Books*, 27 February.
Beard, M., (2015). *SPQR: A history of ancient Rome*. London: Profile.
Fanon, F., (1961). *The wretched of the Earth*. Harmondsworth: Penguin.
Hillman, J., (2004). *A terrible love of war*. New York and London: Penguin.
Mandela, N., (1964). *I am prepared to die*. Houghton, MI: Nelson Mandela Centre of Memory; Nelson Mandela Foundation [Accessed 2 November 2015].
Papadopoulos, R., (1998). Destructiveness, atrocities and healing: Epistemological and clinical reflections. *Journal of Analytical Psychology*, 43, 455–477.
Samuels, A., (1989). *The plural psyche: Personality, morality and the father*. London and New York: Routledge.
Samuels, A., (2001). *Politics on the couch: Citizenship and the internal life*. London: Karnac.
Samuels, A., (2015). *A new therapy for politics?* London: Karnac.
Zizek, S., (2009). *Violence*. London: Profile.
Zoja, L., (2009). *Violence in history, culture, and the psyche*. New Orleans, LA: Spring Journal Books.

Chapter 6

The role of the individual in progressive politics – possibilities and impossibilities of 'making a difference'

Retrospective Introduction: Working with activists who often spoke of feeling burned out, and contemplating my own political trajectory, I found myself oscillating between despair and something more positive. What is the role of an individual? So, without chucking away ideas about context and belonging (and my own pet idea of 'social spirituality', I wanted to see what could be done to bring the idea of the individual to the centre of progressive political process. It gradually became clear that Jung was both an aid and a problem with his positioning of the individual in relation to society. Yet his overall intent was important. The paper was originally published in 2014 and the idea of 'political style' has been found useful in many situations over the intervening years, currently in an NHS context. As often in my work, I end up critiquing ideas that have not found mainstream or majority acceptance – in this case, that people live in particular contexts. It is always an odd feeling for me to be having a go at things that only relatively few believe in.

Talking Points: We live in a groupish era. Everything has a context. Far from encouraging individuality, this Zeitgeist crushes it. When it comes to progressive politics, there is a massive intellectual inhibition on valuing the contribution an individual can male. Using Jung and Albert Camus, the contrary case is made. On the way, Jung's ideas on the individual, a centrepiece of his work, are refashioned for the twenty-first century.

When presenting this material in lecture or workshop format, I begin by playing Ennio Morricone's theme music from the spaghetti western *The Good, the Bad and the Ugly.* (Leone 1966)

The Man with No Name, the Clint Eastwood character, is the consummate individual; hence, he needs no name. The direct and interactive approach of this chapter (as in the preceding one) is maintained also by a series of experiential exercises. I am sure that this article could only have been written by a man in his seventies, enabled by time and its ravages to be less cautious and correct.

It may seem perverse to call for a return to the notion of the individual in progressive political theorising at a time when so many bemoan the collapse of social and communal ties in Western societies. Families don't go bowling any more – and

DOI: 10.4324/9781003598985-9

you (the author) want *more* individualism when everyone is already looking after 'Number 1', in an ethos of *sauve qui peut*?

I hope I may appear less weird if I say that, in a nutshell, I am wondering if there is still a place in radical politics for *individualism* and *the idea of the individual*. My enquiry is into whether or not there can be a theoretical backup to ideas of 'making a difference' via individual entry into political activism. This is a rather emotive topic, as I have encountered it in the clinical situation and in workshops under the general rubric of 'Political Clinics'. Citizens may want to make a difference, and they know that, in order to do so, they must join with other like-minded citizens. In which case, what will become of their individuality? Even actively engaging in political activism cannot really silence doubts about the limits of personal responsibility. Then there are questions of impact and efficacy. Clients speak about these themes, ruefully and sometimes cynically: 'everything seems so complex', so unending. I confess that it was very hard to write this. It came from an inner place and is quite contrary to what I usually think in my roles as a political consultant, activist, and academic. In those situations, how many times have I explained that there is no such thing as an individual and that individuals are socially constructed, even when they believe themselves to be autonomous and inner-directed entities?

I still think the political world and the social class that an individual inhabits are vitally important. In addition, we need also to move beyond the social and the human to consider what is being developed in terms of ecopsychology and eco-criticism (Rust and Totton 2012) – but it is the *experience* of being an individual that interests me at the moment, no matter how illusory that might be on an intellectual plane. Here, much of the contemporary sociological project on the rise of a self-invented identity, cut off from traditional contexts, strikes me as experience-distant, notwithstanding the many ways in which it is challenging and useful. As Layton (2013) has shown, sociologists today, such as Giddens (1991) or Beck and Beck-Gernsheim (2002), have reached the conclusion that the individual needs to be better theorised, though this is usually in order to make a deeper and more fecund contribution to their own discipline of sociology. Nevertheless, the realisation that subjectivity and the individual need to be understood with reference to the social sciences chimes with my project.

Crucially, Layton (2013) has explained how ideas about individuals, collectives, culture, contexts, and constructions have themselves got a particular history and are themselves subject to the relativising they propose for individuals. Reading some of this literature, it has occurred to me that the 'sociological individual' of the past 25 years could be summarised as being interested mainly in her or his life and issues, and not in the life of the times and its issues. As Layton put it:

Rose (1989), for example, has critiqued the work of Giddens and Beck, arguing that 'individualization' has not just been about the expansion of autonomy to an ever-widening portion of the population, but rather has been about the creation and extension of a certain version of subjectivity and autonomy.

(Layton 2013, p. 139)

The problem I am addressing is that the sociologically perceived narcissism and plasticity of that kind of individual actually depotentiates her or him as far as political activism is concerned. I am sure that this is not deliberate but, rather, inadvertent. Hence, in a fresh effort to bridge the gap between the self-invented individual and his or her entry into political activism and engagement, I introduce later in the chapter some material about 'political styles', showing how political activity itself may be explored from an individualistic perspective. The hope is that this kind of contribution will lead to a reconfiguration of 'individual' and 'collective' or 'social'. Then we might be in a position to revisit in contemporary terms the notion of 'organic solidarity' in a society as opposed to 'mechanical' solidarity, to use Durkeim's (1893/1997) words.

Beyond context

In academic discourse – and also in politics, whether mainstream, progressive, or reactionary – the idea of the individual *tout seul* simply does not pass muster these days. Context and construction are all: family, community, society, culture, and nation. This contemporary discourse stresses that individuals are embedded and constructed by and in social relationships, communal networks, task-oriented groups, and ecosystems. This isn't wrong, of course, but has the potential of an individual to contribute actively to what happens in the collective been underestimated by this set of assumptions? Is there an overreaction in which the desire to be intellectually correct has meant that we now refer to contexts within which individuals exist – but not to those individuals themselves?

Among the psychoanalytic writers who most vividly foregrounded the question of the relations between the individual and the collective was Jung (1875–1961). His writings are peppered with iterations of this question. My proposal is that, if Jungian psychology could refashion its approach to the individual, then *it could become a source of support and inspiration to embattled citizens whose experience of their battles is often that they are in it on their own.* Jung was one of the first to explain that 'there is a human desire to "belong", to conform, to relinquish individual responsibility and find a king, a dictator, a boss who will tell you what to do' (Helena Bassil-Morozow, personal communication, July 2012).

Exercise 1. We can all think of individuals who have 'made a difference'. Sometimes, you may feel you have yourself made a difference. Think of times when you personally as an individual have made a difference in some situation or other, whether an important situation or something relatively less important. What happened?

Has the academy gone too far in stressing the contingent and context-bound nature of an individual person? Are the professors saying 'There's no such thing as an individual'? What does it mean that Cushman (1995) titled a book *Constructing the Self, Constructing America*? Is the consensus that the idea of individuals is just another bit of constructivism? Is Levinas right, with his ethical stress on alterity, on the other, on someone other than the individual (Levinas 1995)? I think it is important to explore these questions because many of the horrid conformist features of contemporary Western societies rest on the idea that 'you belong'. This easily becomes 'you *should* belong' and then slips into some variant of 'you belong *to us*'. Society does its bit to get us all to stay in context. Joining the system is more or less compulsory.

The opposites of constructionism and contextualism are essentialism, universality, and eternity. As some Jungian commentators, including myself (Samuels 1993), have noted, these can lead to a kind of archetypal determinism' which, in its own way, can be massively damaging to the idea of the individual whom Jung said he valued so much.

Here's a bit of self-criticism. I have written about and conducted a workshop exercise called 'Where did you get your politics from?' We look at parents, family, ethnicity, class, nationality, and all imaginable other influences, but what about the accidental, or even the constitutional factor, the *individual* factor: some ineluctable and irreducible piece of chance or fate that enters into the realm of political choices and actions, something that cannot be explained by context? Just thinking about what we could call political style enables us to recuperate the idea of the individual with regard to social responsibility. I come back to this question of political style later.

Anyway, the conventional wisdom is that we are always in groups, networks, contexts. By now this may have become banal and, without critique, destructive. Where has the individual gone in progressive discourse? In the spoken version of this chapter, I sing as follows, to the tune of 'Where have all the flowers gone?' (Seeger 1955):

Where have all the individuals gone, long time passing?
Where have all the individuals gone, long time ago?
Where have all the individuals gone?
Professors have banned them every one.
Oh, they will never learn?
Oh, they will never learn

Of course, economic and ethnic factors inform 'subjectivity'. Of course, we are relational beings, and it is important to assert that we are not atomised, split up entities sitting in empty space, but the Shadow aspect of this is that it plays into the ever-increasing centralisation of society. British readers were assuredly not fooled by the fantasy of involvement in 'the Big Society', the flagship policy of the 2010 UK Conservative Party general election campaign, which then formed part of the legislative programme of the Conservative–Liberal Democrat Coalition Agreement, which aimed to create a climate that empowers local people and communities, building a 'big society' that takes power away from politicians and give it to the people. Rather, it's all about central control; individuals are coerced into neighbourhood groups and societies: join or die! Your society needs you!

All of this adherence to 'the context' is the *Zeitgeist* for the industrialisation of psychotherapy that is going on in many countries: they want to legislate, regulate, manualise, and standardise us; they want to get the power to decide which individuals are 'fit to practise' therapy, and which are not. Even the clinical encounter itself seems to exclude individuals. Everyone is 'relational' nowadays. 'It's the relationship, stupid!' was seriously proposed as the banner headline for a national campaign in favour of the talking therapies. Again, it's not my experience that the clinical encounter really excludes individuals; it's the discourses on the clinical that sometimes seem to do so.

Relational intersubjectivity may undermine or exclude individual subjectivity. It's 'the therapeutic relationship' that is supposed to take the strain, not the sweating individuals who compose it. It's all about dyads, dialogue, communication, attachment, attunement, rupture and repair, and transference-countertransference. This refusal of one-person psychology has gone too far. The therapeutic relationship has become an oppressive, conventional, moralistic norm (see Samuels 2014).

I hope my argument becomes clearer: it is that the Shadow of understanding ourselves as group beings living in contexts is that we unwittingly support many of the things we hate. We norm, we conform, but we very rarely storm.

Solidarity becomes a curse as well as a blessing, a *cul-de-sac*, not the way ahead. Although I am a supporter of ecopsychology, I think this Shadow groupishness and enforced belonging stalks many ecosystemic approaches to politics. Where's the individual when the discourse is planetary? Can the Earth really be so hostile to the individual?

Let's explore the old liberal idea of the individual, the individual subject, and root it in a new critical anti-relational discourse. Let's see if we can refresh our idea of political action by engaging with the individual and individualism a bit. Classical individualism stresses the moral worth of the individual who is its focus. The fundamental premise is that the human individual is of primary importance in the struggle for liberation. Individualism is thus also associated with artistic and bohemian interests and lifestyles: self-creation and experimentation as opposed to tradition or mass opinion. This is what analysis and psychotherapy used to be before they got bourgeoisified and subjected to *déformation professionelle* (as I suggested in Chapter 4).

I'd like to suggest that we can revise this monolithic and overly solid approach quite a bit to take in the idea of the individual as fractured. The fact that an individual is fractured is *not* an obstacle to radical politics; rather it is a source of them. The individual is a bridge: between the inner and outer, between the personal and the political, between introverted solitude and being in a network; an individual who is more of an uprooted anti-hero than a hero: a bum, a schlemiel, and a nomad. Someone who *feels* 'self-begotten', just as Milton's (1667/2003) Satan said he was, *pace* the psychoanalytic strictures against parthenogenetic delusion, never mind the ablation of God. Why not be inflated on behalf of the individual? Has there ever been a successful revolutionary who was not necessarily, gloriously, and insanely inflated?

Clearly, there is more to psychology than the isolated individual human being and much has been usefully done to get rid of that idea, but academics have set up a false situation here. If we simplistically equate the idea of the individual with the conscious ego, or with sentimental Jungian, romantic ahistorical trumpeting of the supremacy of the individual, then hurrah for the intellectuals who've got rid of a dangerously misleading conception! This unthinking and reactionary version, however, is not the only possible playing out of the individual.

The individual who needs our attention today has never been like that, has never been solely the product of Puritanism, nor snowy-white, nor a romantic cliché, nor the unified being of orthodox psychology, nor Freudian ego, nor Jungian Self, nor a humanistic ideal. Do those pristine creatures, who would certainly deserve critique, really exist? No. I suggest that the individual who stalks contemporary culture, and who is trying to return to its politics, has *always been* a decentred subject, an actor performing many roles in many scripts, characterised by lack, somewhat faded as well as jaded: jerky, marginalised, alienated, split, guilty, empty, Imaginary. The individual has *always been* a Trickster in his or her practice of politics.

I think there is something we can do with this de-idealised, putrefied, violent and marvellously rebellious individual. The internally pluralistic individual is the *means* to an engagement with politics and culture, not an *obstacle* to it.

Make no mistake, individuals in the West are today in agony. It is an agony that politics is so broken. It is also an agony how political language has collapsed. George Orwell was prescient in his novel *1984* (Orwell 1949) when he tells us that Ingsoc and the Thought Police had a project to *reduce* the size of the dictionary, hence banishing the nuanced conversation needed for intimate and political life alike.

In both clinical work with clients and in political clinics (workshops open to the public), I've found that individual bodies bear this agony just as much as individual minds and psyche – *agon* means to writhe. In a sense, today's body is more than ever a writhing body politic, and is always armoured against attack or loss; people cannot breathe because of pollution, there's a constant state of adrenalisation; consumerist pressures tyrannise us into thinking we are either too fat or too thin, and we are obsessed with medications that we know will fail us.

Recuperating Jung's individual

Those of a Jungian persuasion may be smugly thinking that this argument is preaching to the choir. Such critics would be thinking that they already have a coherent theory of the individual firmly in place, for Jung is well known for having linked the idea of personal individuation and collective phenomena. I have to say that I am not convinced.

What Jung wrote about the individual makes academics turn away and snigger. The Jungian individual doesn't cut the intellectual – or political – mustard. The way in which Jung positioned the individual in relation to society, and the way in which society is reduced to 'the mass' or 'the masses', simply assumes that societies and individuals are inevitably antipathetic. Never mind that, at times, Jung seemed to suggest that a society or a nation is simply made up of the individuals in it, and there is nothing more to be said. In 1956, Jung wrote:

> [T]he agglomeration of huge masses in which the individual disappears anyway . . . the individual [is robbed] of his [sic] foundations and his dignity. As a social unit he has lost his individuality and becomes a mere abstract number in the bureau of statistics, He can only play the role of an interchangeable unit of infinitesimal importance.
>
> (Jung 1956, para 301)

It's hardly surprising then, that he continues in sardonic, sceptical, and depressive vein:

> Looked at rationally and from outside, that is exactly what he is, and from this point of view it seems positively absurd to go on talking about the value or meaning of the individual. Indeed, one can hardly imagine how one ever came to endow human life with so much dignity when the truth to the contrary is as plain as the palm of your hand.
>
> (Jung 1956, paras. 301–302)

I think that this sense of the impossibility of the individual in relation to society represents a premature concession by Jung; it is just too pessimistic and melancholic, though the rhetoric is splendid: 'an interchangeable unit of infinitesimal importance'.

Can we recuperate the Jungian idea of the individual? To do so would involve critiquing the relationship between individual and society as Jung set it out. In a recent discussion, Tacey (2012) succinctly summarised Jung from his book *The Undiscovered Self* (Jung 1957/1956)) as making 'a romantic defence of individuality and a warning against collectivism – [but] it makes for an odd kind of sociology if Jung sees the social mass only as something that wants to swallow the individual'.

Commenting on the draft doctoral manuscript that eventually became Ira Progoff's (1952) *Jung's Psychology and Its Social Meaning*, Jung (1978) said: 'the individual in society may be understood as a piece of the archetype. . . . The archetype of the individual is the Self. The Self is all-embracing' (p. 211). Tacey is correct: it is an odd approach to the social.

The way I see the same passage, Jung also got a lot of it right, and specifically the way in which the individual is ruined and controlled by the state: 'It is small wonder that individual judgement grows increasingly uncertain of itself and that *responsibility is collectivised as much as possible, i.e., is shuffled off by the individual and delegated to a corporate body*' (Jung 1978, p. 118, emphasis added).

Unfortunately, there is more than Jung's 'odd sociology' to hold back the evolving of links between his ideas and a progressive, humane politics. Jung's ideas on the individual are aristocratic, elitist, and supercilious. I am thinking here about this awful reference to 'stunted individuals':

> It is obvious that a social group consisting of stunted individuals cannot be a viable and healthy institution; only a society that can preserve its internal cohesion and collective values, while at the same time granting the individual the greatest possible freedom, has any prospect of enduring vitality. As the individual is not just a single, separate being, but by his very existence presupposes a collective relationship, it follows that the process of individuation must lead to more intense and broader collective relationships and not to isolation.
>
> (Jung 1921, para 758)

I want to go head to head with Jung here:

> Look, CG, the stunted individual is the only bloody individual that there is. Just as you taught us about alchemy, we begin political struggle with base materials: citizens who are far from individuated, who inhabit a world you've told us does not want them to individuate.

Similarly, from his paper on 'Adaptation, Individuation, Collectivity' (Jung 1916/1977):

> 'Whoever is not creative enough [to individuate] must re-establish collective conformity with a group of his own choice, otherwise he remains an empty waster and a windbag' (para. 1098).

So we have stunted individuals here, wasters and windbags over there, and truly individuated people in the first-class cabin. No wonder Shamdasani (2003) summarised Jung as saying 'individuation was for the few' (p. 307), but there are a lot of people in the world, not just 'the few', and not just the Jungian 0.1%.

Here Jung is like Marx; that is, the Marx who considered that the lowest of the low, the lumpenproletariat, were incapable of making a revolution. We should join the liberation theologians in their challenge to this Marxian elitism. For Boff (1988), it is the poorest, most downtrodden, most out-of-it who will make the revolution: 'God is in the poor who cry out. And God is the one who listens to the cry and liberates, so that the poor no longer need to cry out' (p. 166).

Orwell (1949) got it too: 'If there is hope, it lies in the proles' (p. 89), as did the Psalmist: 'The stone that the builders rejected has now become the cornerstone of the Temple' (Psalms, 118: 22).

Rebels and individuals

To this point, I have discussed whether contextualism and constructivism have gone too far; the 'fractured' and 'stunted' individual; and considered the advantages and disadvantages of Jung's conception of the individual for a progressive politics.

I now turn to Albert Camus and his working out of the intricate connections between existence, oppression, freedom, action – and the individual. I draw for the most part on Camus's (1951/1953) *The Rebel*, a book I first read at school, when aged 16, and used as a base for numerous attempts to get out of my cage; *plus ça change . . .*

Camus stated succinctly that rebellion and revolt are critically important to the making of meaning and hence to what we could call the birth of an individual. He reaches no conclusions about the purpose and meaning of life. He is relentlessly sceptical. Hence his position is that there is a fundamental absurdity to life and that attempts to create meaning, which are innate and valuable, are also – crucially – attempts to avoid the unavoidable absurdity of existence. Here Camus's twinning of despair and a kind of ironic hope reminds us of Beckett, but he is also, suggestively, very like Jung, as this quote from *The Red Book* shows: 'Meaning is a moment and a transition from absurdity to absurdity and absurdity only a moment and a transition from meaning to meaning' (Jung 2009, p. 242).

The Rebel is a history of humanity in revolt. Over time, humans have displayed a basic rejection of injustice; hence they rebel. All one can believe in is the value of protest and the protester's life. Crucially, for Camus (1951/1953), the impulse to rebel is inborn! 'To breathe is to judge' (p. 8). The act of rebellion is a primary given of human life. Revolt creates dignity and the ethical life – and solidarity. Individuals who rebel against oppressive state are transformed into a collective force: '*I rebel, therefore we are*' (ibid., p. 111; original emphasis). The rebellious individual is the progenitor of the social movement.

Now, if the impulse to rebel is inborn and hence archetypal, then any idea that Jung and Camus are total opposites may not be the case. Camus's default position is that human nature is made by decisions and acts whereas Jung's conception of human nature is different – but Jung is not only about archetypal determinism either. Remember: 'every confrontation with the archetype is a moral confrontation' – and there are many references to 'free will' throughout Jung's *Collected Works*.

I find Jung and Camus as writers rather similar: neither is rational or linear; both use metaphor and are interested in psychological experience; both write in the face of the catastrophes of the twentieth century. Camus, however, rejects the collective as a given; for him, personal rebellion creates whatever is more-than-personal.

What I take from Camus for this discussion on the individual' is that, while the original motivation to rebel may be inborn and individual, it becomes buried because of social and other repressions. Political individuality arises from rebellion which then may lead to joining others in solidarity. Camus admitted that people have a longing for something *social*, but also in the *spiritual* area. He called it 'religion' or 'philosophy' (Camus 1953, p. 237), but I think it is more accurately termed 'social spirituality'.

In social spirituality, individuals come together to take action in the social sphere, doing this in concert with other people. When this happens, something spiritual comes into being. Being actively engaged in a social, political, cultural, or ethical issue, together with others, initiates the spiritual. This is a very different perspective from one that would see social spirituality as being something done in the social domain by spiritual, that is, individuated, people. On the contrary, there is a kind of spiritual rain that can descend on ordinary individuals who get involved in politics and social issues with others, and hence 'social' spirituality (see Samuels 2001).

The difference from Jung's elitist conception of the individual should be clear: this is by no means an elitist perspective. Social spirituality embraces people who get involved with other people in political and social action: for example, the Occupy movement or other protests against global capitalism. Some participate in a general resacralisation of culture (Samuels 1993). To play on the word 'politicised', many of them are becoming 'spiritualised'. When one gets involved in idealistic politics, sometimes, not always, one gets spiritualised, and so anti-capitalist movements create their own spirituality and, in turn, is being informed by the spirituality that it creates. Political action leads to spirituality of some kind and spirituality informs political action. Of course, eventually it all falls to pieces: either the police wreck it or people (allegedly) 'grow up', but there is a basic resacralising tendency worth recognising.

Exercise 2. Think of times you feel someone or something was trying to prevent you from being an individual – family, society, peer pressure, shame, whatever. Did you rebel – or not? In either case, what happened?

Political style

Now, as promised, I introduce a frankly individual and experiential element into the discussion. I mentioned that there are questions of *individual political style* to consider.

What follows was first fashioned out of working with a mixed group of Israeli Palestinians and Israelis Jews in Jerusalem in the early 1990s. It became clear that, aside from the obvious irreconcilable differences in how the Middle East political scene was understood, there were individuals on both sides of the divide who were participating in the group in very similar or identical ways. I pointed this out and divided the larger group differently along style and type lines rather than content lines. I put the warlike with the warlike, the historically minded with the historically minded, the diplomatic with the diplomatic, the visionaries with the visionaries. The basic disagreements were there but the participants were now in groups with others whose political style resembled their own. There were discernible improvements in comprehension and even in goodwill.

The warring factions were presented not with an analysis of what they were saying (that came later), but with a panorama of *the ways in which they were saying it*, that is to say, with the style or type of politics they were using – for it isn't what you *say* but the *way* that you say it.

So the various people in conflict are operating in very different political styles or types. My inspiration for this was, in general terms, Jung's model of psychological types: extraversion, introversion, thinking, feeling, sensation, intuition. As in life generally, for a variety of reasons, some of them to do with their personal backgrounds, some to do with their inborn political constitutions, people will live out the political aspects of their lives in different ways. Over time, I've developed a list of images of differing political types as follows, in a spectrum ranging from active styles to passive ones: *warrior, terrorist, exhibitionist, leader, activist, parent, follower, child, martyr, victim, trickster, healer, analyst, negotiator, bridge-builder, diplomat, philosopher, mystic, and ostrich.*

Some individuals will be violent terrorists; some pacifists. Some will want empirical backup for their ideas; others will fly by the seat of their pants. Some will definitely enjoy cooperative political activity; others will suffer the nightmare of trying to accomplish things in a group only because they passionately believe in the ends being pursued. Let's not make the mistake of insisting that everyone do it in precisely the same way. If we are to promote political creativity, we need to value and honour individual political styles and types, and to think of ways of protecting such diversity.

As described, the notion of political type is particularly useful when addressing conflict, whether interpersonal or within organisations or even between nations or between parts of nations. Just as introverts and extraverts suffer from mutual incomprehension, individuals or groups that employ a particular political type often have very little idea about how the other person or group is actually 'doing' their politics. This is not to say that political content per se is irrelevant, only that there may be more that divides opponents than their different views. When working on questions of political style, it isn't necessary to encourage anyone to stick to just one style. In fact, the opposite holds true. Some individuals will use one political style in one setting and quite another in a different one. A *negotiator* at work may be a *terrorist* at home, or people may have, to borrow Jung's words, a 'superior' political type, an 'inferior' political type and 'auxiliary' styles; thus a *warrior* may have neglected his *philosopher*, or a *diplomat* his *activist*.

Over the past decade, I have been working on the Top Manager Programme run by the King's Fund, a National Health Service-oriented think tank. The idea is that participants become comfortable with as vast a range of political types as possible. Jung said that individuation involved activating all the types, and both extraversion and introversion.

Exercise 3. Reflecting on the political styles listed above, (a) choose the one you do the best/more often; (b) choose the one you are poor or ineffective at and might work on in order to develop; and (c) reflect on whether there are any you cannot imagine using.

The limits of individual responsibility

It is now time to probe the limits of individual responsibility – to think about making a difference and about not making a difference.

What is the scope of an individual's responsibility for others and for the world? The roots of the word 'responsibility' lie in *spondere*, to promise or pledge. What happens if we promise too much? In politics – and, I suppose, in life – there is a problem of people being too demanding of themselves. If we cannot live up to these demands, our idealism and energy go underground and are self-suppressed. We seem politically apathetic but, secretly, we are not: secretly, we are in touch with our 'inner politician'.

Let us think about how this banishing of political energy and idealism affects *Tikkun Olam* – Hebrew for the repair and restoration of the world. We are back to the problem of 'the stunted individual'. If one tries to do *Tikkun* from too perfect a self-state, it won't work because the only possible way to approach and engage with a broken and fractured world of which one is a part is, surely, as a broken and fractured, stunted individual: an individual with death in mind.

I call the broken and fractured one the 'good-enough individual', using Winnicott's epithet, albeit out of context but not overlooking his interest in how the parent helps the baby to steer a path between idealisation and denigration of the parent. Here, we are talking of the individual's own path between self-idealisation and self-denigration.

Winnicott said that 'the mother will fail the baby but in the baby's own way' (Rodman 1987, p. 8). Thus the individual will fail him or himself but in his or his own way – and failure to make a difference in the world to the extent one hopes becomes much less shameful, one becomes less self-denigrating. This is important because shame at failure is what leads to depression and guilt and so destroys the impulse and the capacity for action.

Individuals need a different attitude to their failure, particularly the failure of their political hopes and aspirations and projects.

Perhaps this is the kind of thing Camus (1953) meant when he wrote: 'The rebel can never find peace. He knows what is good, and despite himself, does evil. The value which supports him is never given to him once and for all – he must fight to support it, unceasingly' (p. 206)

Exercise 4. Think of times when you yourself made a difference and also of times when you wanted to but failed in the attempt.

Before we exit this chapter, having packed up in despair, and go home let us recall that the official politicians and the governments of the world, with all possible resources at their disposal, have not done such a terrific job of managing things. Governments constantly try to improve things in the political world, usually by redistributing wealth or changing legislative and constitutional structures or defusing warlike situations. It is *not* that nothing is being tried to make things better, but a materialist approach deriving exclusively from economics, or one that depends solely on altering the structures of the state, will not refresh those parts of the individual citizen that a psychological perspective can reach. There is disappointment at societies that fail to deliver the spiritual goods and a sense of meaning and purpose. We can change the clothes, shift the pieces around, but the spectre that haunts materialist and constitutional moves in the political world is that they only ruffle the surface. They do not – because, alone, they cannot – bring about the transformations for which the individual political soul yearns. For that we may have to turn to 'the man with no name'.

I end with an untitled poem by Jerzy Ficowski (1979), working on the theme of the Holocaust and with individual responsibility in mind:

> [I] did not succeed in saving
> even a single life
> i did not have the ability to stop
> even a single bullet
> so i wander, trying to find cemeteries
> that do not exist
> i search for words
> i run
> for help that no one called for
> for rescue that got delayed
> i want to come on time
> even when i am too late.

References

Beck, U. and Beck-Gernsheim, E., (2002). *Individualization: Institutionalized individualism and its social and political consequences.* London: SAGE.

Boff, L., (1988). *When theologians listen to the poor.* San Francisco, CA: Harper & Row.

Camus, A., (1951/1953). *In:* J. Laredo, trans. *The rebel.* London: Hamish Hamilton.

Cushman, P., (1995). *Constructing the self, constructing America.* Reading, MA: Addison-Wesley.

Durkheim, E., (1893/1997). *In*: L. A. Coser, trans. *The division of labor in society.* New York: Free Press.

Ficowski, J., (1979). *Untitled poem from Odczytanie Popiołów.* Jason Francisco, trans. jasonfrancisco.net/poems-of-ficowski

Giddens, A., (1991). *Modernity and self-identity: Self and society in the late modern age.* Stanford, CA: Stanford University Press.

The good, the bad and the ugly, (1966). Film. Directed by S. Leone. Italy.

Jung, C. G., (1921/1926). Definitions. *In*: R. F. C. Hull, trans. *The collected works of C. G. Jung.* Vol. 6. London: Routledge and Kegan Paul, 408–486.

Jung, C. G., (1953). The relations between the ego and the unconscious. *CW7.*

Jung, C. G., (1956). The undiscovered self. *CW10.*

Jung, C. G., (1977). Adaptation, individuation, collectivity. *CW18.*

Jung, C. G., (1978). *C. G. Jung speaking: Interviews and encounters.* W. McGuire and R. F. C. Hull, eds. London: Thames & Hudson.

Jung, C. G., (1916/1977). Adaptation, individuation, collectivity. *CW18*.

Jung, C. G., (2009). *The red book: Liber Novus*. S. Shamdasani, ed. New York: W.W. Norton.

Layton, L., (2013). Dialectical constructivism in historical context: Expertise and the subject of late modernity. *Psychoanalytic Dialogues*, 23, 126–149.

Levinas, E., (1995). *Alterity and transcendence*. B. Michael, trans. New York: Columbia University Press.

Milton, J., (1667/2003). *Paradise lost*. Harmondsworth: Penguin.

Orwell, G., (1949). *1984*. Harmondsworth: Penguin.

Progoff, I., (1952). *Jung's psychology and its social meaning*. New York: Julian Press.

Rodman, F. R., ed., (1987). *The spontaneous gesture: Selected letters of D. W. Winnicott*. Cambridge, MA: Harvard University Press.

Rose, N., (1989). *Governing the soul: The shaping of the private self*. London: Free Association Books.

Rust, M.-J. and Totton, N., eds., (2012). *Vital signs: Psychological responses to ecological crisis*. London: Karnac.

Samuels, A., (1993). *The political psyche*. London: Routledge.

Samuels, A., (2001). *Politics on the couch: Citizenship and the internal life*. London: Karnac.

Samuels, A., (2014). Shadows of the relational. *In*: D. Loewenthal and A. Samuels, eds. *Relational psychotherapy, psychoanalysis and counselling*. London: Routledge, 184–192.

Seeger, P., (1955). Where have all the flowers gone. *Sing Out*, 11 (5), 4–5.

Shamdasani, S., (2003). *Jung and the making of modern psychology: The dream of a science*. Cambridge: Cambridge University Press.

Tacey, D., (2012). *Jung and sociology*, 29 June. On-line discussion group of the International Association for Jungian Studies. Available from: http://jungianstudies.org/iajs-online-discussion-forum/

Chapter 7

Taking the green agenda out of the margins – psychological strategies

Retrospective Introduction: I have been playing with these ideas for over 30 years, and this is the latest version. In short, I think that efforts to manage the climate crisis will fail because of the shaming and pessimistic way in which they are communicated. This involves too much blame levelled against humanity and too little focused on our achievements. The whole thing is complexified by an idealisation of nature. The material on 'apocalypticism' was also useful during the lock-down period of the still ongoing COVID pandemic.

Talking Points: The question is whether the green movements really want to be in the centre of political activity. Assuming for the moment that they do, then there is a need to stop hammering humanity for what it has done to the planet. Celebrate our achievements: cities, trains and planes, coffee, and perfume. Artifice is natural for us! Nature is not natural; it has a history! The chapter also looks at the secret desire many people have to be punished for damaging Mother Earth. We want to perish. This is called 'apocalypticism'.

Here's a summary of the chapter which follows. First, I will link up some aspects of what I call 'therapy thinking' and climate change – with reference to the question of 'mainstreaming' political actions and ideas in this area. Can this be achieved, I ask? Then, in the second section, still in pursuit of the elusive goal of bringing the green agenda out of the margins, I will assert it's time to praise humanity and human artifice, not to bury them, and pick out some items well deserving of praise. Third, I discuss salient aspects of green politics. In the fourth section, I take a look at the political desirability and advocacy of sacrifice-in-the-service-of-the-planet by those able to manage it, and set this in an economic context. Finally, I will probe what I see as a sort of addiction to apocalypse operating in the West just now.

Here's the summary of the chapter: first section – therapy; second section – praise; third section – politics; fourth section – sacrifice; final section – apocalypse.

Therapy and climate change

Do climate activists ever really want to be in the centre? To be part of the people as a real mass movement? To capture universal and enthusiastic support? In the mordant and suspicious vein of a therapist engaging with what may lie below the

DOI: 10.4324/9781003598985-10

surface, I ask is it possibly the case they cannot be happy anywhere save on the margins? Or, if they do struggle to move into the mainstream, aren't they inevitably going to betray their values and ideals? Or waste their time?

I realise this is a controversial thing to write. Yet isn't it clear that mainstreaming has become the goal of youth-led movements like Extinction Rebellion? Consider its three goals as listed on its website at the time of writing (Winter 2019), and note that the word 'Government' appears in all of them. What could be more mainstream than to call on the Government to do such-and-such a thing?

> Government must tell the truth by declaring a climate and ecological emergency, working with other institutions to communicate the urgency for change.
> Government must act now to halt biodiversity loss and reduce greenhouse gas emissions to net zero by 2025.
> Government must create and be led by the decisions of a Citizens' Assembly on climate and ecological justice.

Is it wise for Extinction Rebellion to be as mainstream as this? Is the Government really the key here? Yes and no . . . .

It is interesting to review how climate change figured in the 2019 and 2024 elections. Professor Sir John Curtice, who interprets the polls for the BBC, wrote, 'The attention given by all of the parties to the issue of climate change seems to have resulted in an increase in concern about the environment, although it is still relatively low down in the pecking order'.

What about Labour's Green New Deal? It got massively diluted. My first reflection is that it simply didn't resonate with mass audiences. My impression is that this was not because the policy was wrong – but it was presented in an overly detailed and intellectualised way. I mean, who knew what the 'new deal' was, from the 1930s in the United States?

This chapter plunges into both of these issues: that the climate crisis is still relatively low down the political pecking order – and that policies are over-detailed and intellectualised.

The link between the climate emergency and our own lives has never seemed clearer. Finally, after decades of activists struggling to push the crisis into the larger consciousness, poll after poll shows that public concern, and desire for action, is at an all-time high.

The question that becomes clearer as the year went on was: having achieved what the climate movement always wanted – prominent and positive media coverage, widespread public support, audiences with world leaders – was it possible to effect any actual political change? The spectacle of Greta Thunberg and the larger youth climate movement arriving at international meetings and parliaments and accusing heads of state of hypocrisy to their faces is undoubtedly thrilling. But climate politics itself still seems far from any genuine watershed moment.

Additionally, as the British environmental campaigner George Marshall noted in his critique of Leonardo Di Caprio's environmental film 'Before the Flood', those celebrities and big names warning ever so articulately of the climate change catastrophe which looms are making things worse. Why? According to Marshall, they simply 'ignore entirely the global zeitgeist of popular cynicism about political leaders and institutions' (2015).

So, if the facts – 'the truth' – are known by now, why is it proving so difficult to get majority buy-in for the policies and actions needed? Is there a collective psychological problem? Or is the language and rhetoric being used by climate change campaigners not really working? Answering these questions is what I am struggling with in the chapter.

With others, I have been developing what I call 'therapy thinking' in relation to politics for more than 30 years in too many books for comfort. I have pointed out such an activity is truly transpersonal; for politics, like spirit and soul, links people to each other and to everything else is on the planet.

Therapy thinking in the context of climate change has become suspiciously easy. Therapists find it easy to be right when it comes to politics– because one invokes the 'maddening rectitude of the psychotherapist' in which the goal is to prove one's cherished theories – of archetypes, object relations, self-actualisation – to prove them correct above all else. That is why every single psychoanalytic comment on Donald Trump or Boris Johnson is 100% correct, even when they contradict. It is easy to be right.

However, some of the recent history of therapists' engagement with climate change has not been inspiring or reassuring. When I held the elected office of Chair of United Kingdom Council for Psychotherapy (UKCP), I encouraged the creation of a climate change policy for the organisation as part of its diversity, equality, and social responsibility agenda. I can only regret and deplore what seemed to have happened when the proposed climate change policy went to the next Board under a new Chair. It was said that this is a minority view without sufficient grassroots support. 'What does this have to with psychotherapy?' was asked, and the Board was told that 'Political ideologies have no place in our work'.

So, although UKCP recently held a conference on climate crisis, there are many questions left unresolved. For example, if a member takes part in a demonstration and is thereby arrested, do they have to report such a thing to an ethics committee? When it comes to politics, sadly and still, it may be a case of 'put not thy faith in therapists'.

This brief opening section is coming to an end. It consisted of some critical comments on the role of therapists and therapy thinking in relation to climate change. The next section makes a positive proposal of what could be done to bring climate activism in from the margins.

It's time to praise human artifice

If we really, truly, and seriously want to mainstream ecopsychology and other psychological approaches to climate change, then now may also be the time to praise human achievement and human artifice. On one level, I am thinking of praise, not judgement, for the entire dynamic range of human emotions – positive ones such as joy, hope, and inspiration, and the negative and more difficult ones such as lust, greed, and envy. It's impossible to pick and choose; to select only what is nice and appealing. Vitality is not the same as morality, after all.

But it is also time to praise our cities, those achievements of human creativity, aesthetics, and social organisation. To praise our squares and piazzas, to praise our restaurants and rejoice in the drinking of alcohol or of coffee, to praise traffic and modern communications. To praise, too, brothels and hospitals, banks, and schools.

Such celebration has, over time, gone missing from much current environmental discourse. The need to celebrate, to dance, and to chant is being more recognised. Yet this needs to be offset against another tendency and maybe stronger. For I don't think it is helpful to use the language of psychopathology – for example, as George Monbiot often does. Here's an example: 'We need to kick our *addiction* to driving' (2016, emphasis added).

Alongside praise of artifice, it is also time to guard against any lingering idealisation of Nature – for this is politically useless and intellectually weak. No one really knows what 'Nature' means.

In his seminal book, *Man and the Natural World* (1983), the historian Keith Thomas showed that our present conception of Nature has a complicated history. But it has a history. Nature changes its nature, so to speak. Thomas sets out the trajectory wherein by around 1800 the world was so irradiated by science, technology and industry that people felt 'begrimed, endarkened and smelly' (p. 96). So they sought a sunny, clean, and fresh antidote. If they could afford it, they bought country estates. If not, they merely dreamed of pastures and sang hymns about them. This swing to the opposite end of the spectrum – what Heraclitus and Jung called enantiodromia – created the modern, romantic notion of Nature. We created Nature!

The snowball of industrialism, Enlightenment, and modernity introduced a profound anxiety in European cultural consciousness, to the point of neurosis, over what was being done by civilised humans to the natural world. Between 1500 and 1800, massive doubts emerged over the changes brought about by science and technology in the ways the natural world was perceived. There were many romantic and artistic expressions of this counter-cultural sentiment. Theologians altered their notions about the relations between humanity and the rest of creation so as to gentle those relations and accommodate a certain decentring of humanity. Naturalists tried to understand and classify other species in non-anthropomorphic terms, thereby respecting their separate existence. Scientists explored links between humans and animals. Moral philosophers urged kindness to animals. In the city, the land came to be regarded as a thing of beauty, fit for contemplation, not only as a useful resource.

In sum, by 1800, people had responded to the anxiety engendered by the brutalising path on which the world seemed embarked.

Today's concerns over the limits to economic growth, animal welfare, and the fate of the environment may be regarded as descended from these earlier expressions of cultural anxiety. Yet we should temper our admiration for those who could not stomach 'progress'. They did not actually stop its march. Today, animal experimentation and factory-farming have to coexist with the supreme idealisation of the animal: The child's toy furry animal. As Thomas says, these cuddly creatures 'enshrine the values by which society as a whole cannot afford to live' – an observation he extends to include nature parks and conservation areas (p. 238).

The revolution in consciousness that Thomas writes about constituted a kind of underground resistance to what was being done to the natural world. This resistance went beyond a reaction to the ruination of nature. The perception of slaves, non-Europeans, children, and women also underwent profound changes. As far as women were concerned, the form that liberal anxiety about modernity's denigration of women took was of an oppressive (and convenient) idealisation that restricted women to private and domestic roles. The idealisation of women and the idealisation of nature share similar roots in cultural history in the West: They are both reaction formations. But women and nature remain deeply threatening because the idealisations of them are based on such flimsy and anxiety-ridden foundations.

But by the end of the nineteenth century, we see another swing. This time against Nature. The fight back was led by Nature's great opponent Artifice. My favourite novel in this direction is *A Rebours* (Against Nature), written by the French novelist (and influence on Oscar Wilde) J.-K. Huysmans in 1884. This book, in all its imaginative perversity and impossible elaboration, is a paean of praise to artifice and I want to propose Huysmans's thoughts like these for us to play with now:

> Nature has had her day; she has finally and utterly exhausted the patience of sensitive observers by the revolting uniformity of her landscapes and skyscapes. In fact, there is not a single one of her inventions, deemed so subtle and sublime, that human ingenuity cannot manufacture. Does there exist, anywhere on this earth, a being conceived in the throes of motherhood who is more dazzlingly, more outstandingly beautiful than the two locomotives recently put into service on the Northern Railway?
>
> (Huysmans 1884/1959, p. 125)

I shall conclude this section with an anecdote on the topic of human artifice, which is what I have chosen to praise.

At an ecopsychology conference in Oxford in 2009, I gave a workshop also titled 'Against nature'. In it, I distributed sample phials of many perfumes that Selfridges very kindly gave me. In pairs and threes, participants used the perfumes, applied them to each other, and compared notes. It was a smelly old exercise and a lot of fun.

Before we did the exercise, I asked who in the audience of around 150 ecopsychologists wore perfume or its male equivalents. Only one person said that she did. I asked who read fashion magazines in which perfumes are widely advertised. None, though one person said guiltily that she did it in the dentist's waiting room.

I then said that this showed why environmental activism might possibly fail and why ecopsychology had truncated itself. For those in the room had, at least as it seemed to me in the moment, got completely cut off from the role artifice plays in ordinary human life. Cut off, when you get down to it, from humanity itself. As far from the mainstream as one can get.

I am as frightened of the destruction of the planet as anyone in the ecopsychology world. But I am also convinced that, if you look in the right way, there is much of value in the fripperies of fashion and consumerism and it is elitist to deny it. Depth is hidden on the surface.

Green politics substance and shadow

From a political point of view, my sense is that the environmental movement is neither truly 'for' nor secretly 'against' change. It may be both. In the sense that environmentalism represents an opposition to the forms of social organisation established in the industrially advanced countries during the past two centuries, the environmental movement supports change. But in the sense that some environmentalists have not caught up in consciousness with the techno-industrial revolutions of the past 200 years and may wish to revert to a pre-industrial cultural matrix, environmentalism may be seen as being against the very changes that have already happened. Maybe, paradoxically, some environmentalism may be regarded as both deeply conservative and wildly radical.

The key question, in all its school debating society naivety, remains: Does, or can, human nature change? Oscar Wilde, as mentioned profoundly influenced by Huysmans, wrote in his tract 'The soul of man under socialism':

> The only thing we know about human nature is that it changes. Change is the one quality we can predict of it. . . . The systems that fail are those that rely on the permanency of human nature, and not on its growth and development.
>
> (1895/1978, p. 1010)

In the chapter, I have been asking must the environmental movement fail? I have been suggesting it will fail politically unless the idealisation of nature is somehow moderated. Now I move on to propose further it will fail socially unless it becomes more conscious of certain strands of authoritarianism and depression within it.

A lot of what follows rests on what constitutes 'the real world'. Is the real world the world of the hard-bitten businesspeople who say that only corporate capitalism instituting changes can anything be done about the climate emergency? Or is the real world that of the activists of Extinction Rebellion, which I support and some of whom have come to see me as a therapist. For me the way in which the XR youth conduct their politics reminds of what I was trying to work out in 1993, in *The Political Psyche*, when I wrote the chapter on the 'Political Trickster' (pp. 78–102).

Criticisms in the right-wing press of the authoritarianism of the environmental movement, referring to its 'eco-terrorism' and recent examples of stopping traffic moving in big cities as part of a demonstration, can be frighteningly effective. The latent function of such broad brush attack is that entrenched industrial and financial institutions gain succour. As I say, we saw this in the negative reactions in Britain to the rise of a plethora of non-violent and violent direct action movements, mostly in connection with climate change. Extinction Rebellion, occupying London's bridges and public spaces, is the best known. British readers may recall that there were those who cheered when drones – allegedly flown by these 'eco-terrorists' – closed down Gatwick airport at Christmas 2018, stopping people from getting away on holiday. Are these things helpful to the cause of mainstreaming climate change and other planetary issues? Or do they simple demonstrate that there is a not-so-hidden authoritarianism in much of the new environmental politics, which could be seen as the latest manifestation of the Enlightenment belief in perfectibility.

Whether this takes the form of equating humanity to the level of fauna (or flora) in a scale of what is valuable or of issuing of a whole set of edicts about what is 'good', the tendency is clear to see. And already a backlash is going on. I think that, if it is fair to say there is environmentalist authoritarianism, stemming from a deeply buried misanthropy, it will be horrendously destructive to the movement. In Jungian terms, this is the shadow of the environmental movement and it would be helpful to become more conscious of it. Then the advantages of the unquenchable human thirst for a better world can be enjoyed – for only things of substance cast a shadow.

Casting an analyst's eye over the information and education material put out by organisations like Greenpeace and Friends of the Earth, I am struck by the one-sided portrait of humanity they present. Certainly, there is much to feel guilty about, much thoughtlessness and destructive behaviour to be owned, much acquiescence in horrid developments to be confessed. But the unremitting litany of humanity's destructiveness may not be the way to spur movement in a more creative direction. The result of too much self-disgust may be the cultivation of a deadening cultural depression that would interfere with environmental action. This is because fantasies of being all-bad and all-destructive usually lie at the heart of depressive illness. Therefore environmentalists should try to avoid any presentation of ideas about the environment that reflects humanity in an exclusively harsh light. It is not just that guilt-tripping is ineffective politics. My concern is what the one-sidedness obscures.

Going back to the perspectives introduced by Keith Thomas (above), instead, we might also celebrate what careful tending of the earth there has been over millennia. As I have been saying, we might reaffirm the goodness, gentleness, and aesthetic sensibility of humanity's artificial, cultural productions – our buildings, cities, art works, and so forth.

Politically speaking, it is vital not to represent environmentalism as a concern of the privileged classes or regions, cut off from wider issues of social justice. To begin with, we have already seen that the greening of politics is going to be painful, both within Western societies and in terms of the relations between the developed and the undeveloped worlds. A whole host of moral decisions arises when we in the industrially advanced countries call for limits on deforestation in poor countries or advocate their controlling of their birth rates. We need an educational programme that faces people with these decisions and choices rather than letting them to be made for them by experts who will offer protection from the moral implications of what is being done. Otherwise we will end up with a new Western hegemony: We will be more or less OK – but the poor of the earth will be radically worse off as the temperatures and the seas rise.

What is more, we must see through the desirability and efficacy of changes in consumer spending patterns, recycling, and veganism to bring about improvement. Are we to say that when the going gets tough, the greens go shopping? If substantive issues of social justice are not addressed, then we *will* just be doing a mere landscaping job.

The question of economic redistribution within advanced societies is going to have to be addressed. If polluters are to pay, prices will rise enormously. The knock-on effects will be dramatic. Many goods that we take for granted will be priced out of reach. *I want to suggest this is a marvellous opportunity!* We are going to have to think about how we live and about how resources are distributed within our more advanced societies – and this will challenge the awesome power structures which exist. The problems confronting the world force a critical engagement with the banks, the multinational corporations, the IMF and with governments. Without this, poorer people will suffer intolerably. They may – they will -rise up.

Nevertheless, calls for a return to traditional forms of homeworking or the setting up of *ersatz* agrarian-style communities should be treated with caution. In such situations, the lot of women has been and would continue to be an unhappy one. Instead, we should think of greening the cities we already have, making them safer and more pleasant for the groups they oppress – women, children, the elderly. For it has never been demonstrated that agrarian, parochial life is inherently superior to urban, cosmopolitan life. Advocating the tearing down of cities so as to foster the triumph of nature would be the way of a Khmer Vert.

Younger people will see through any educational campaign that idealises nature, leaving out its frightening, harsh, and bloody aspects and our ambivalence towards it. Such a campaign would resemble those commissioned portraits of the eighteenth century in which the lady of the manor is pictured dressed up as a milkmaid. The effect was to make nature an acceptable decorative element in the salons of the rich. We must not do this again.

Politically speaking, the environmental movement still has to work on a balance between its 'anthropocentric' middle-of-the-roaders and its extreme wing – sometimes called 'ecologism'. Are we doing this for ourselves, for our own benefit and that of our children and other humans? Or is that simply a new gloss on the old exploitative attitude to nature? Should we not be acting for the benefit of an entire planetary organism? Battle lines are even now being drawn up between green extremists and the rest of the community, including 'ordinary' environmentalists.

The argument that trees and rivers have rights needs to be assessed so that we can distinguish between its potential to inspire action and its gross oversimplifications. Does the HIV virus have 'rights'? Is it ethical to destroy dams or insert into trees spikes that injure loggers?

I hope it's clear that I am not repeating the nostrum, more honoured in the breach than in the observance, which climate changers need to stop telling people that they are being very bad boys and girls indeed. Of course, this won't work. But what I am adding is something positive that can be conveyed about aspects of life everyone shares in to some extent or other.

There are some connections between climate change and racial justice that some – but not all – writers overlook and omit. Global warming affects disadvantaged groups that in any given society. We saw how, when collective disasters like Hurricane Katrina occur, they disproportionately affect people of colour. And it is in the lands of 'the South' that the effects of our addiction to fossil fuels are most strikingly visible and experienced. With intersectionality in mind, the correlation of race and environment is of huge importance.

Here, it is extremely interesting to note that Indigenous communities, such as Native Americans or Aboriginal people in Australia, often lead the fight against carbon and all its derivatives, such as deforestation and open mining. Nevertheless, we should be careful not to Orientalise such people (in the sense of marvelling in a buried, patronising manner) that such 'primitives' can manage to see clearly what is happening, it is noteworthy. Assigning 'nature' to them is not a friendly or socially just thing to do, just as was the case when nature was assigned to women.

Allow me to contradict myself. I have been saying that we need to praise cities. True enough. But am I as guilty of an idealisation of the urban as some commentators are of the natural? For, if we have racial and economic justice in mind, then we must admit that cities are not only propitious containers for equality. They could be – but for that to happen something huge needs to change in urban consciousness.

That is the end of an exploration of green politics. Next, we move on to consider the idea of sacrifice in search of the change in urban consciousness I just mentioned.

Sacrificial politics

In this much more depth psychological section, I am in effect linking the psychology of climate change with the whole question of sacrifice.

As I have been saying, it is becoming a consensus among those who write about climate change and sustainability that the climate crisis and imbalances of wealth under capitalism and globalisation are linked. Economic sacrifices are needed.

Because of this consensus, I have been wondering what some ideas about sacrifice might contribute, with climate change and economic justice in mind. We know that people will make sacrifices for their children, or for the sake of a cause they believe in, or in the hope of greater benefits in the future (what the economists call 'opportunity costs').

However, sacrifice is a much deeper and wider psychological and historical theme. Sacrifice lies at the heart of the Abrahamic religions (the aborted sacrifice of Isaac in Genesis 22) but is much, much older as a propitiation of the Gods. Asceticism has a long cultural history as does martyrdom.

In Jungian psychology, we talk of the sacrifice of the ego for the flowering of the wider personality in individuation. In art and religion, we contemplate the sacrifice of autonomy and control to something experienced as 'other', whether inside or outside the self.

Maybe the time has arrived for psychologically minded people to begin to find an emotional basis for a psychologically considered programme of *economic* sacrifice, calling and naming it as such, rather than waiting for governments to bring it about by fiscal legislation or some other compulsory method – which they are anyway reluctant to do for electoral reasons.

I think it is important, if we are thinking of changing the thrust of climate change or any other environmental campaigning, to find a new way of conveying the value, not only the desirability, of sacrifice. Now we come to the promised last section on catastrophe and apocalypse.

Addiction to apocalypse

I want to discuss why, when it comes to climate change, it is still quite often a case of 'Eat, drink and be merry, for tomorrow we die'. Or 'drill, baby, drill'. I want to give my own suggestions as to why there is the denial, disavowal, and despair so many climate change psychologists write about in such interesting ways.

Yes, what follows is exaggerated – but exaggeration is at the heart of satire, and much research shows the usefulness of a Trickster element when it comes to communicating scientific information. Here's an example:

'We do not care about planet Earth', four French scientists declared in February in the journal *Trends in Ecology and Evolution*. If humans are exhausting the planet's resources, they wrote, it's Earth that needs to adapt – not us. The authors issued a warning: 'Should planet Earth stick with its hardline ideological stance . . . we will seek a second planet' (Preston 2018, n.p.). This got a lot of attention.

The use of satire to defuse anxiety-driven rejection of the already existing planetary catastrophe is a contribution to what I called in *The Political Psyche* (1993, pp. 78–102) the 'political Trickster'. The politics of Trickster are often still overlooked. We perform our environmental politics within a fantasy of our own seriousness. For the Greeks, the arch-Trickster was Hermes, with his tendency to play jokes, to lie, to cheat, to steal, to deny reality, and to engage in grandiose fantasy.

Genuine Tricksters, from Coyote in North America to Ananse or Eshu in West Africa, follow that pattern, undermining the prevailing organisation of power and even the perceived structure of reality itself. Tricksters can certainly be seen as personifications of primary process activity, challenging and disregarding the laws of time, space, and place.

Rather than judge and condemn, let us speculate about why Trickster mounts this challenge. He does it *precisely to test the limits of those laws,* the bounds of their applicability, and, hence, the possibility of altering them. At the moment we say this, the political referents of the Trickster are revealed. He enters the arena of climate change and environmental despoliation. Challenging the limits of laws, their applicability and the possibility of altering them – and doing this in an ideological climate which is hostile to such a challenge – is *the* classic progressive political project.

Claiming the Trickster for environmental politics might seem like the most crass over-interpretation. But if Trickster's political theorising can retain his own capacity for shock and irony, then no more than a little damage will have been done to him.

If involving the Trickster in political discourse does not injure the Trickster, then what does it do to our conception of politics, and environmental politics in particular? There is a conventionally moralistic nature of most depth psychological analysis of the fate of the planet. For example, the front page of the estimable Climate Psychology Alliance carries the slogan 'Facing Difficult Truths'. Well, what could be more conventional than to advocate the facing of difficult truths? The language is so middle aged, middlebrow, and middle class.

From this perspective, driven as it happens by psychoanalysis, Trickster's mendaciousness and self-deception are misunderstood as immature, obscuring his transformative and generative aspects.

We need to be both sensible and other-than-sensible. Green politics requires a ceaseless dynamic between a passionately expressed, codified, legally sanctioned set of principles and certitudes (original morality) – and a more open, flexible, improvised, tolerant morality which is basically code-free (moral imagination). These two aspects of political morality are present in varying degrees in any political problematic. It is important to resist the temptation to see one of them as somehow more advanced, rising from the ashes of the other. Certitude and improvisation are *equally* valuable, and, even assessed from a conventional psychodynamic perspective, they are equally mature.

It is easy to see that a political morality based exclusively on improvisation would be too slippery by far and would contribute to a culture in which anything goes. But a political morality based exclusively on principle, law, and certitude would be equally problematic (in psychological language, equally 'primitive'). To begin with, laws are not politically effective on their own; legal codes reflect and depend on the distribution of wealth and power. Moreover, political principle easily becomes ossified and used to gain control over others. Finally, codified political and moral prohibitions do not always work, as the prevalence of theft or adultery demonstrates.

I accept Trickster's discourse may seem like garbage to some readers. Yet his refusal to say definitively *this* is the only reality (e.g. economic growth, fracking, coal-mining and industrialisation), and *this* is Utopian fantasy (i.e. radical reform or even revolution in planetary politics) is in itself a profound, political statement.

Viewed this way, Tricksters contribute to the abolition of every kind of exploitation or oppression, be it directed against a class, a party, a sex, a race – or a planet.

I now turn to 'Apocalypticism' – the belief there will assuredly be an apocalypse. When deployed by Puritan sects, the term apocalypse originally referred to a revelation of God's will, but now usually refers to the belief that the world will come to an end very soon, even within one's own lifetime.

This belief is usually accompanied by the idea that civilisation will soon come to a tumultuous end due to some sort of catastrophic global event.

The notion that the world is coming to an end is fairly called 'archetypal', found in many religions, paths, and 'ways'. This is what gives apocalypse the power to possess groups and individuals who do not belong to Puritan sects. To possess all of us, perhaps? Is this what has happened in relation to climate change? If so, then we have the beginnings of a theory as to why so many people in the Western countries have so little interest in the matters we are discussing today. They prefer not to.

Climate change and planetary degradation inspire images of an apocalypse which one would imagine to be horrid but which may be oddly pleasing and reassuring. The breakdown will happen, nothing to be done about it. And that could be for some people an oddly reassuring thought – because it justifies inaction.

Fantasies of an apocalyptic end are rooted in reality and it is right to point them out. But these may be deep signs of a self-punishing contempt for ourselves. Apocalypticism is not based on fear of an end but rather on desire of it.

Perhaps some people think we deserve to perish like this. Perhaps this is why many people don't talk about climate change?

Perhaps this self-loathing is a shadow element for many people, including me, with concerns about climate change. It exists alongside our excitement at witnessing the rise of a responsible tending for the planet, and the flowering of depth psychological interpretation of climate change denial, disavowal, and despair. We desire, we actually want the whole terran temple to crash down. It is a tad exciting, a macabre spectator sport, a form of political pornography, masochism in an environmental setting.

Why do I end my chapter on this note? Because I feel obliged to say, in inflated and prophetic mode, it is *the very love of catastrophe* that contributes to our paralysis. What do we want? Apocalypse. When do we want it? NOW. We climate change campaigners can never move to the centre if we don't think about this thing of darkness that is holding us back. Hamlet got it:

> To die: – to sleep:
> No more; and, by a sleep to say we end
> The heart-ache and the thousand natural shocks
> That flesh is heir to, 'tis a consummation
> Devoutly to be wished.
>   (Act 3, Scene 1, lines 21–26)

References

Huysmans, J.-K., (1884/1959). *Against nature*. R. Baldick, trans. Harmondsworth: Penguin.

Marshall, G., (2015). Engage centre-right voters to put climate change on the political platform. *The Guardian*, 15 April.

Monbiot, G., (2016). Our roads are choked. We're on the verge of carmageddon. *The Guardian*, 21 September.

Preston, E., (2018). Using satire in science communication. *Undark: Truth, Beauty and Science* (no page).

Samuels, A., (1993). The *political p*syche. London and New York: Routledge.

Thomas, K., (1983). *Man and the natural world: Changing attitudes in England 1500–1800*. London: Allen Lane.

Wilde, O., (1895/1978). The soul of man under socialism. *In: Complete works of Oscar Wilde*. London: London Book Club.

Part III

Therapy

Chapter 8

Pluralism and psychotherapy – what is a good training?

Retrospective Introduction: I hardly know where to begin with the retrospective intro-duction to this chapter. I have been engaged with the issue of pluralism all my career. I have noted with interest that a new approach to therapy called pluralistic psychother-apy has arisen since about 2020. For me, this new approach is very muddled between pluralism and eclecticism, never mind integration. These are all rather different. In the chapter, I try to be as down to earth as possible with clinical vignettes illustrating the ideas. I also draw on my experiences when I became the elected chair of the United Kingdom Council for Psychotherapy in 2009. That was a huge surprise because I only stood so as to promote opposition to the Government's ideas to statutorily regulate psy-chotherapy in the UK. Once elected, I took the job mega-seriously, and we made some advances, especially in relation to the banning of conversion therapy for sexual diversity.

Talking Points: Pluralism is having a vogue in the therapy world. But it is basically just integration or eclecticism in disguise. A little bit of this and a little bit of that. Pluralism does not just mean having many viewpoints. It means getting a balance between 'the many' and 'the one'. Pluralism can make use of the clash of viewpoints so characteristic of the 'psy' field. We have to bargain and negotiate, just as political theory tells us. When it comes to organising training, why not structure things around dispute and polemic, rather than the historical or thematic approach that is usually taken? Starting at the beginning is no guarantee of comprehension.

Politics of/and psychotherapy

Psychotherapists can learn a good deal from politics as it is practised and theorised these days. Much of what I have to say about pluralism and psychotherapy is taken directly from political theory and praxis. One political theme that seems to me to be very relevant is what the political philosophers call the 'identity/difference theme'. This means that, in some ways, every psychotherapist or counsellor is identical, and in some ways different. Now, there are no votes in such an unsexy formulation. But I invite my readers to consider it at the outset for its very complexity and ambiguity.

The professional concerns raised in this chapter are directly connected to my own ongoing work in the psychology–politics field. I am attempting to bring a psycholog-ical perspective to the political issues of the day, and to a re-invention of the political

DOI: 10.4324/9781003598985-12

itself. In the 1990s, I was a founder of Psychotherapists and Counsellors for Social Responsibility (PCSR) and of Antidote, the psychotherapy-based think tank. In 2014, I co-founded (with Emilija Kiehl) the Jungian Analysis and Activism movement.

On a more clinical level, I am involved in working out the details of what I call the 'politicisation of therapy practice'. Everybody these days says they want to work with the political and social dimensions in therapy. It has become a kind of cocktail-party truism or slogan. Yet there are absolutely no detailed texts on how to do this. So I am trying to write such detailed texts that explicate the political person as he or she appears in the clinical situation (see Samuels 1993).

My interest in pluralism and psychotherapy dates from the publication of *Jung and the Post-Jungians* in 1985. In that book, I commented that it was not easy to find one's way around in the contemporary Jungian world. This was because very little had been written on the various competing schools of analytical psychology that have grown up. The book and my whole approach rest on a fundamental paradox – that by concentrating on debate, dispute, and difference, we can get the best possible conception of what psychotherapy as a whole really is.

Traditionally, the ways in which one defines a field involve looking for that which everybody agrees with – the consensus approach. These core values and core practices are usually regarded as defining the field. This is old-fashioned thinking. We need, instead, to think of a radical way of defining the field by reference to the differences of opinion in and around it. What defines the field of psychotherapy in my view is dispute. How does this actually work in experience?

If some psychotherapists, of whatever orientations, are having an argument about what psychotherapy really is, and you have some idea what they are talking about, and you are in some way stirred by their argument, then you are in a sense in the field. The field can be defined by the emotional ripples its arguments generate. This is a very complex and difficult idea that lies at the heart of much that I shall be proposing in this chapter. We should start our profession-defining work at the outer limits of the envelope. We should stay with dispute, argument, disagreement, miscommunication, misunderstanding, betrayal, and onslaughts on the other, rather than staying with the core, the centre, the consensus. The philosopher A. N. Whitehead put this beautifully in a nutshell when he said: 'A clash of doctrines is not a disaster, it is an opportunity.' But first you have to find the clash and then use the clash to define what you are doing.

There is a cultural change to consider here, as well. I want to mention this, lest my stress on dispute sound-like an exclusively male perspective. I do not like the term, but there is what could be called a 'feminisation of knowledge' going on in the West today involving a boundary blurring between disciplines and within disciplines. There is a new valuing of subjectivity and intuition even within the hard sciences, and certainly within the social sciences and the humanities. It is my belief that altering the angle from which we define the field to one of difference and dispute, and away from one of consensus and agreement, is in an unexpected sense aligned with such new approaches to knowledge.

So, what is 'pluralism'?

On pluralism

Pluralism is an attitude to conflict which tries to reconcile differences without imposing a false resolution on them or losing sight of the unique value of each position. Hence, pluralism is not the same as 'multiplicity' or 'diversity'. Rather, pluralism is an attempt to hold unity and diversity in balance – humanity's age-old struggle, in religion, philosophy, and politics, to hold the tension between the One and the Many. My use of the term 'pluralism' is also supposed to be different from 'eclecticism' or 'synthesis'. As the chapter unfolds, the distinctions should become clearer. Here, at the beginning, I would merely say that the trademark of pluralism is competition, and its way of life is bargaining.

We need a psychological working out of the idea of pluralism, and, in order to do this, I will make two suggestions.

First, on a personal level, each of us is faced with the pluralistic task of aligning our many internal voices and images of ourselves with our need and wish to speak with one voice and recognise ourselves as integrated beings. So it is an issue of intense feeling. But it is also an issue of thinking – for psychological theory also seeks to see how the various conflicts, complexes, attitudes, functions, self-objects, part-selves, sub-personalities, deintegrates, internal objects, psychic *dramatis personae*, areas of the mind, sub-phrases, and gods – how all of these relate to the personality as a whole. The extent of the list demonstrates the universality of the problem and its inherent fascination.

My second suggestion is that a pluralistic approach may be of immense help in dealing with issues of unity and diversity as they affect psychotherapy, with its massive ideological differences. By 'psychotherapy', I mean all psychological endeavours which seek to help individuals and small groups. We need a term which refers to the social context of the whole field – psychoanalytic, Jungian, integrative, humanistic, body, family and marital, cognitive-behaviourist, etc. – and, at the same time, to the divisions within the field. Of course, we should not forget that the field itself is composed of individual psychotherapists.

The fragmentation and dispute within psychotherapy, as each group fights for the general acceptance of its viewpoint, seem, on the surface, to be the very opposite of what is usually regarded as pluralism. However, as I said earlier, this competitive aggression is at the heart of any attempt to build up a pluralistic approach. The idea of unconscious compensation (in Jungian terms) or the idea of reaction formation (in Freudian terms) suggest that we should look a little more deeply into the warlike situation. If we do so, then it is possible to see psychotherapy as struggling, and as having always struggled, towards pluralism. As Heraclitus put it, 'that which alone is wish both wishes and does not wish to be called Zeus'. What seems like a flight from pluralism may also be a yearning for it and an acceptance at some level of a pluralistic destiny for psychotherapy.

A pluralistic attitude can hold the tension between the claims of and tendencies towards unity and claims of and tendencies towards diversity. Psychotherapy is a cohesive discipline with right and wrong approaches – and psychotherapy as containing a multiplicity of valuable approaches. It would not be pluralistic, as I understand it, to assert that there are many diverse truths but that these are but aspects of one greater Truth. In that religious and elitist approach, entry into the greater Truth, which would do away with all the lesser and seemingly contradictory truths, is reserved for the elect. This is not pluralistic, it is condescendingly casuistic. From a pluralist standpoint, Truth (with a capital T) and truth have to compete. Sometimes passionate and aggressive expressions of, and adherence to, the Truth can (even should) be the right way to live and function. But sometimes we need a more partial and pragmatic vision, equally passionate and aggressive in its way. Aggression, which is so characteristic of debates between psychotherapists, often contains the deepest needs for contact, dialogue, playback, and affirmation.

Now, many psychotherapists are probably committed to dialogue, but the psychological difficulties associated with maintaining a tolerant attitude cannot be minimised. Psychotherapists, being human, will continually fail to be as tolerant as they would like to be. In part, this is because of their passionate devotion to their own psychological approach, to their own particular vision, or 'personal confession'. But where is a programme to combine passion and tolerance in psychotherapy? We know about and concentrate on the opposites of tolerance – envy, denigration, power, control, and so forth. But we usually pathologise these. My intent is to do something positive and realistic with the incorrigible competitiveness and argumentativeness, mining the envious shit for the tension-rich gold it might contain. Competition that is open, competition that is brought into the open, and into consciousness, competition that is psychologically integrated and valued, could lead to a new tough-minded tolerance. My approach is psychologically realistic here, staying close to and trading off what Jung called the shadow – the thing each of us has no wish to be. To mimic Lacan, if the unconscious is indeed structured like anything, it may be structured like an argument!

Through competition and argument with others, we may come to know ourselves and our ideas better and more deeply. This is an example of the importance of the mirroring other whose presence glimmers in so many dialectical psychologies – Jung's, Winnicott's, Neumann's, Lacan's, Kohut's, and Mitchell's. This other is a creative other and needs nurturing. What is more – and I mention this as an example of the realism of pluralism – you cannot annihilate the other who is your opponent. He or she will not go away. The opponent is omnipresent and indestructible. The opponent resists the false way in which we all try to describe him or her. Sure, you can describe your opponent as narcissistic, religiose, mechanistic, idealistic, transference-bound, and badly trained – but he or she will bounce back, rejecting that distortion and returning to the argument: *la lutta continua*. Like it or not, the dialogue and confrontation go on, as they always have in psychotherapy. And, amidst the seemingly ridiculous institutional splits, a kind of exchange is constantly being crafted. Let us not forget that when we project on to an other, it is often the good or positive things about ourselves that are projected (for whatever reason). Re-collection of projected contents is vital for the health and integrity of the self.

Psychotherapy is a social phenomenon which, viewed over time, has shown itself able to withstand clashes and splits and generate new ideas out of them. This capacity lies alongside the far better-known tendency for the splits to become institutional and concrete, and hence somewhat unproductive. Psychotherapy continues to be desirous of entering a pluralistic state but lacks the ideological and methodological means to do it. It could even be possible that we are all pluralists but the prevailing ideology in the world we live in forces us to deny it. The tendency towards multiplicity and diversity is as strong – and creative – as the search for unity or a striving for hegemony.

As we proceed, we shall see again and again how these two suggestions of mine are really the same suggestion. That is to say, the experience of the One and the Many in relation to one's own psyche and personality and the argument about the One and Many in relation to disputes in the professional area of psychotherapy are, in a sense, the same thing. However, the vicissitudes of psychotherapy as a cultural movement – the splits, plots, alliances, gossip, and power struggles – all these reveal that, in their professional lives, therapists are participating in a mighty projection of the objective psyche. When therapists argue, it is the psyche that is speaking. Differing points of view reflect the multiplicity of the psyche itself. And when therapists recognise what they have in common, often through discussions of clinical experiences, then it is psyche in its monistic, unified vein that is revealed.

My point is that when therapists look at themselves – and they should always be looking at themselves – how they think, feel, behave, and organise themselves, they are, perhaps without knowing it, also gazing at and participating in the world of the psyche.

Similarly, the books that therapists write, and candidates and colleagues read, are not what they seem to be. Texts of psychological theory can constitute for us what alchemical texts constituted for Jung. A deconstruction of psychotherapy parallels his of alchemy. Just as the alchemists projected the workings of the unconscious into chemical elements and processes, becoming caught up in the pervasive symbolism of it all, so the texts of the psychotherapists, taken as a whole and understood psychologically, may unwittingly provide us with documents of the soul. I think this is a radical re-reading of what books on psychotherapy are about. What was intended to be about psyche is *of* psyche. The conscious aim may be to plumb the past for its truths, or to connect past and present, or to reveal the workings of cumulative psychopathology. But what gets revealed, according to this analysis, are the central characteristics of psyche itself. This is where clashes between theories are so useful, because the actual clash itself contains the definitive psychic issue, not the specific ideas which are in conflict. Not psychological dialectics, but psyche's discourse given dialectical form. The warring theories and the particular points of conflict speak directly of what is at war in the psyche and of what the points of conflict might be therein.

Now, sometimes it is claimed that differences of opinion could not have such deep implications because they only show differences in the psychological type of the disputants. I agree that some therapists will tend constitutionally to prefer, see, and search for multiplicity and differentiation. Others will be more inclined to favour and to find integration and unity. But this typological approach contains the seeds of its own contradiction. As with typology, to become truly himself or herself, the psychotherapist cannot 'belong' to one school alone. There is an interdependence, with all possible manner of divergence and convergence.

Pluralism is a perspective in which various therapists or the various schools of psychotherapy have to take note of each other, without necessarily having unity as a goal, a modular, conversational approach in which different worldviews meet but do not try to take each other over.

When theories and fantasies of the psyche are in competition, what attitudes are possible? None seems really satisfactory. We can choose between theories – but that may lead to blind partisanship and possibly to tyranny. We can synthesise theories – but that may lead to omnipotence and an avoidance of the hard edges of disagreement rather than to transcendence. We can be indifferent to the dispute, but that leads to ennui and a subtle form of 'clinical' inflation in which the relevance of theory is denied. Of course we could be pluralistic – but that leads to fragmentation and anxiety (as we shall see). It is hard to act upon, this idea of pluralism!

Political thinkers and philosophers have addressed many of the questions we shall try to answer, and we can learn from that. Later, I will use pluralistic political thinking as a metaphor to further our understanding of psychological processes and of the social organisation of psychotherapy.

Let us consider how pluralism conceives of the state. This will be a useful model for a subsequent discussion of the role of national or trans-national umbrella psychotherapy organisations. Many people see the state as the container of everything in a society. But it is not. A state may also be regarded as a special interest group within society. Political process in a single society consists of arguments, competitions, bargaining, between the various interest groups in society, and perhaps the state has a regulatory role. But the regulatory role of the state itself also constitutes a special interest. The state may indeed be special when we are talking about regulation. But when we are talking about other things – art, trade, or maybe education – then the state does not necessarily have a particularly special place. What I am trying to communicate is a vision of the state in which what we usually think of as the unifying factor, the container, the core, the regulator, is also one of the parts. In human psychology, the ego (and even the self), often regarded as fulfilling the functions of 'the state' for an individual, is, as many theorists have pointed out, nothing more than one part of the psyche competing with the other parts. In modern societies, increasingly, the state has to argue for its place in the sun. The state can be as vulnerable to competitive pressures as any other interest group in a society.

Pluralism and the organisation of psychotherapy

We can move this argument on or over to the question of psychotherapy organisations I referred to earlier. In the case of organisations like the UK Council for Psychotherapy (UKCP), the implication of what I have been saying is that the organisation as a whole, with its central committees, is not in fact only a container or regulator of everything going on in it. They (the organisation and its central committees) are special interest groups. The centre ('ego') of UKCP is only a special interest group! The Annual General Meeting, supposedly the container of everything, is only a special interest group. There is a paradox here. *What looks like the big thing is only in certain respects and at certain moments the big thing.* For much of the time, the big thing is only one of a number of little things. This is political pluralism applied to our understanding of umbrella psychotherapy organisations.

The manyness – the sections, the organisations, and the individual psychotherapists – and the oneness – the UKCP as a whole – are in a competitive relationship. It is important to re-imagine and re-vision the centre or the conference as a whole also as parts. The centre, the Governing Board, and the Registration Board are not above the fray. They have their own state-like interests at stake. They, too, are involved in the bargaining process – as parts relating to parts, not as a whole relating to parts.

I think what I want us to do is to get beyond either maternal or paternal models for our professional organisations. In the maternal model, the big thing, the UKCP as a whole (to continue with the British example), 'holds' everything else in it. Holding as in Winnicott's idea of maternal function. In the paternal model, the UKCP sets standards and guidelines, makes regulations which everyone has to adhere to. A pluralistic model moves beyond the family altogether to try to find a new way to approach this organisational problem, which everybody is worried about: the relations between the organisation as a whole (and its central committees) and the rest. By this simple and yet oh-so-complex device of reconceiving the whole as a part, we can at least make a psychologically valid beginning in working out new models – pluralistic models – for psychotherapy organisations.

Can diversity be analysed so as to reveal its special requirements and guidelines? And can we develop a vision of diversity which makes a place for unity? For, as I have said, pluralism, as I use the term, does not simply mean diversity or multiplicity, not just the Many.

We know from politics that freedom does not guarantee diversity, for freedom can lead to a part of a system expanding to take a tyrannical hold over the whole. If I am free to do or be what I like, this will produce an unequal state of affairs between you and me. To make sure that does not happen, we may be required by political consensus or law to be more equal in some or all respects. But then an inhibition has been placed on my freedom. Exactly the same conundrum faces the psychotherapist today. If I act on, live out, hold dear, fight for my ideas, what am I to do with the differing points of view of which I am aware? I can't just deny that these points of view exist! My freedom to have a particular point of view may lead to an unhelpful, destructive denigration and abandonment of other people's ideas to the ultimate detriment of my own position and personal psychological well-being.

Equality doesn't guarantee diversity either, for equality may lead to the perils of indifference and boredom stemming from an unreal and infinite tolerance that lacks passion, is flat, bland, and mediocre. This ennui can be seen in the attitude some practitioners have towards theoretical differences: they don't matter when compared to clinical inevitabilities. This myopic, clinical triumphalism overlooks the fact that everything in one's practice is suffused with theory (and, hopefully, vice versa). But if all views are considered to be of equal worth, what is to become of the freedom to feel a special value attaching to one's own view?

So, surprising to psychotherapists, perhaps, but not to political theorists, neither the freedom to think nor an egalitarian approach to thought can be said to guarantee diversity in a way that permits a unified view to coexist with it. Perhaps there is a problem with the way I have formulated things, and so I want to make a most radical suggestion. Instead of advancing pluralism as a desirable state or goal, let us begin instead to use it as a tool or instrument whose purpose is to make sure that diversity does not lead to schism and that differences between particular points of view are not smoothed over. Pluralism can function as an instrument which monitors the mosaic of the psyche or of the psychotherapy profession, rather than as a governing ideal.

One last brief point concerns pluralism and clinical practice. It seems to me that we have to start thinking in terms of what I call 'plural interpretation'. Plural interpretation is not the same as offering the patient a kind of multiple-choice interpretation, letting them choose the interpretation they fancy or think is right. Plural interpretation makes the existence in the therapist's mind of competing alternative interpretations a central plank of some interpretations that he or she may want to make. As we all know, it is often the case that there are a number of different ways in which material can be understood. These exist simultaneously in the mind of the therapist and often all of them have an equal, or nearly equal, weight. I would advocate that questions arising from the idea of plural interpretation, whether it is adopted as a technique or not, should be being discussed with any good-enough training, especially within the supervision situation, which carries this particular burden of multiple understanding.

Pluralism and psychotherapy training

Now, I hope we are in a position to use pluralism as an instrument or tool to help us look at the topic of dispute and disagreement in psychotherapy. This subject is, I suggest, of the greatest importance to anyone concerned with the training and formation of the psychotherapists of the future, seniors, and candidates alike.

A pluralistic approach to psychotherapy, as I have explained it, means that a person interested in any particular area of knowledge should seek out the conflict and, above all, the competition between practitioners and ideologues in the discipline. The main implication is that even a so-called beginner should try to discover what the contemporary debate is all about. This approach differs fundamentally and profoundly from the conventional, linear style of training and education in psychotherapy. There, one is supposed to start 'at the beginning', and when the 'basics' have been mastered and one is 'grounded', exposure to more grown-up disagreements is permitted. The point I am advancing, backed up by a good deal of teaching experience, is that starting at the beginning is no guarantee of comprehension. However, if a person were to focus on the up-to-the-minute ideological conflict, then he or she cannot avoid discovering what has gone before; book learning is replaced by a living process. In a way, this is an educational philosophy derived from psychotherapy itself. In therapy, the focus of interest is where the internal 'debate' is at its most virulent; and in therapy, the participants do not follow a linear 'course'.

The debates within psychotherapy give it life. They also serve to define the discipline generally, as I suggested earlier, and act as access routes for those who want to learn. What is important is not so much whether people are right or wrong, though it is vital to have views about that, but whether you know what they are talking about. For it is really rather hard to be completely wrong in psychotherapy. Or, as Kafka put it, 'the correct perception of a matter and a complete misunderstanding of the matter do not totally exclude one another'.

I am suggesting that, instead of searching for one guiding theory, we consider several competing theories together and organise our training around such theoretical competition using papers and books written with polemical intent. Actually, if you think about it, that includes a high proportion of the literary output of psychotherapists! What holds these theories together is that the subject – the psyche – holds together; just as for modern sub-atomic physicists, their subject, the universe, holds together. In this viewpoint, passion for one approach is replaced by passion for a plurality of approaches.

Problems of pluralism

Let's consider now some of the problems with pluralism. For all manner of psychological reasons, it is very hard to get worked up about being tolerant, to be a radical centrist in psychotherapy, to go in for what has been called 'animated moderation'. Does pluralism condemn us to losing the excitement of breakthrough ideas, which are more likely to be held with a passionate conviction? My view is that such a worry rests on a misunderstanding and an idealisation of the cycle of creativity. So-called new ideas emerge from a pluralistic matrix and are re-absorbed into such a matrix. As Winnicott put it paraphrasing T. S. Eliot: 'It is not possible to be original except on the basis of a tradition' (Winnicott 1971, p. 117). Ideas do not come into being outside of a context; nor does the new necessarily destroy the old but often co-exists with it. So, what looks like inspirational conviction arises from a plural *mise en scene* but it is convenient for the debt not to be acknowledged. And before we hail the man or woman of vision, let us not forget Yeats's words: 'the worst are full of passionate intensity'. The well-known clinical benefits of having conviction in one's ideas can still be available, but together with open communication, and the chance to learn from diversity.

This is not a dry or woolly perspective; passion abides in dialogue and tolerance as much as it does in monologue and fanaticism. The psychotherapist has never been able to work in isolation from others in the same field who have a different viewpoint. That's the conclusion I draw from the history of splits and struggles. People have to fight with one another because they cannot ignore one another. Leaving aside the never-settled question of whether any one clinical approach is more 'successful' than the others, the arrogance of isolation was never a viable option. The rows within psychotherapy cannot be ignored in a serene, Olympian fashion.

Even those who feel uncomfortable with pluralism, and seek to render it inaccurately as 'eclecticism', need to recall that their own theories arose from a pluralistic matrix and from a competitive diversity of views. For instance, Hillman's archetypal psychology was not a single, time-bound, unchallenged, piercing vision of the future of Jungian analysis. This was also something Winnicott noted in relation to Melanie Klein. In November 1952, he wrote her a remarkable, long, and agonised letter protesting strongly against 'giving the impression that there is a jigsaw of which all the pieces exist' (Winnicott 1987, p. 35).

Psychotherapy's secret desires

So far, I have been trying to establish that pluralism can be seen as an extremely useful metaphorical approach to the interplay of the One and the Many in the psyche and in psychotherapy generally. I have also suggested that pluralism can keep diversity alive in the face of threats from both tyranny and ennui or boredom. I have tried to show that pluralism enables us to harness the competitive and aggressive energy trapped in theoretical dispute and competition. My overall position is that psychotherapy wants to become, needs to be, and, ironically, already is pluralistic.

In spite of all this, pluralism is threatened and under attack from all manner of entrenched interests. I would almost say, thank God that pluralism is under attack, for what would pluralism be without its opponents? There are several branches to this attack which it is possible to identify. First, holism, which tends to impose a false unity on our thinking, ignoring diversity. Second, numinosity, which forms the unavoidable heart of intolerance, for we become overwhelmingly fascinated by our own ideas and correspondingly threatened by other people's. Third, hierarchy, which sets up selected categories as pre-judged good things or goals. But the enemy of pluralism upon which I want to focus is consensus.

Clearly, for there to be any communication at all, some assumptions have to be permitted and agreed, though consensus can become like airline food – just acceptable to everyone but truly pleasurable to none. However, blandness is not what I perceive as problematic with consensus – for consensus is not really cuddly, cosy, friendly, and bland at all. It can be quite violent. In psychotherapy, and perhaps even in science as well, personal allegiance and power dynamics play a part. Orthodoxy, heterodoxy, and heresy come into being. I do not see us as being able to get rid of vested interests, but I would like us to do something creative with the vested interests we have.

This highly politicised state of affairs can be seen most vividly in relation to training for psychotherapy and therefore lies at the very root of psychotherapy as a social institution. Though the candidate is an adult, a degree of regression seems inherent in the training situation due to the continuing entanglements of the candidate's personal therapy and supervision/control work. It has been claimed that the training posture actually fosters regression in general, and persecutory anxiety in particular, and that this is exacerbated by a confusion that often exists in the trainers' mind between therapy and training. My concern is different. It is that the whole range of careful, thoughtful experiences most therapists have been through in their training might inadvertently have removed the creative sting. I am thinking of syllabi, seminar themes, reading lists, feedback sessions, and so forth. The more integrated and professional the training programme, the greater the denial of pluralism.

I think that the denial of pluralism has contributed to the formation of cult-like bodies within our little world of psychotherapy. Being in a cult implies obedience. There may be too much obedience in psychotherapy today. There is a serious danger that training programmes will become obedience cults, and that this will be rationalised by reference to the advantages of practising on the basis of a system in which one has conviction. It is striking how many of the groups which are active in psychotherapy today either are or were in the recent past dominated by leader figures. The leaders may be remarkable people, with a comprehensive vision, which would partially account for the tendency, but I think there is more to it than that. I do not think this pattern results from conscious fostering, but I would argue that its effect is to shield the candidate from the stress and anxiety of pluralism. And then the benefits of pluralism are lost as well. The need for strong leader figures has a lot to do with the desire to avoid the anomalous. The leader sorts things out by arranging competing ideas in a hierarchical schema of acceptability, protecting, or advancing his own ideas in the process. The desire to avoid anxiety and confusion when confronted with something which feels strange and new strengthens the tendency of groups to select leaders as a combination of leader and safety net.

Perhaps it is a case of taking it in turns to be the dominant theorist, accepting that, in some ways and in some situations, the other person has a more utilisable (more 'correct', from a pragmatic viewpoint) theory. Then we may make bilateral and multilateral agreements to sing each other's song – not the same as agreeing to disagree and different, too, from eclecticism. For eclecticism means singing selected verses only. Eclecticism ignores the contradictions between systems of thought, whereas pluralism celebrates their competition. Eclecticism is intolerant in that parts of a theory are wrenched from the whole. In a pluralistic approach, the whole theory is used, as faithfully as possible, and together with other theories, until inconsistencies lead to breakdown. Then the breakdown itself becomes the object of study.

What is a good training?

My short answer to this deliberately naive question is: a good training is an open training.

I want to talk about openness as a criterion for a good training under a number of different headings. These are (1) sexual orientation, (2) gender issues, and (3) socio-economic factors. These can contribute to a discussion on what constitutes a good training.

First of all, sexual orientation. Here is a brief vignette from 1990 concerning a patient of mine (who has given permission for publication). The patient, in his mid-thirties, who is homosexual, was interested in training at the Institute of Psychoanalysis in London. This man was, perhaps, a little naive. Prior to his analysis with me, he had been to see a very distinguished training analyst to discuss the possibilities. Not only was the patient given the information that there was no chance at all, but he was given a whole bundle of gratuitous interpretations about the infantile origins of his homosexuality in terms of the dynamics of the relationship with the father. Now, I think it is very important, if we are considering a good training, that we assert that a training cannot be a good training if it is not open in the area of sexual orientation, given that depth psychological theorising about homosexuality has been shown to be, for the most part, compounded of prejudice, fear, and ignorance (Lewes 1988).

[Note added in 2024: Everything I wrote above is also true in relation to transgender issues.]

The second criterion for openness concerns gender issues. Again, I am going to illustrate this with a very brief vignette which I have permission to publish. A patient of mine was being interviewed for admission to a training course in psychotherapy. She had two interviews. She had a baby who was at the time about six months old; she herself was 40 years old. At the first interview, she was asked about her child-care arrangements which happened to utilise a child-minder. She was asked the following questions: is the child-minder you have employed qualified? What is the size of the group the child-minder has in her house? How much do you pay? At the second interview, when she explained her child-minding arrangements, the interviewer said: 'Ah, so you've found a mother for her.' Now, obviously, this account has been filtered and maybe distorted through the analytical situation. However, I believe it is justifiable to introduce such material so as to illustrate that there is a really oppressive issue here concerning openness which must be addressed. A training cannot be a good training if it is not open in the area of gender issues.

The third aspect of openness is founded on socio-economic issues. Here is another vignette which I have permission to publish. This particular patient left school at 15 and was, to be frank, not particularly literate. So he had enormous trouble in writing the course paper. (I am not intending to raise the more general question about whether or not there should be papers to indicate that a therapist has achieved a certain level of intellectual development.) Here was somebody who, through no fault of their own, for socio-economic reasons, was simply not able to manage what was involved in writing the paper. Yet the patient was apparently getting pretty good reports from supervisors and seminar leaders. On the basis of accounts like this, I think there is a crucial question concerning openness that needs to be examined in socio-economic terms. I am not forgetting racial and ethnic factors as issues of special concern over and above economics, and I discuss ethnicity in/and psychotherapy elsewhere (Samuels 1993, pp. 299–312; see Chapters 12 and 13 in this book).

I would not want these ideas about openness to cease to be applicable once admission to training has been achieved. It is a far more important matter than a mere admissions policy. My vision is of the production of psychotherapists who have the values and perspectives I have summarised under the rubric of 'openness'. Let us try, in our quest for a good training, to turn out socially and politically aware psychotherapists who can bring a sense of openness to what they do and how they think about it. Matters of sexual orientation, gender issues, and socio-economic factors should be addressed during the training and after graduation, as well as in connection with admission to training.

Concluding reflections

To summarise again, I have outlined what I mean by pluralism and suggested that we use it as an instrument. I have suggested what psychotherapy can learn from political theory. An ideology and a methodology for the organisation of the profession are beginning to emerge. Some problems with pluralism have been discussed, and 'consensus' has been attacked.

The general impression I have of psychotherapy is that there was a golden age that is now past. The broad outlines of the enterprise are firmly drawn. If that is so, then the fertilising challenge presented by the arrival on the scene of all-inclusive theories, forcing a person to work out his or her response, has been lost. If our generation's job is not to be restricted to 'professionalisation', institutionalisation, or historical recovery of the happenings of the earlier days, it is necessary to highlight the one thing we can do that the founding parents and brilliant second-generation consolidators cannot. This is to be reflexive in relation to psychotherapy, to focus on the psychology of psychology, a deliberate navel-gazing, a healthily narcissistic trip to the fantastic reaches of our discipline; a post-modern psychological outlook, redolent with the assumption that psychology and psychotherapy are not 'natural', but made by psychologists and psychotherapists. After that, but only after that, we can turn towards the world.

I will conclude with four aphorisms. These are crafted out of an internal dialogue between C. G. Jung and myself about some of these matters. Some words are his and some words are mine:

The art of psychotherapy requires that you be in possession of avowable, credible and defensible convictions.

Too much agreement spells onesidedness and desiccation.

We need many theories before we get even a rough picture of the complexity of the psyche.

Behind every fanaticism lurks a secret doubt.

References

Lewes, K., (1988). *The psychoanalytic theory of male homosexuality*. New York: Penguin.

Samuels, A., (1985). *Jung and the Post-Jungians*. London and Boston, MA: Routledge and Kegan Paul.

Samuels, A., (1993). *The political psyche*. London and New York: Routledge.

Winnicott, D. W., (1971). *Playing and reality*. New York: Penguin.

Winnicott, D. W. and Rodman, F. R., (1987). *The spontaneous gesture: Selected letters of D. W. Winnicott*. Cambridge, MA: Harvard University Press.

Chapter 9

Everything you always wanted to know about therapy (but were afraid to ask)

Social, political, economic, and clinical fragments of a critical psychotherapy

Retrospective Introduction: This chapter, published originally in 2014 and revised for this book, is really a credo. In it, I set out my late-career reflections about many differing aspects of the practice and institution of psychotherapy. I manage to work in many intensely personal and often deeply upsetting professional experiences along the way – for example, my prominent involvement in the campaign in the mid-1990s to overturn the ban in psychoanalytic and some other organisations against lesbians and gay men undertaking training. I have often been asked why I have not written very much on this campaign. The reason is that as an 'ally', I try not to claim leadership but let those directly affected direct how things are managed.

Talking Points: This chapter proposes that therapy and freedom are far from bedfellows. Rather, what therapists and analysts do is heavily conditioned by the rules, systems, and traditions within which they function. There is a need to think about some of the huge fights (about sexuality in particular) in psychotherapy, not as isolated incidents but as indicative of core problems with the whole business. The author was there, so he knows! The title of the chapter references Woody Allen's film on sex.

Introduction

To be critical without reference to the critic would be fatuous. This chapter attempts to share some of what I have learned in the past 50 or so years about the challenges and crises facing psychotherapy and counselling. Prominent experiences have been the founding and successful operation of the Alliance for Counselling and Psychotherapy which led the campaign in 2006–2010 to thwart the Government's plans for state regulation of counselling and psychotherapy in Britain. The minister responsible for regulation of health professionals was kind enough to say to the Alliance that we had 'won the argument'. It was not all due to a change of Government. Indeed, it is fascinating to observe, as with whites in apartheid South Africa, that for a period of time, it was hard to find anyone who supported the absurd and overblown regulatory plans of the then Health Professions Council. Nevertheless, attempts continue to be made to bring counselling and psychotherapy into statutory regulation. It could that the whole divisive battle will be fought all over again.

DOI: 10.4324/9781003598985-13

Created in 2006, the Alliance brought together progressive thinkers from all the modalities and traditions of psychotherapy. We had Lacanian analysts working alongside libertarian humanistic people who rejected the very term 'psychotherapist'. Putting aside considerable distrust of legal process, the Alliance strongly supported the successful application for Judicial Review that a group of psychoanalysts mounted. Although this was by no means my first exposure to working harmoniously via difference in the professional field – a similar pluralism characterised the earlier formation (by Judy Ryde and myself) in 1994 of PCSR – it was a memorable experience (see Samuels 1993).

PCSR had also tangled with the Government by drawing the attention of the then health ministers to discrimination against members of sexual minorities with regard to training at a number of psychoanalytic institutes and also in some important NHS centres of excellence in psychotherapy. The campaign was greatly helped by what some have called the idiocy of the most prominent theoretician Charles Socarides, who had been invited to give an important NHS lecture and to get an award. The dressing-up of his out-of-date prejudices as psychoanalytic theory was so obvious that even a Conservative politician was incredulous. It has been amusing to see how the institutes I referred to above nowadays stroke themselves with pride at having scrapped their discriminatory practices. But what is actually taught on those trainings regarding sexuality may be another matter entirely.

A second relevant experience was my unexpected (though overwhelming) election as the chair of the UKCP in 2009, mentioned in the previous chapter. In my three years in office, I was made forcefully aware of the destructive threats facing psychotherapy, especially but not exclusively in the public sector – and also of the significant extent to which psychotherapy had contributed to its own crisis: by incorrigible infighting, pathological deference to authority, adoption of a falsely 'deep' perspective on issues that inhibited action and, generally, living in a series of interconnected bubbles. There was a failure to engage with new thinking on therapy provision, such as national low-cost schemes, community-based endeavours, and ideas about there being a psychological 'commons' (Postle 2013, 2014). Sometimes, it was clear to me that, despite the overall goodness of the project to defend and extend psychotherapy in the NHS, much of what existed prior to the cuts was difficult to justify. For example, certain modalities had 'captured' certain localities, and people with different training backgrounds could not get jobs. People reading this may be interested to note that, where UKCP and its sister organisations were successful in campaigning against cuts, the support of the local community and its elected councillors was decisive.

On a more personal level, finding myself established in the profession, I have been more able, in recent years, to reconnect to the earlier passions of my life: to political activism, to an ongoing love affair with the theatre, and to humanistic psychology. My first work as anything resembling a therapist was in the context of theatre work with massively deprived young people. Then, followed a time, as an encounter group leader, leading, in an epiphany, to training as a Jungian analyst. Subsequent extra periods in body psychotherapy, marital therapy and systemic therapy on an individual basis have helped to give me a sense of proportion with regard to many of the issues that upset colleagues.

For years, I quoted the French writer on religious themes, Charles Péguy, who claimed that 'Everything starts in mysticism and ends in politics'. Perhaps now, as I enter my mid-sixties, the poles of that aphorism are starting to reverse. Hence, these fragments of a critical psychotherapy are intended to be compassionate as well – and to look to the future as well as bemoaning and slashing the present.

I write as an insider so, if there is a bubble in place, enveloping the world of counselling and psychotherapy, I am probably in it. Hence, what I and many others in the bubble see as radical will, to someone who believes themselves to be outside of the bubble, seem rather conservative. While this may be so, I doubt that anyone is so free of their context as to be 100% outside of a bubble. (See Chapter 6 for a discussion about the limits of 'context'.) One way of reconciling this is to say that the bubble will benefit if ideas developed externally penetrate into it.

In the chapter, I discuss three assertions about psychotherapy that, as far as I can tell, would find substantial if not universal support. (You never will find unanimity in the therapy field.) Then, as stated, I will discuss each of them critically, compassionately, and with an eye to the future.

(1) Counselling and psychotherapy can be free and independent professions, provided we, acting together, fight for them to be that way (the one word tag for this topic is 'Freedom').
(2) Counselling and psychotherapy are private and personal activities, operating in the realms of feelings and emotions – the psyche, the unconscious, and affects rooted in the body. Above all other factors, the single most important thing is the therapy relationship between two people ('Relationship').
(3) Counselling and psychotherapy are vocations, not jobs. Therapists are not only motivated by money ('Vocation').

Freedom

Much of what follows derives from reflection after the successful campaigns to remove discrimination against sexual minorities in terms of psychoanalytic training and to stop the project of state regulation. While I am pleased that all of it happened, I have come to see that a notion has developed that, provided we are organised and energetic enough, we can 'save' psychotherapy, and can recuperate its independence and its awkward nature (awkward from the point of view of the powerful, that is). Now, painfully, I am not sure.

These are never going to be free and independent professions (and nor are any of the other professions in our society). Some would say that psychotherapy isn't really a profession at all. But the point is that the state is omnipresent, and this is true even if its mode of regulation is said to be 'voluntary'. The legal system, including legislation about 'equality', sets parameters for clinical work. Therapy takes place within what sometimes seems like an immutable economic system with its concomitant values of an anti-humanistic nature. We are all subject to ethics codes, sometimes called Fitness to Practise, and even supervision and peer supervision temper any illusion of freedom. There is no free association, in all senses.

The 'supervisor on your shoulder' is a phrase with which every therapist is familiar. I have often wondered if the old-fashioned term 'control analysis' doesn't describe the supervisory process more precisely. There is a politics of supervision, to do with power generally, but also with clashes of values and experiences. Also, your supervisor has desire too. I do not refer here to the erotics of supervision, a powerful phenomenon that has yet to be written about very much. I am referring to the manifold ways in which supervisors seek mirroring that they are good and even brilliant supervisors. It would then mean that they are good and even brilliant therapists. This requires, au fond, agreement – and it remains true even when the official line is that robust differences of opinion are welcomed. One learns pretty quickly, if one's supervisor is psychoanalytically oriented, that you must not see your work as educative, that you must not reassure or promise the client that things will be OK, and that you really need to think extremely carefully and reflect deeply and discuss with the supervisor before you disclose any personal information. If you make a mistake, then saying sorry is not the default position.

I turn now to what could be called 'the profession in the mind of the therapist' – a serious inhibitor of freedom. The various experiences described in the introduction have made me sensitive to the internalised professional hierarchies that exist in the therapy world. Though things are changing, one can still discern, by interpreting the intensity of cries of protest that it is not so, that psychoanalysis remains at the top of the therapy pile, something that belies its general cultural decline. It is clear that when therapists undertake second therapies wherein they can choose the modality of their therapist, they go to psychoanalysts. Jungians can tell you a lot about the hierarchy. I said, many years ago, aping Avis in its battle with behemoth Hertz: 'We're number two – we try harder'.

Humanistic and integrative psychotherapists have tended to welcome government projects to map the skills of therapy practice and even to welcome regulation, because it would 'level the playing field'. All state-regulated therapists would be equal. I have always said that, in this particular regard, such humanistic and integrative supporters of regulation have got a point. But the fact that some people are complaining that the playing field is not level means, surely, that they are admitting that the playing field is not level – which is the point I am developing here.

Finally, therapists do not strike me as wanting to be free. I have already noted a deference to authority, and given unconscious dynamics, this deference may also be present in some shadowy form when therapists seem rabidly against authority of any kind. We are, for the most part, a conventional and conformist group of people. Generally, the highest clinical value is attached to settled long-term relationships that produce children, to 'normal' families and not to lone-parent families or families headed by two parents of the same sex. The profession is not as reprehensibly homophobic as it used to be, but the plumb-line for the majority remains heteronormative.

We know now how much the composition of the therapy pair or group matters and that it profoundly affects the therapy process – as does everything in society such as violence, war, ecological disaster, unemployment and poverty, and major state-sponsored surveillance intrusions into privacy. Therapy is not hygienically insulated from the infection of such phenomena, and, if we continue in a critical vein, we find that it means that therapy is not really free to define itself in any way. Differing cultural and ethical specifics may make an approach based on the therapy relationship or the therapeutic alliance inappropriate or damaging in some instances. In a sense, the client may have to resist the way in which the therapist predefines their joint activity.

Let me pose a few relevant questions at this juncture. The matter of therapists from minorities working with clients, and not from those minorities (i.e. so-called majority clients), is important. How white clients feel when confronted with black therapists, or straight clients with a therapist from a sexual minority (yes, such things can sometimes be visible or are acknowledged/disclosed), are not talked or written about very much. Yet, in conversation with Black and ethnic-minority therapists, there is a considerable fear that one will be sequestered into working only with clients who resemble the therapist.

We know, too, that the history of relations between the groups the two participants come from is important. There are ancestral as well as here-and-now dynamics when a black person and a white person work therapeutically together, or when a German and a Jew find themselves in the same therapy room.

In addition, economic inequality, and its concomitant envy and sense of failure or success, skew the transference-countertransference. Sometimes, the client has more wealth, and sometimes the therapist. Money is always a hot issue (see Samuels 2014b). Much the same can be said about the physical health and disability characteristics of both participants.

What about similars working together as therapist and client? Of course, it is a truism that apparent cultural and identity similarities mask deeper differences in culture and background, so there is always cultural difference in the room. But to focus on it avoids the sharp point I wish to make here: palpable difference and inequality inevitably impact on the level of professional freedom that can exist.

Relationship

'It's the relationship, stupid!' Taking off from ex-U.S. President Bill Clinton's famous 'it's the economy, stupid!', this slogan was seriously considered for use in an advertising and PR campaign in support of psychotherapy and counselling. This was possible because it was the therapy relationship that was considered the unique selling point of psychotherapy and counselling. This is stated to be what the clients want, and it is what the therapists want to offer. It has become a marker of difference between psychotherapy and Cognitive Behaviour Therapy (CBT) – which may be one rhetorical reason why CBT practitioners these days emphasise that there, too, the client will find a relationship. We're all relational now (see Loewenthal and Samuels 2014).

Hence, I have asked (Samuels 2014a) whether relationality in therapy was still cutting edge or had become conformist. I said it could well be both. But I also argued that the emphasis on relationship, with notions of safety, containment, holding, and diminution of risk, tended in the conformist direction. Without going so far as to say that making therapy safe is all done in the interests of the therapist, I think we have to consider what our professional expectation – that safety is what clients need – has done to the way we work. Does it not reinforce the idea of the client as needy, dependent, and infantile, caught between flight and fight? Such clients exist. Perhaps every client is like this at some time. But pushed just a little bit further, this apparently profoundly psychotherapeutic set of assumptions about clients comes perilously close to imitating what the government's state therapy scheme (Improving Access to Psychological Therapies [IAPT]) wants to see in its clients. The clients of state therapy are to be compliant and grateful, do what the therapist wants them to do, and, above all, get off state benefits and back to work. The therapist is situated as an expert, working out of an evidence base, something like a surgeon whose recommendations one would be very misguided to disobey. When psychotherapists and counsellors say to clients, 'You must relate to me', they are as mistrustful of the client's autonomy as anyone working as a state therapist would be.

What we are seeing in the literature, and hence we may assume is taking place in practice, is the emergence of a wholly different conception of the client, a perspective that sees the client as the motor of therapy (summarised in Norcross 2011). This client is a heroic client, a client who knows what she needs, a client who can manage her own distress. As Postle (personal communication 2013) has pointed out, there is also a client who engages less in a process of healing or cure and more in a process of ongoing enquiry. This multifaceted new client is potentially a healer of others, especially the therapist, and, in a sense, of the world. Client as a healer.

Summarising a mass of research findings, Norcross (2011) has forced us to consider whether it truly is the therapy relationship that is the decisive factor. Is the private and highly personal therapy relationship the main thing that makes therapy work? Not really. Unexplained and extra-therapeutic factors amount to some 40% of efficacy variance, the client accounts for 30%, the therapy relationship 12%, the actual therapist 8% and the school or tradition or modality of the therapist 7%. Of course, Norcross would be the first to admit that therapy is a melange of all of these, and I would add that the findings do not do more than force us to consider our ideas about our clients. These figures are far from veridical. But let us take them as heuristic, stimulants to critical thinking about clients. Who they are, what do they want and what point in their life journey have they reached? What stage have they reached in what Norcross calls their 'trajectory of change'?

There are some clients from whom one learns great lessons. My first training 'case' had a dream early on in the analysis. She dreamt: 'I visit a doctor who is ill in bed. He begs me to stay'. Her associations to 'bed' were of illness, not of sexuality. How else could we understand this dream? Was the doctor in fact me?! Or was this an assumption, intended to justify what has been called a 'you mean me' interpretation (also known as a here-and-now transference interpretation)? Was there denial here, in that she is the ill one and I am truly the doctor? Or is she in the grip of an inflation, of herself as the one who brings life and succour, more than a human mother? Or was this dream, perhaps, an accurate perception? I did need something from her, and not just that she stick with me so I could get through the training. Crucially, there would be a further accurate perception in the dream: that she could in fact help/heal this doctor. This was in 1974, and at that time, it would have been difficult to think of the client as healer. Has much changed? (I write at length and with permission about working with this client, 'D', in Samuels 1985.)

Thinking of the client as a healer, we see that recent thinking about the client has moved in that general direction. From the person-centred approach, we find Bohart and Tallman (1999) referring to the 'active client'. Rogers (1951), in the era when the discourse was of 'client-centred' therapy, makes it clear that the client knows for herself what is needed, where she wants to go. Jung (1946) writes of entropy in the client, an innate process of self-regulation. From relational psychoanalysis, we read that Hoffman (2006) regards the client as having responsibilities to the analyst and the analysis, more than just for the co-creation of the therapy relationship.

So the therapist is, in a way, adjunct to the therapy process. But she is also a contingent figure, product of a particular social circumstance. Franks (1961) suggested that what makes the therapist is not only training, techniques, and wounds but also being socially sanctioned as a therapist, a sort of overarching placebo effect. The therapist is being socially sanctioned, granted permission to be a therapist – by society and by the client. This is a new version of the client who does not want the analyst to be the one who knows, or even one who is supposed to know.

Let us see what happens if we revision the therapy relationship with all of these thoughts about the client in mind. I am putting it like this because it has gradually dawned on me that clients sometimes do not dare to deploy their tacit knowledge and emotional literacy. We therapists are cool with this because it leaves us free to do our work. But that could, and, from a critical perspective, perhaps should change.

Almost no one argues for discarding the idea of the therapy relationship completely, such unanimity being a rare phenomenon in our field. As already mentioned, even CBT therapists are now aware of it and work with it these days. But the therapy relationship is a limited lens through which to view therapy. It is also far too monolithic. Based on Jung's alchemical metaphor for transference-countertransference, I suggested (in Samuels 1985) that the question we should ask is: 'One therapy relationship or many?' Similarly, Clarkson (1986) acutely delineated five levels of the therapy relationship. So what gets called 'the therapy relationship' is in fact only one aspect or level of the therapy relationship. Sticking my neck out, and aware that I am generalising, could it be that we have conflated all the others into what is accurately termed the therapeutic alliance or working alliance? If there is co-creation, it stems from the alliance. If there is an inter-subjective process, it is sustained by the therapeutic alliance. But there are problems with the idea of the therapeutic alliance and these are not much discussed.

Focus on the therapeutic alliance can also be a very one-sided perspective on therapy. For it is as if the therapist is the one who is ready, willing, and able to enter the alliance, whereas the client has to struggle to enter it. 'Well done, client, for getting to where I, your therapist, have already got!' Now, I expect some people who are therapists to object to this and say that they do sometimes struggle to enter the alliance. But be honest about it – don't you usually regard your struggle to enter the alliance as more to do with the client or type of client you are with? The client is a sort of obstacle to your entering the therapeutic alliance? How can borderline clients or traumatised clients or regressed clients do what their therapists have done, reach the level of therapeutic alliance-readiness?

If what I am saying is at all reasonable, then the very attempt to have a kind of ethical equality in therapy – the stress on the therapeutic alliance – can lead to a radical inequality. Herein, the therapist is the one who is 'sorted' about the project of therapy, and the client as having to 'commit' to it. Not fair. I do not think that much of what is regarded as the therapy relationship can achieve what Jung (1946, p. 219) meant when he wrote: 'The meeting of two personalities is like the contact of two chemical substances: if there is any reaction, both are transformed'.

A number of specific critiques of the proposition that it is 'the relationship' that is central to the therapy process will now be outlined.

(1) Social critiques: therapy is an induced relationship, not a natural one. The therapy relationship is imbued with the history, power dynamics, and authority structures of therapy itself.

(2) Systemic critiques: focus on the therapy relationship misses out the presence and impact of the wider human systems in which client and therapist are embedded: families, friends, other people at work, and so on. Just to give a simple example, it has been illuminating to listen to the answers when I ask a potential new client what their partner or family thinks about their having therapy. Paradoxically, nothing is more potent in this regard than to be told that the client has not told anyone.

(3) Reality critiques: this is a critique of those, mainly but not only in psychoanalysis, who see hints and references to the therapist in the discourse of the client. Sometimes, as I mentioned earlier, these are called 'you mean me' interpretations', so the inefficient car mechanic is the inadequate therapist in disguised form. Or, there is simply a symbolic interpretation made. Mrs. Thatcher is your Mum, David Cameron (or Saddam Hussein) your shadow. But sometimes the car mechanic (or the boss at work) is just the mechanic or the boss, Mrs. Thatcher is Mrs. Thatcher and David Cameron plays himself. (And sometimes clients are late because there really has been a body on the line.)

(4) Ecological and political critiques: emphasis on the therapy relationship makes it even more difficult for the client to express the impact on herself of planetary/environmental crisis or any other collective field of emotional distress. When I first began to advocate the therapist picking up on political aspects of the client's material, I was told that I might be depriving the client of the

opportunity to talk about her mother if I kept her references to Mrs. Thatcher on the level of Mrs. Thatcher. I replied that I was worried about the opposite: that a client who needed to talk about Mrs. Thatcher would be definitely if indirectly discouraged from so doing because talking about mother is what one does in therapy. In principle, any political theme can be taken under the umbrella of the therapy relationship and it is an important development in our field that people are doing that to an ever-increasing extent. But whether the focus moves off the two humans in the room is another question, one that deserves a fuller discussion at some point (see Samuels 2006).

(5) Ethical and epistemological critiques: without intending it, proponents of the centrality of the therapy relationship are buying into a particular view of human relationships. In this view, people are regarded as atomised, isolated beings who have to struggle into relationship and when they achieve relationship with a therapist, the two people in the relationship 'own' it. But this is not the only narrative of relationality. What about those narratives in which people are always already in connection and relationship? They do not meet each other via the hurling of projections (from the Latin *proicere*, to throw a spear) across empty space. For there does not exist any empty space between people, even though it may look that way. What if we conceive of a rhizome, or nutrient to be, buried out of sight, which throws up separate stalks that are, nevertheless, already connected? What if we understand the two people as linked by their citizenship, their membership of the polis, no matter how different that experience might be for them? Or, as Totton has suggested (personal communication 2013), perhaps we should understand the members of the therapy pair as linked via their experiencing and perhaps exploring the manifold bodily, physical phenomena present in the therapy room?

(6) It would be ironic as well as tragic if, just as we discover the importance of the created therapy relationship, we omit to recognise (and experience) the ordinary and 'natural' relationship that is always there. One need hardly add that the autonomous, separate, 'individuated' person is exactly the person that capitalism and free market theorising assumes to exist. So, relationality in therapy is not a politically neutral notion.

This observation on the politics of the idea of therapy relationship leads me to suggest that the new model client, the client as the motor of therapy, is increasingly a politically active and aware client. One possible goal of therapy might be that, during the work, the client may develop her capacity for alterity, meaning, among other things, an empathic concern for the other. Yes, this does mean other people – but there is a more-than-personal version of alterity to consider. For example, in a multicultural world, meeting one's inner diversity could lead to support for outer (cultural) diversity and hence to support for those hitherto subjects to social inclusion. To the idea that a client is also a healer, we can now add that clients have the potential to be citizen-therapists for the wider world, with its environmental problems, economic injustice and ubiquitous violence. The therapy client, revisioned as a healer, may now be understood to be a socially responsible agent of *Tikkun Olam*, the drive to repair and restore the world.

My research (2006) shows that, in many countries, clients bring political, social, and cultural material to therapy much more than they did (and, I would add, they will bring even more when they know it is permitted to do so). Therapy becomes a place where, in political dialogue, client and therapist work out their political attitudes and engagements. This can be as transformative as a more personal alchemy, and can be done even when one of them finds the political position of the other to be horrid or reprehensible.

As so often, when one thinks one is gathering in some new ideas in the therapy field, one finds that there is a back story. In 1957, Racker stressed that analysis is not something done by a sane person to a neurotic one. In 1975, Searles wrote his paper 'The patient as therapist of his analyst'. If part of 'mental health' is to want and be able to help and heal others, then it is not this something to work on in analysis? If so, then is not the obvious relationship within which the client can develop skills as a healer the one with the analyst? (Searles 1975).

A few years earlier, in *Power in the Helping Professions*, the Jungian analyst Guggenbühl-Craig (1971) pointed out that the sharp split in Western culture between health and woundedness impacts on psychotherapy. Therapists get assigned health and clients left with their woundedness. But in the inner worlds of each resides the opposite. We know about wounded therapists (and I will soon devote a whole section of this chapter to them). But even Guggenbühl-Craig does not write much about clients as healers.

The word 'healing' is much used, and I suppose, there is intended a contradistinction to curing and cure. This was developed in some detail by Gordon (1978) in her book *Dying and Creating: A Search for Meaning*. But, with healing in mind, perhaps one does not have to do very much. Meier (1949) showed this in his account of classical Greek healing practices in *Ancient Incubation and Modern Healing*: If you are ill, enter the temenos, the sacred temple precinct, lie down, sleep, and take your dreams to the priests.

Vocation

This section is written with students and recently qualified therapists in mind, though the concerns raised apply to all of us. Therapy is not only a vocation but also a job! This brings up the usual range of Trades Union issues: money, job security, and status. Conventionally, money is the shadow of vocation but, as Stone suggests (personal communication 2013), there is a complicated relationship between vocation and money.

New entrants into the profession find themselves in what I have called a 'battle for the soul'. This is the context in which today's therapy is being practised. In the United States and Britain, with resonances in other Western countries, a full-scale war has broken out regarding emotional distress (and 'illness'): how we talk about it, whether we try to measure it or not and – crucially – what we do about it. Behind this battle for ownership of the soul lies contemporary culture's profound ambivalence regarding psychotherapy and counselling. Many countries have now opted for what they believe to be a quick and effective form of therapy, CBT, which, proponents maintain, has been scientifically measured to have proven effects in relation to those suffering from anxiety and depression.

But if you read the previous sentence again, you will see just below its surface the main grounds upon which the war is being fought. Are there really separate illnesses or diseases called 'anxiety' and 'depression'? No one in the field seriously believes that – hence the coinage 'co-morbidity'. And whether or not one can measure either the illness or the cure is such a hot topic that it will be keeping university philosophy of science departments busy for years. Is there such a thing as an 'effective' therapy? Don't people keep coming back?

Recently, a further front opened up in connection with the fifth version of the Diagnostic and Statistical Manual of the American Psychiatric Association (DSM-V). Many established professional bodies are concerned that 'the psychiatrists' bible' adopts an over-easy pathologisation of what are really ordinary – if difficult and painful – human experiences, such as grief. Others have protested that DSM-V is not scientific enough, failing to consider genetic determinants of mental illness. At the time of writing, it seems that the DSM psychiatrists have seen off the opposition. What is your problem, they say, with taking a systematic approach to mental illness? How can that fail to help? The media agreed.

But will they actually win? The stock-in-trade of psychiatry remains drug treatments and, recently, a series of books and scholarly papers have appeared (notably Irwin Kirsch's *The Emperor's New Drugs: Exploding the Antidepressant Myth* 2010) that cast doubt on the reliability of the research that seems to support such treatments. Kirsch's point, made by many others as well, is that the methodology that underpins such research – randomised controlled trials (RCTs) – is liable to many kinds of distortion. For example, if a patient is given a placebo with a mild irritant in it, she/he will assume they have been given the actual drug being trialled (everyone knows that drugs have side effects, you see), and Hey Presto! – they get better.

In Britain, there is always great interest in discussing the pros and cons of RCTs because they are used to ration therapy on the National Health Service (NHS). Well-established approaches, such as humanistic, integrative, family systemic, and psychodynamic, are vanishing from the NHS. Either CBT or a watered-down version of it that I call 'state therapy' secures the funding. This has led some to say that we should do RCTs of our own. I understand the tactic of 'If you can't beat them join them' but what if it doesn't work?!

Others point to the fact that there is a huge amount of non-RCT evidence for the efficacy of psychotherapy and counselling. But the government agency that draws up guidelines for treatments on the NHS does not recognise the methodologies that underpin this research. At times, this National Institute for Healthcare Excellence (NICE) does seem to have been captured by the proponents of RCTs and – due to the way in which it has been researched via RCTs – CBT. The Department of Health claims that NICE is beyond its control, which has left many observers speechless.

That is the world a new therapist is going to encounter. But there is worse to consider. We also need to ask about what it means to train to be a therapist in the age of austerity. Where are the jobs going to come from? If courses in counselling and psychotherapy are not transparent and honest, is there not a risk of a scandal of mis-selling?

Ending: the future, failure and the Trickster-therapist

I said I would be compassionate and look to the future.

Here are a few intuitive suggestions for the themes of the future: deconstructing the idea of trauma, deepening our understanding about how one variant of masculinity has shaped our world, debating whether or not the past really does shape the present, how we apprehend relations between individual and collective – can individuals make a contribution to social and political change? Above all, it would be constructive to engage with these themes as a cohesive profession, putting aside preciously held in-house ideas and assumptions. If we are going to arrest the decline of psychotherapy in our society, we had better do it from as united a base as possible.

In terms of compassion, I think it is very important not to be too hard on ourselves. However, we will fail to be self-compassionate. Yet failure is at the centre of what we do and what we deal with. But it is hard to let 1,000 flowers bloom if we are frightened that the garden is going to get untidy and overgrown. I am not sure there is a solution to many of the problems I have been writing 'critically' about in this paper.

Hence, even a critical project has the most severe limitations, and is subject to critique.

I wish that therapists were more spontaneous, trusting more in the revelatory aspects of their own minds. Perhaps, we should be less frightened of embracing contradictory positions. And perhaps, we should show more respect for people's pet ideas, the bees in their bonnets, the idees fixe, today's bright ideas. Do not be afraid to be foolish, do not seek to avoid shame, let it all hang out, for no one in our profession is all wise, all deep, all spiritual, always reflective or always related.

This lacklustre characterisation of today's therapist brings me to some thoughts about the legendary figure of the Trickster in general, and to Hermes in particular. These personifications are intended to jazz things up a bit in our field. What attracts me to the Trickster-therapist is his very lack of a coherent psychological project. In fact, he lacks ambition to do good. If he does good, it is often by accident. This is how I have come to think of healing and cure in psychotherapy. There can be little or no cleaning up of our Trickster-therapist. His primitivity makes him what he is. And 'he' is not only a 'he'.

The Greek Trickster God was Hermes – responsible for trade and commerce, maintenance, and penetration of boundaries and for carrying the messages of the Gods, as well as carrying out practical jokes and mockery of the powerful. Can this coarsely energetic figure be re-fashioned so as to speak to therapists? This is perhaps the deeper project of the paper.

On this note, let me end by providing a brief summary of the overall thrust of this essay in critical psychotherapy. I wanted to show how many of the core ideals, values, and practices of psychotherapy are not what they seem, not as valuable as they seem, and even capable of doing harm to whatever therapeutic project might exist. It was not a comfortable paper to write because there is so much self-criticism in it – but that's my punishment at Trickster's hands, I should think.

References

Bohart, A. and Tallman, K., (1999). Empathy and the active client: An integrative, cognitive-experiential approach. *In*: A. Bohart and L. Greenberg, eds. *Empathy reconsidered: New directions in psychotherapy*. Washington, DC: American Psychological Association, 97–111.

Clarkson, P., (1986). *The therapy relationship*. London: Whurr.

Frank, J., (1961). *Persuasion and healing*. New York: Basic Books.

Gordon, R., (1978). *Dying and creating: A search for meaning*. London: Society of Analytical Psychology.

Guggenbühl-Craig, A., (1971). *Power in the helping professions*. New York: Spring Publications.

Hoffman, I., (2006). The myths of free association and the potentials of the analytical relationship. *International Journal of Psychoanalysis*, 87.

Jung, C. G., (1946). The psychology of the transference. *CW16*.

Kirsch, I., (2010). *The emperor's new drugs: Exploding the antidepressant myth*. New York: Basic Books.

Loewenthal, D. and Samuels, A., eds., (2014). *Relational psychotherapy, psychoanalysis and counselling appraisals and reappraisals*. London: Routledge.

Meier, C. A., (1949). *Ancient incubation and modern psychotherapy*. Evanston, IL: Northwestern University Press.

Norcross, J., (2011). *Psychotherapy relationships that work*. Oxford: Oxford University Press.

Postle, D., (2013). *The PsyCommons-ordinary wisdom and shared power*. Available from: www.youtube.com/watch?v=5lipKokm5-A

Postle, D., (2014). *The PsyCommons and its enclosures-professionalized wisdom and the abuse of power*. Available from: www.youtube.com/watch?v=pxuFnUuLqyc

Rogers, C., (1951). *Client-centered therapy*. Cambridge, MA: Riverside.

Samuels, A., (1985). *Jung and the post-Jungians*. London: Routledge and Kegan Paul.

Samuels, A., (1993). *The political psyche*. London: Routledge.

Samuels, A., (2006). Working directly with political, social and cultural material in the therapy session. *In*: L. Layton, N. Hollander and S. Gutwill, eds. *Psychoanalysis, class and politics: Encounters in the clinical setting*. London: Routledge.

Samuels, A., (2014a). Shadows of the therapy relationship. *In*: D. Loewenthal and A. Samuels, eds. *Relational psychotherapy, psychoanalysis and counselling*. London: Routledge, 222–237.

Samuels, A., (2014b). Economics, psychotherapy and politics. *International Review of Sociology*, 24, 77–90.

Searles, H., (1975/1979). The patient as therapist to his analyst. *In*: *Countertransference and related subjects: Selected papers*. New York: International Universities Press.

Part IV

Jungian

Chapter 10

Political and clinical developments in analytical psychology since 1972

Subjectivity, equality, and diversity – inside and outside the consulting room

Retrospective Introduction: I think this chapter is as much about what I wanted to see happen as it is about what has happened. In that sense, it is manifesto as much as history. I think there remains a lack of historical overview work in the Jungian field. I think that when the bulk of this chapter was written, I was seething with a kind of anticipatory anger over what was even then in my mind as the Open Letter on Jung and 'Africans' which will appear in Chapters 12 and 13.

Talking Points: Biographical, but not only biographical in tone, the chapter looks at the tensions between analytical psychology as a unified body of ideas and practices and as a manifold activity. What can those of us working in the old areas such as Europe and North America learn from people in the former Soviet world, Latin America, and Asia? Is the spread of Jungian (and psychoanalytic) ideas around the globe only a good thing? Who benefits? Is it colonial? Missionary work? Can it be done, actually because the ideas and practices are quite out of context? Again, the author has lived and worked through these developments. So the chapter is also a late-career reflection on the/his/their history.

This chapter began life as a paper dedicated to my friend Fred Plaut. The original title of the paper as published in 2014 was 'My evolutions, revolutions and convolutions 1972–2014 (and what would Fred Plaut say about it is he were here today?'

Dedication

No paper exists in a vacuum. I had never before offered a paper for the *Journal of Analytical Psychology* conferences, due to some historical frictions between me and the *Journal* as an institution – differences that we have finally managed to resolve (as of August 2024!) The fact that the conference was in Berlin was decisive. 2014 was the first time I had returned to the city since Fred Plaut died in 2009. Born in 1913, he was a training analyst of both the British and German Jungian societies and a former editor of the *Journal* – elected, as he often recalled, in a bitterly contested election. My relationship with him lasted most of my adult life and I dedicate this paper to his memory. Despite the 36 year age gap, we often joked that we fathered each other. Fred wrote in his autobiography

DOI: 10.4324/9781003598985-15

(2004) that I was his 'best friend' and I wrote in the margin when I was editing the book the one word 'ditto'.

In that underappreciated book, Fred wrote:

> [I]f the evolution of analytical theory and practice over [more than] a century demonstrates anything, it is that the theory and practice of analysis not only changes in time but also that it is at no time the same for everybody and everywhere.
>
> (p. 70)

Fred's apercu is one reason why I suggested to the IAAP that a good title for a Congress would be 'One analytical psychology or many?'

I am interested in discussing the meaning for our profession of the migration of Jungian analysis from its European heartlands – including the forced migration from the European base – to other places, including to the United States which, as Jung would agree, is by no means 'European'. As we expand the boundaries of the Jungian world south and east, are we IAAP Jungian missionaries, Western imperialists, shadowy salesmen and saleswomen – or are we praiseworthy conveyors of things that are good beyond dispute, rather like vaccines?

Structure of the chapter

Here is how I am planning to proceed following this Dedication. The *first* section concerns the personal context in which the paper is written.

Then, in the *second* section, I will discuss critically how and why we use the concepts of transference and countertransference in analysis. Then, still in the second section, I go on to take an equally critical look at the possibilities of a more 'relational' approach to the analytical process.

The *third* section looks at some aspects of the relationship between analytical psychology and politics and goes on to consider the massive problematic of diversity and equality in our profession. I see this as far from being a matter for minorities or marginal people. Rather, it is something that impacts with massive force on the majority.

As the chapter proceeds, I will be asking readers to join in three carefully constructed experiential exercises, privately in feelings and thoughts. I hope you will not mind participating in this attempt to bring a more experiential, dimension to the experience of reading and to allow the roots of the paper in a live conference to be apparent.

Personal confessions

Jung famously wrote that 'every psychology is a personal confession' and that remark guides me here. The editors of the *Journal* specifically invited me to be personal and so I'd like to show why – to the best of my conscious knowledge – some of the themes in my work came to be there from a personal angle.

In 1967, at about the age of 18, I was a highly political young man but trying to realise my political dreams through the arts – specifically, theatre. We were a radical theatre company, in those remarkable days at the end of the 1960s when you could get money from the English Arts Council for radical theatre companies. Then, after becoming a youth worker and a counsellor working with young people, an encounter with humanistic psychology – and that was a serious option career-wise for a while – led me into analysis, and I dropped out of the political world for a decade. So, when Thatcherism came in in the 1980s, there was I, former Trotskyist and student radical, busy writing Jungian books!

Gradually, the political side of my personality, and my interest in society, came back in and merged with my clinical concerns, leading to the formation in 1994 of Psychotherapists and Counsellors for Social Responsibility. Then, when I began to have children, as often seems to happen with men, a third strand came in, which we could call 'spiritual'. Psychotherapy, politics, and spirituality – three sides of a coin! Charles Pēguy said that 'everything starts in mysticism and ends in politics'.

The account up to now is somewhat external and avoids my beginnings in the family. I have always struggled to find a vigorous to-and-fro in my image of my parents' marriage. I am not saying it was never there, only that I had an image of a conventional togetherness without much passion or risk taking. They were kind to each other but never went near (in my fantasy anyway) the grotesque and divine experimentations I found a need to write about in my paper on 'The image of the parents in bed' (Samuels 1989).

I will talk about my mother in a moment. My father was a gentleman, and I mean this in two senses. First is that he was well educated, had been through the war (ending up in both Italian and German prisoner of war camps), and enjoyed a cultivated and comfortable lifestyle ranging from golf to classical music. But he was also, for me, what I came to call in my writings (e.g. 2001) a 'dry' father, not using his body to give out much erotic or aggressive playback – but a decent and polite man. In fact, I felt he depended on me to provide a kind of excitement and, via my rebellious, bad, and rejecting behaviour that is what I did. His father was a self-made immigrant tycoon type, though the family business went bankrupt in the end.

My concern – even obsession – with relations between women and men stems, I believe, from this respectable but emotionally constrained background. Hence, I found it hard to buy into Jungian essentialist approaches to gender because they felt so limiting. That was why I wrote 'Beyond the feminine principle' (1989). And I have been strongly influenced by feminism in what I wrote over the years about the relations between women and men.

I am a competitive person, who takes delights in the principles of negotiation and bargaining. But over time I have become able to agree with Gerhard Adler that there is an additional 'principle of complementarity' at work in life: some people are better than others at some things. When it comes to other things, other people are more adept. These three principles, stemming from my personal psychology, also lie at the heart of pluralism: competition, negotiation and bargaining, and complementarity. Pluralism gave me an opportunity to be aggressive and tolerant at the same time.

Although my classification (1985) of the schools of post-Jungian analytical psychology was developed before I developed pluralism as a theory in 1989, it was the former project (post-Jungians) that got me going. In 1985, the Jungian analytical field was even less cohesive than it is today – I mean in terms of any beginner being able to find their way around in it. There were huge differences in approach and things only held because each segment of the field claimed to derive something from the connection to Jung.

I experienced it all differently from most of my friends and fellow students. I really liked the fragmented nature of the field, with its dispute, polemic, and lack of clarity. What looked like totally inimical perspectives were in fact linked by their desire *to go beyond Jung* while *retaining a critical connection to him*. This meant that each of the revisionary or revolutionary tendencies (Developmental, Archetypal) could be seen as having a similar relation to the more settled centre (Classical). But the model did not rule out evolutions within Jungian classicism.

For a novice analyst to write an overview of the field into which he had just arrived was, of course, an inflation. But I certainly made a name for myself. This leads me to comment a bit on my mother's influence on me. It was she who spotted, with her down to earth intuition and generally savvy approach to life, that writing could be a way for me to make my mark. She went on and on about this, and, unusually and amazingly, I listened even though I knew that my success was for her glory.

This brings me to the not inconsiderable matter of my relationship, on all levels, to Tricksters in general and to Hermes in particular. What attracts me to the Trickster actually is his very lack of a political or psychological project. In fact, he lacks integrity or ambition. If he does good, it is entirely by accident. There can be no 'cleaning up' of the Trickster act. His primitivity makes him what he is. And 'he' is not only a 'he'. I do not really know why I was the first to spot the potential of the idea of the 'female Trickster' (1993).

I deplore that there is these days so much idealistic, sentimental, and romantic writing on the Trickster as a creative and constructive force (especially the female version).

Nevertheless, Hermes speaks to me, as to many analysts I suspect, because he links the base, corrupt, grotesque aspects of the Trickster ('dirty tricks' in politics) with some kind of skill at making creative connections. But the story of Hermes/Andrew remains resistant to a wholly positive reading because the shadow of being an emissary of the Gods is that the messenger becomes (or seeks to become?) more important than the message. A power trip, then? So, behind my pluralistic tendency to pop up in many fields of psychotherapy beyond the post-Jungian one (humanistic psychology, body psychotherapy, relational psychoanalysis), and in both mainstream and activist politics, there is, like there was for Hermes, assuredly a quest for power.

Be that as it may, I don't think it was only the need for power that motivated my controversial work on Jung and anti-Semitism from the mid-1980s until the publication of *The Political Psyche* (1993). This material and other later discoveries were originally published in the *Journal*. If there was a personal background to this project, it was simply to do with the plain fact of being Jewish in a community whose founder had written objectionable things about my people. Fred and I discussed this all the time. In addition, there was also some kind of background wish to be more accepted as a contributor to academic, psychoanalytic, and political discourses that was undermined by being seen as an adherent of that notorious anti-Semite Jung.

The reactions to my early essays into the allegations of Jung's anti-Semitism really pissed me off, though on a good day I could also empathise with them. It did feel like being in my family in which I was always the 'black sheep', the *Rosha* – the wicked son who seeks to opt out of the Passover Seder ceremony. In the early stages of our community's engagement with our problem, there was a closing of the Jungian ranks, a repetitious argument that Jung was merely a man of his time, and even some pathologising of me as a Jew with a complex.

Well, Jung was not exactly a man of his time (as you can see from the detailed research I and others did), and it is those kinds of knee-jerk defences that even today sometimes represent our problem (the Jungians' problem) and not Jung's problem. Nevertheless, gradually, the Jungian community realised that apology and reparation was needed and the informal alliance of concerned people that emerged has done a pretty good job in this regard. Of course, for those who need us as a tribal enemy, such as some psychoanalysts, the unfortunate legacy provides a marvellous base.

Nevertheless, much explicatory and reparative work still needs to be done on Jung's racial attitudes and his theories and utterances about 'Africans', and I return to this in my third section on diversity and equality (and see Chapters 12 and 13 herein).

Exercise 1: Examine, to the best of your conscious knowledge, how the personality of your mother or your father (or both) has impacted on your attitudes to clinical work and to your values as an analyst or therapist.

Clinical work: a via negativa – problems with transference-countertransference – and with the relational approach

In this part of the paper, I want to say a few things about *transference and countertransference* that are of a critical nature. Later, I will discuss *relational approaches* to the analytical process in equally critical vein. While no one is going to say that these are alternatives to each other or that they are mutually exclusive, or that you have to choose, all analysts will know, broadly speaking, why I might want to discuss them separately. Colman (2013) and Meredith-Owen (2013) have done a good job in opening up debate here. As Fred and I used to say, what is as important as agreement or disagreement is whether or not you know what I am talking about! To be honest, I am not sure that their debate (between two past editors of *JAP* shows that they do know what the other is talking about.

I apologise for following a *via negativa* in which neither transference-countertransference nor relational approaches emerge unscathed. I hope it is not too depressing. But what we mean when we refer to being 'critical' does indeed often bring us down.

Critical transference-countertransference

Here are some specific critiques of the clinical usage of the ideas of transference and countertransference:

(1) Social critiques: Therapy and analysis involve an induced relationship not a natural one. The analytical relationship is imbued with the history, power dynamics and authority structures of analysis itself. The relationship is an unequal one in an unhelpful way. (Please note that this is the first of a number of references to inequality running through the paper like a red thread.) Anyway, many transference phenomena are therefore very largely the result of suggestion and have less to do with the psychic reality of the patient than we sometimes think.

(2) Systemic critiques: Focus on transference-countertransference misses out the presence and impact of the wider human and non-human systems in which patient and analyst are embedded: families, friends, other people at work, and so on. Just to give a simple example, it has been illuminating to listen to the answers when I ask a potential new client what their partner or family thinks about their having therapy. Paradoxically, nothing is more potent in this regard than to be told that the client has not told anyone.

(3) Reality critiques: This is a critique of those, mainly but not only in psychoanalysis, who see hints and references to the analyst in the discourse of the patient. Sometimes, these are called 'you mean me' interpretations', so the inefficient car mechanic is the useless therapist in disguised form. Or there is simply a symbolic interpretation made. Mrs Thatcher is your Mum, David Cameron (or Saddam Hussein) your shadow. But sometimes the car mechanic (or the boss at work) is just the mechanic or the boss, Mrs Thatcher is Mrs Thatcher, and David Cameron plays himself. (And sometimes clients are late because there really has been a suicide on the underground railway line.)

(4) Ecological and political critiques: Stress on the transference-countertransference relationship makes it even more difficult for the client to express the impact on herself of planetary/environmental crisis or any other collective field of emotional distress. When I first began to advocate that therapist pick up on political aspects of the client's material, I was told that I might be depriving the client of the chance to talk about her mother if I kept her references to Mrs Thatcher on the level of Mrs Thatcher. I replied that I was worried about the opposite: that a client who needed to talk about Mrs Thatcher would be definitely, albeit indirectly, discouraged from so doing, because talking about mother is what you do in therapy. In principle, any political theme can be taken under the

umbrella of the therapy relationship, and it is an important development in our field that people are doing that to an ever-increasing extent.

(5) *Ethical and epistemological critiques:* Without intending it, proponents of the centrality of the transference-countertransference relationship are buying into a particular view of human relationships. In this view, people are regarded as atomised, isolated beings that have to *struggle* into relationship and, when they achieve relationship with a therapist, the two people in the relationship 'own' it. But this is not the only narrative of relationality. What about those narratives in which people are always already in connection and relationship? They do not meet each other via the hurling of projections (from the Latin *proicere*, to throw a spear) across empty space. For there isn't any empty space between people, even though it may look that way.

I'd like to develop this particular critique a bit. What if we conceive of a rhizome, or nutrient tube, buried out of sight which throws up separate stalks that are, nevertheless, already connected? What if we understand the two people as linked by their citizenship, their membership of the polis, no matter how different that experience might be for them? Or maybe we should understand the members of the therapy pair as linked via manifold bodily, physical phenomena?

One need hardly add that the autonomous, separate, 'individuated' person is exactly the person that capitalism and free market theorising assumes to exist. This is the 'neoliberal subject' – self-governing, enterprising, calculating. So the notion of transference-countertransference is not politically neutral, nor, as I've been suggesting, problem free. But nor, too, are relational approaches to the work, to which I now turn my attention.

Relational analysis and therapy: cutting edge or cliché?

As I mentioned in Chapter 9, the slogan 'it's the relationship, stupid' was seriously considered for use in an advertising and PR campaign in support of psychotherapy and counselling. This was believed by its advocates to be an accurate slogan because it was the therapy relationship that was considered the unique selling point of analysis, psychotherapy, and counselling. The therapy relationship is what the clients want, and it is what the therapists want to offer. Hence, relationality or 'the relational' or 'the therapy relationship' has become markers of difference between 'real' psychotherapy and most Cognitive Behaviour Therapies.

Hence, I have asked whether relationality in therapy was still cutting edge or had become clichéd and conformist. I said it could well be both. But I also argued that the stress on relationship, with associated notions of safety, containment, holding, and diminution of risk, tended in the conformist direction. Without going to so far as to say that making therapy safe is all done in the interests of the therapist, I think we have to consider what the professional expectation of many of us – that safety is what clients need – has done to the way we work. Does it not reinforce the idea of the client as needy, dependent, infantile, caught between fight and flight?

Such clients exist and maybe every client is like this at some time or other. But to make this the default position is to wire inequality into everything that we do. (The second mention on the red thread of inequality.)

But pushed just a little bit further this apparently profoundly psychotherapeutic set of assumptions about clients comes perilously close to imitating what more directive, cognitively oriented therapists want to see in their clients. The clients of such therapy, especially when, as in Britain, it is funded by the state, are supposed to be compliant and grateful, to do what the therapist wishes them to do, and, above all, get off welfare benefits and back to work. The therapist is situated as an expert, working out of an evidence base, something like a surgeon whose recommendations one would be crazy to disobey. When analytical psychotherapists and counsellors say to clients (in effect) 'Your well-being depends on relating to me', they are as mistrustful of the client's autonomy as anyone working as a 'state therapist' would be.

What we are beginning to see in the literature, and hence we may assume is being witnessed in practice, is the emergence of a wholly different conception of the client, a perspective that sees *the client as the motor of therapy*. This client is a heroic client (in a good sense), a client who knows what she needs, a client who can manage her own distress. A client who engages less in a process of cure or even of healing and more in a process of ongoing enquiry. This multifaceted new client is potentially a healer of others, especially the therapist, and, in a sense, of the world.

Client as healer

There are some clients from whom one learns great lessons. My first training 'case' had a dream early on in the analysis. She dreamt: *I visit a doctor who is ill in bed. He begs me to stay.* Her associations to 'bed' were of illness not only of sexuality. How else might we understand this dream? Was the doctor in fact me so this could be a Wounded Healer dream? Or was it a here-and-now transference involving denial that she is not well? Or is she in the grip of an inflation, of herself as the anima or mother who brings life and succour to the doctor who is ill in bed?

Or was this dream, perhaps, *an accurate perception*? I did need something psychological from her, not just that she stick with me so I could get through the training. Crucially, I would say now that there was a further accurate perception in the dream: that she could in fact help/heal this doctor. This work took place in 1974 and, at that time, it would have been difficult to think of the client as healer. Has much changed? (I write at length about working with this client, 'D', in Samuels [1985] and am always grateful to her for the open permission she has given me to write about our work together.)

Thinking of the client as a healer, we see that recent thinking about the client has moved in that general direction. From the person-centred approach, we find Bohart and Tallman referring to the 'active client' (1999). The 'other Carl', Rogers (1951), in the era when the discourse was of 'client-centred' therapy, makes it clear that the client knows for herself what is needed, where she wants to go.

Jung (*CW*16), as ever a clinical pioneer, writes of entropy in the client, an innate process of self-regulation. Guggenbühl-Craig was also a pioneer in this area. From relational psychoanalysis, we read that Hoffman (2006) regards the client as having responsibilities to the analyst and the analysis, more than just for the co-creation of the therapy relationship.

One positive aspect of the new developments in research that involve asking clients regularly (or even after every session) to give feedback to and evaluation of the work is that it chimes with this more active version of our clients.

So the therapist is, in a way, adjunct to the therapy process. But she is also a contingent figure, product of a particular social circumstance. Franks (1961) suggested that what makes the therapist is not only training, techniques, and wounds but also being *socially sanctioned as a therapist*, a sort of overarching collective, placebo effect. The therapist is being socially sanctioned, granted permission to be a therapist – by society, and specifically by the client. This is a new version of the client who does not want the analyst to be the one who knows or even 'the one who is supposed to know' (in Lacan's oft-quoted aphorism).

Let's see what happens if we revision the therapy relationship with all of these thoughts about the client in mind. I am putting it like this because it has gradually dawned on me that clients sometimes *do not dare* to deploy their tacit (or even actual) knowledge and emotional literacy. We therapists are content with this because it leaves us with a job to do. But that could, and, from a critical perspective, maybe should change.

These observations on the politics of therapy relationships lead me to try to sketch a new model of the client, one that I'm calling 'client as healer'. It concerns the 'activist' client. I offer this in a tentative spirit, looking for discussion and dialogue about it. Would people agree that one possible goal of therapy might be that, during the work, some clients may develop their capacity for alterity, including, among other things, an empathic concern for the other? Yes, this would certainly mean active concern for other people – but I think there is a more-than-personal version of alterity to consider.

For example, in a multicultural world, meeting one's inner diversity could lead to support for outer (cultural) diversity and hence to support for those hitherto subject to social and political exclusion. To the idea that a client is also a healer, we could then add that activist clients have the potential to be citizen-therapists for the wider world with its environmental problems, economic injustice and ubiquitous violence. The therapy client, revisioned as a healer, may now be understood to be a socially responsible agent of *Tikkun Olam*, the Hebrew term for the drive to repair and restore the world.

My research (Samuels 2006) shows that, in many countries, clients bring political, social, and cultural material to therapy much more than they did (and, I would add, they will bring even more when they know it is permitted to do so). Therapy becomes a place where, in political dialogue, client and therapist work out and on the admixtures of their political attitudes and engagements. This can be as transformative as a more personal alchemy and can be done even when one of them finds the political positions of the other to be horrid or reprehensible. The professional task remains to develop responsible ways of working with political, social, and cultural material in the session.

Exercise 2: Which of your clients/patients has done the most to heal you personally, whether deliberately or not? Then ask yourself which of your clients/patients has done the most to bring some kind or degree of healing or improvement to the wider world (i.e. on the societal or collective level).

Analytical psychology and politics/the politics of analytical psychology

These remarks about the activist client lead us into the third and final section of the paper on some political considerations facing analytical psychology, with a particular focus on questions of diversity and equality.

Jungian analysts, Jungian psychotherapists, and their organisations have got involved in political crises and situations in ways in which you could not have imagined 35 years or possibly even 20 years ago. I am thinking of Jungian therapists who take sand tray work to the Chinese earthquake zone and also Jungians going to work with earthquake survivors in Japan. In South Africa, you will find Jungian therapists and analysts in the townships. In Brazil, you can find Jungian therapists and analysts working in community settings and they've done so for many, many years. I remember going with the Jungian analyst Walter Boechat to a community centre in Rio devoted to psychotic people from poor backgrounds where they were using Jungian art therapy. Jungians are now leading authorities on psychological questions to do with refugees and with people seeking asylum. In Israel, although in some ways problematic, you find Jungian analysts engaging with Palestinians inside and outside Israel. At the moment, I think it's a question of the Israelis teaching and putting on courses and seminars but I already detect that there's something happening the other way: that the highly westernised Israeli experts are learning something when they go onto the West Bank, into the occupied territories.

So we can celebrate the fact that in all likelihood no school of psychotherapy is making a greater contribution to the alleviation of the suffering of the world than Jungian analysis and analytical psychology. How wonderful to be able to say such a thing, with hand on heart!

Here we are, supposedly the most unworldly, introverted, even mystically inclined group of therapists on the planet, getting passionately involved in a huge range of cultural, social, and political problems. We are part of the attempt to recover the political from the swamps into which it has sunk in many countries, not just detached commentators upon such an attempt. This turnaround probably derives its energy from a sense that the change of direction was urgently needed, perhaps as reparation for past misjudgements. Anyway, the job is well started and is carried out these days by so many of us that I don't think I can produce a list of names. There are so many of you in the field who have sensed the danger of losing the revolutionary idealism of Jung's pioneering work if we stand still and rest on our laurels. You know that our common interests will collapse if we only pursue our common interests, if we only invest in what advantages us.

Looking at what is going on, I think one thing to say is that we are in the middle of developing Jung's radical intuition, floated in the 1930s, of the need to create a culturally sensitive psychology. A culturally sensitive psychology does not level out all differences in the psyche that stem from ethnicity, religion, nation, social class, gender, and sexual orientation. Jung was against the universal imposition of a single system of psychology. Inevitably, so-called universal psychologies (like Freud's) are in fact context-bound, limited, personal confessions writ unhelpfully large. So Jung was perhaps the first to anticipate the ethical and political disaster of a one-size-fits-all colonial psychology. Hence he is one of the founding fathers of transcultural and intercultural psychotherapy – and I'll say more about this in a moment.

Jung was also one of the first to understand that we cannot insulate clinical practice from contemporary history, saying that the analyst 'feels the violence of its impact even in the quiet of his consulting room' (1946b, p. 177). And he goes on in the same passage (which is from the Preface to *Essays on Contemporary Events*) to make a suggestive and evocative reference to the analyst's having 'duties as a citizen'.

Politics in many countries is broken and in a mess; we urgently need new ideas and approaches. Jungian analysts, working alongside other psychotherapists, economists, social scientists, religious people, environmentalists, and others, can contribute to a general transformation of politics and, step by stumbling step over many years, to an alleviation of the suffering of the world.

But it is far from certain that we have mustered the necessary humility of interdisciplinary work when it comes to politics. By all means, let's have an analyst on every committee – but please God not a committee of analysts! If we are to organise more conferences on political themes, let's involve people from the political world, mainstream big names if we can get them, but also activists and political visionaries.

The right tools for the job

I have been attempting to bring the insights and practices of analysis (what I call 'therapy thinking') into the political world since the early 1980s. One thing that I have learned is that it's necessary to find and choose the right tool for the job. This should be driven by the nature of the problem under consideration as well as by one's preferences and knowledge. What it does not mean is using one huge concept, such as the paranoid-schizoid position or the cultural complex as if this could settle everything. Psychological analysis of political problematics needs to be a bit more detailed and fragmented. It needs to accept that such analysis might be wrong or fail. Saying there is a cultural complex at work or that the paranoid-schizoid position is the problem or that we need to see more of the Feminine in our world – these are statements that will never, ever be wrong. I try not to go for the temptation of a massive single explanation, seeking instead to be a *bricoleur*, promiscuous in owing loyalty to no one specific concept or one particular school of psychology.

Here are some illustrative examples from my work:

In terms of leadership, I have found (Samuels 2001) Winnicott's notion of 'good enough' very useful – the good-enough leader for whom the binary divide success/ failure is less rigid than is usually considered to be the case. Additionally, thinking derived from contemporary revisions of the father's role has been illuminating as regards leadership (see below).

In terms of the economy, I turn to Freud's account of sadism as a backdrop to the state we are in and to relational psychoanalytic ideas as the (admittedly Utopic) way ahead.

Nationhood and national character may be understood more deeply by Jung's writings in the 1930s on national psychology – the valuable (and overlooked) part of his work on cultural psychology during that period (see Samuels 1993).

When we consider foreign policy, all that has been written on empathy and the obstacles to empathy is relevant, plus up to the moment ideas like the notion of the moral third in geopolitics.

Finally, when it comes to vision in politics, what could be more apt than the Trickster, who models the denial of the realities of time, space, and place just as any revolutionary or social reformer has to defy the social and cultural realities of her or his present moment.

James Hillman famously claimed that we've had 100 years of psychotherapy and the world is getting worse. But, as I've shown, this claim was ahistorical and ill-informed (Samuels 1993). There's no need to give up on clinical work after all! Totton (2000) has also shown that a better title might be 'we've had much more than a hundred years of all the schools of psychotherapy trying to change the world – but the world has stayed pretty much the same'. The world just didn't turn up for its first session with us. All the pioneers of psychoanalysis (and humanistic psychology as well) were deeply committed to improving the world. *Pace* Hillman, it is by no means a new thing. The problem is how little impact the psychotherapy and politics project has had. Sorry to have to say this. I am an enthusiast for linking therapy thinking and politics – but I am also sceptical.

Exercise 3: Think of the problem in the world that concerns and interests you the most. Then do your best to imagine a solution to this problem. Finally, ask yourself why your solution won't happen!

Aspects of diversity

In South Africa, at the IAAP congress in 2007, I suggested that we offer a public apology for some of the things Jung said about Africans and other non-Europeans along the lines of the very successful public apology that John Beebe and others elicited from the Analytical Psychology Club of Zurich which, in a sense, was an apology on everyone's behalf in relation to allegations of Jung's anti-Semitism. But unfortunately my proposal for a public apology about Jung and Africans wasn't taken up. (The whole matter got very complicated and is entered into in

Chapters 12 and 13.) Now it could be that I put it badly. It could be that people were fed up with me saying things like that. But I don't think that was the only set of reasons. It was just too difficult to get our minds round something as huge as Jung's relation to what we now call 'diversity'. Maybe it was right not to apologise. But I think the absence of an apology is one of a number of factors that will restrict diversity in our profession.

Readers may be interested to know that the most downloaded article from the *British Journal of Psychotherapy* is Farhad Dalal's 'Jung – a Racist' (1988). With numerous quotes from the *Collected Works* and *Memories, Dreams, Reflections*, the writer details Jung's claim that Africans lack an entire layer of conscious-ness compared to Europeans. Dalal asserts that Jung has produced three specific pseudo-scientific equations: The modern Black person with the prehistoric human, modern Black consciousness with the white unconscious, and the modern Black adult with the white child. Dalal also documents a series of comparisons between Africans and monkeys that Jung made.

I do not want, in this chapter, to discuss this matter in detail: for example, the inevitable debate about how 'normal' Jung's views were for the time. That can wait (though it should have happened). But if it is still true that there are few American Black Jungian analysts (as Polly Young-Eisendrath noted decades ago in 1987), then might this kind of statement not be a reason? We may need to go through the same kind of public reparative process concerning Jung's attitudes to Black people that was so moving and important with regard to anti-Semitism.

The notion of diversity is an elastic one. It can refer to the composition of a professional grouping. But diversity also leads to thoughts of working with patients and clients from diverse backgrounds – meaning backgrounds different to those of the analyst. What is the state of the art regarding intercultural and transcultural work? Does immersing oneself in the culture of the other help? Or is it better to remain curious and admit one's ignorance?

Diversity is closely linked to considerations of power and, while everyone notes that power dynamics are terribly important in clinical work, we are slow to adapt our actual practices – the things we do with clients – to take account of such dynamics.

I want to return to what I was saying earlier about looking to Jung, not only as our problem but also as a source of possible solutions, or at least of a move in the right direction. In spite of the invention or the discovery of the collective uncon-scious, Jung rejects a universal psychology. He saw this as a major problem with psychoanalysis. It's quite clear that in some of the controversial things he says about so many sections of humanity – Slavs, Jews, Americans, 'Negroes', South-ern Europeans, Indians, Chinese, and so on – he is feeling his clumsy way towards something that is very far from a universal psychology. Why have we ignored this aspect of Jung's legacy in favour of the universality of the archetypes?

As far as the composition of the profession is concerned, the sea of white, elderly faces that you see at most professional analytical conferences (and actually also in the areas of humanistic and body and art therapies as well) tells its own story. In Britain, the situation in counselling is a little different from the situation in psychoanalysis and Jungian analysis. The counselling trainings are accessible and cheap and come across as places where persons of colour feel they will not have to defend who they are. They will take those trainings – but where the analytical trainings strike them as expensive, enclosed, elitist, and inaccessible, as requiring qualifications that it is often quite difficult to see the relevance of in relation to therapeutic work, then, of course, they reject those offerings. Such 'high-level' trainings are thereby diminished. Similarly, in the United States, the percentage of non-white counselling psychologists is way higher than the percentage of non-white psychoanalysts which is of course extremely low.

Thinking of diversity and equality in relation to clinical work, there are many things to consider. We know now how much the composition of the therapy pair or group matters and that it profoundly affects the therapy process – as does everything in society such as violence, war, ecological disaster, unemployment and poverty, and major state-sponsored surveillance intrusions into privacy. Therapy is not hygienically insulated from the infection of such things, and, if we continue in critical vein, we find that it means that therapy is not really free to define itself in any way. Differing cultural and ethical specifics may make an approach based on the therapy relationship or the therapeutic alliance inappropriate or damaging in some instances. In a sense, the client may have to resist the way in which the therapist predefines their joint activity.

Let me pose a few relevant questions. The matter of therapists from minorities working with clients not from those minorities (i.e. so-called majority clients) is important. How White clients feel when confronted with Black therapists, or straight clients with a therapist from a sexual minority (yes, such things can sometimes be visible or are acknowledged/disclosed) are not talked or written about very much. Yet, in conversation with Black and ethnic-minority therapists, there is a considerable fear that one will be sequestered into working only with clients who resemble their therapist.

We know, too, that the history of relations between the groups the two participants come from is important. There are ancestral as well as here-and-now dynamics when a Black person and a white person work therapeutically together, or when a German and a Jew find themselves in the same therapy room.

In addition, economic inequality, and the relative envy and sense of failure or success, distorts and skews the transference-countertransference. The massive and increasing differences in wealth that we see within countries and between countries has led activists and protesters, such as the Occupy movement, to coin the formula of the 1% and the 99%, to underscore the way wealth is concentrated. The 85 richest individuals in the world have wealth equivalent to that of half of the world's population, 3.5 billion people. In Britain, 1% of the population possesses 14% of the wealth.

Elsewhere (Samuels 2014a, 2014b, 2014c), I have written of the psychology and the politics of both economic inequality – a major factor in 'mental illness' and of inherited wealth. A recent well-respected academic study shows how flows of inherited wealth have returned to nineteenth-century levels. Inequality does not appear to ebb as economies mature (Piketty 2014). Neither should we expect the share of income flowing to capital to stay roughly constant over time. There is therefore no reason to think that capitalism will 'naturally' reverse rising inequality. The point is that all this economic thinking is at work in the therapy session – it's the economic psyche – *it's the inequality, stupid!* Sometimes, the client has more wealth, and sometimes the therapist. Money is always a hot issue. Is analysis only for the wealthy?

Much the same combination of factors and dynamics is present when it comes to the physical health and disability characteristics of both participants. Often one or the other (or both) are injured and ill and this complicates the red thread of vulnerability inherent in all psychological work.

Exercise 4: Reflect on times when you yourself felt in a minority – in the family, in society, or in the profession? Did you ever get out of this state of mind? If so, then how? If not, then why not?

Concluding remarks

Fred Plaut felt himself to be in a minority all his life. He was in a minority in the Jewish community in Dusseldorf in spotting the Nazi danger very early. He was then in the white minority in South Africa (and a German among the British and Afrikaners as well). In London, he remained an immigrant, and he was never in the majority grouping in the Society of Analytical Psychology (SAP). When he went back to Berlin in 1985, he was clearly in a minority, again as an immigrant and as a Jew. But there's a lot to be said for being in the minority in our profession and I'd like to end by generalising, a little wildly perhaps, from Fred's experience. These are just a few brief reflections on what it means to be a Jungian analyst in today's world.

I suggest that the Jungian analyst who stalks contemporary culture, and who is trying to engage with its politics, has *always been* marginal and decentred, not at all integrated but rather an actor performing many roles in many scripts, characterised by lack, somewhat faded as well as jaded, jerky, marginalised, alienated, split, guilty, empty, nomadic. *A minority figure.* I think there is something we can do with this vision of a marvellously rebellious Jungian analyst: the misfit, the rebel, the troublemaker, and the round peg in a square hole?

To embrace this vision of ourselves, we have to firmly reject Jung's aristocratic, elitist, and supercilious ideas (see Sherry 2010). Here's a by-no-means unusual quote from 1921: 'It is obvious that a social group consisting of stunted individuals cannot be a viable and healthy institution' (Jung 1920/1949, para. 758). Or try this quote, from the 1916 paper 'Adaptation, individuation, collectivity': 'Whoever is not creative enough [to individuate] must re-establish collective conformity with a group of his own choice, otherwise he remains an empty waster and a windbag' (1916, para. 1098). So we have stunted individuals here, wasters and windbags over there, and truly individuated people in the first-class cabin.

Don't Jungian analysts, along with others in the liberal professions, have to question whether or not we really want to live in gated communities, sending our children to elite schools and colleges, employing servants – and, in general feeling, ourselves to be better than average human beings? Better, I say, to be 'stunted', remembering that in alchemical process, the lapis can't be reached without the assembly of perfectly ordinary, base elements found everywhere and every day.

References

Bohart, A. and Tallman, K., (1999). Empathy and the active client: An integrative, cognitive-experiential approach. *In*: A. Bohart and L. Greenberg, eds. *Empathy reconsidered: New directions in psychotherapy*. Washington, DC: American Psychological Association.

Colman, W., (2013). Bringing it all back home: How I became a relational analyst. *Journal of Analytical Psychology*, 58 (4), 470–490.

Dalal, F., (1988). Jung: A racist. *British Journal of Psychotherapy* (March), 263–279.

Frank, J., (1961). *Persuasion and healing*. New York: Basic Books.

Hoffman, I., (2006). The myths of free association and the potentials of the analytical relationship. *International Journal of Psychoanalysis*, 87.

Jung, C. G., (1916). Adaptation, individuation, collectivity. *CW18*.

Jung, C. G., (1920/1949). Psychological types. *CW6*.

Jung, C. G., (1946a). The psychology of the transference. *CW16*.

Jung, C. G., (1946b). Preface to essays on contemporary events. *CW10*.

Meredith-Owen, W., (2013), Are waves of relational assumptions eroding traditional analysis? *Journal of Analytical Psychology*, 58 (5), 593–614.

Piketty, T., (2014). *Capital in the twenty-first century*. Cambridge, MA: Belknap Press.

Plaut, A., (2004). *Between losing and finding: The life of an analyst*. London: Free Association Books.

Rogers, C., (1951). *Client-centered therapy*. Cambridge, MA: Riverside.

Samuels, A., (1985). *Jung and the post-Jungians*. London and Boston, MA: Routledge and Kegan Paul.

Samuels, A., (1989). *The plural psyche: Personality, morality and the father*. London and New York: Routledge.

Samuels, A., (1993). *The political psyche*. London and New York: Routledge.

Samuels, A., (2006). Working directly with political, social and cultural material in the therapy session. *In*: L. Layton, N. C. Hollander and S. Gutwill, eds. *Psychoanalysis, class and politics: Encounters in the clinical setting*. London and New York: Routledge.

Samuels, A., (2014a). Shadows of the therapy relationship. *In*: D. Lowenthal and A. Samuels, eds. *Relational psychotherapy, psychoanalysis and counselling*. London and New York: Routledge.

Samuels, A., (2014b). Everything you always wanted to know about therapy (but were afraid to ask): Fragments of a critical psychotherapy. *European Journal of Counselling and Psychotherapy*, 26 (4), 7–24.

Samuels, A., (2014c). Economics, psychotherapy, politics. *International Review of Sociology*, 24 (1), 77–90.

Sherry, J., (2010). *Carl Gustav Jung: Avant-Garde conservative*. New York: Palgrave Macmillan.

Totton, N., (2000). *Psychotherapy and politics*. London: SAGE.

Young-Eisendrath, P., (1987). The absence of black Americans as Jungian analysts. *Quadrant*, 19, 47–59.

Chapter 11

The future of Jungian analysis

Strengths, weaknesses, opportunities, threats ('SWOT')

Retrospective Introduction: The conceit of a sort of 'balance sheet' for Jungian analysis and analytical psychology is both tasteless and useful. In numerous settings, it has enabled constructive and unpolarised discussion. The chapter was published in 2017, and I have updated details. I enjoy working on this material because it exactly gets what I wanted when I set out on Jung and the Post-Jungians 40 years ago. The aim was connection to and critical distance from Jung. I hope it is not too arrogant to say that this desideratum has spread and has morphed into a new mainstream approach.

Talking Points: Imagine you are an investor contemplating investing in Jungian analysis. Would you take a punt? What does your due diligence show? So a balance sheet is drawn up in which strengths of Jungian analysis (such as its clinical excellence) are set against weaknesses (such as its failure to distance from Jung's prejudices). This is controversial stuff but presented humorously and generously. For example, 'Jung the man' is stated to be both a strength and a weakness of Jungian analysis.

Introduction

Of course, these ideas are entirely personal and, though presented originally as the 2017 annual lecture of the SAP, do not represent the SAP's views – nor, obviously, those of the *Journal of Analytical Psychology*. It is an example of someone shooting from the hip and maybe shooting his mouth off in a fit of prophetic vigour. Justification may be found in the fact that I qualified as a Jungian analyst in 1974, so, in a sense, now aged 76, I have spent my whole adult life in the Jungian and post-Jungian world. I care very deeply about its future.

I have been fortunate enough to visit many countries over the years to lecture and give workshops. Recently, I served on the IAAP Organizational and Advisory Working Party on the state of Jungian analysis worldwide, a truly representative group chaired by Martin Stone, and this experience also informs what I have to say today. So maybe my outlook isn't totally a British one.

Although the paper is full of contrarian opinions and is intended to spark debate, I am using a serious methodology in it. This is called 'SWOT': strengths, weaknesses, opportunities, threats. Developed in the organisational and business world, it is a tried and tested method of assessing the state of any organisation (usually a

DOI: 10.4324/9781003598985-16

corporation or division of a company – or even, in these days of the irresistible rise of coaching, of a single individual person). https://en.wikipedia.org/wiki/SWOT_analysis

Here it is being used in relation to a professional field. The great thing about a SWOT analysis is that it enables us to look at both internal and external factors and also to list the same thing in more than one of the lists. Something can be *both* a strength *and* a weakness. SWOT organises matters, and SWOT helps in keeping anxiety at bay so there is a space for reflection. After all, a lecture on 'the future of' anything will create anxiety immediately. As a good Jungian, I also like the fact that there are four headings, the *quaternio* so frequently found in Jung's writings.

Perhaps some readers will be a little surprised that a methodology derived from the commercial world was used in the SAP Annual Lecture. As an academic in psychosocial studies, I do see analytical psychology as a sort of commercial enterprise, in competition with other modalities of psychotherapy, and subject not only to the *Zeitgeist* but also to the laws and regulations of the health professions and of the state. We pay tax on our incomes, remember!

In addition to being a global business organisation, there are signs that Jungian psychology, as represented by the IAAP, is still in some respects a kind of Western imperialistic entity complete with salesmen and saleswomen. At our worst, we may look like missionaries, bringing our faith to the faithless, on a 'civilising' mission as colonialists claimed to be. But perhaps we prefer to identify simply as praiseworthy conveyors of things that are good beyond dispute, rather like vaccines.

But whether we are a business, a church, or a medical charity (*psyche sans frontières*), the SWOT analysis works pretty well.

One important thing to bear in mind is that all the positive and valuable things we as Jungians know to be true about Jungian analysis may not really be strengths when examined more deeply. Or they are disputed as strengths by people outside our world. So, our perspectives derived from soul or spirit, and our search for meaning and purpose in life are not strengths when viewed from an external perspective. We see them as strengths, of course. Similarly, many of the weaknesses I will be reviewing will strike Jungians as untrue, unfair, personalistic, and ignorant propaganda. But remember they are still weaknesses in the eyes of our critics whatever we think.

Before getting further into the paper, I'd like to ask readers to play the same little game played by the audience at the lecture. You are asked to try to imagine that you are considering investing in a business entity called 'analytical psychology'. What I mean is a play version of a financial investment. On a scale of 1–10, how would you rate the viability of such an investment, where 1 indicates you'd keep out, and 10 indicates you've seen the most marvellous opportunity and intend to seize it. At the end, I will ask you to review your score. Just a game to play alone or with your colleagues. . .

Strengths

For the purpose of my SWOT analysis, I identified four strengths: *clinical, trans(gender), polyamory, and Jung the man.* Of course, there could have been more, but a focus was needed. I will discuss these in turn.

The *first* strength is the clinical one. Jungian analysis and psychotherapy occupy a very interesting and significant middle position in today's spectrum of therapies. (I am not going to spend time on things that divide us Jungians: the number of sessions per week, couch or chair, transference, and so on.)

In general terms, the strength of the Jungian approach is that it straddles a broad spectrum of therapies. For example, the relations between analytical psychology and neuroscience are often noted these days and sometimes even by the neuroscientists not just the self-congratulatory Jungians! The links between Jungian and humanistic approaches are so well known and exciting that the UK Confederation of Analytical Psychology held a sell-out conference on them a couple of years ago. The conference demonstrated the seminal importance of Jungian analysis in relation to body psychotherapy, psychosynthesis, the expressive art therapies, and transpersonal psychotherapy. Several of the founders of body psychotherapy and the art therapies in this country had Jungian analysis.

The relationship with psychoanalysis is too complicated to summarise in a few words and deserves more attention. In psychoanalysis (and this is true about a wider range of today's therapies as well), there has been a 'relational turn'. Starting in New York, the growth of relational psychoanalysis is remarkable to behold. I have been fortunate to be in on the ground floor, having been a founder board member of the International Association for Relational Psychoanalysis and Psychotherapy (IARPP) serving as such for 15 years. Starting in 2000.

Jung's standing as a pioneer of relational approaches is gradually being recognised. This is a serious strength of present-day Jungian analytic approaches. Like today's New York relational theorists, Jung asserted that analysis involved mutual transformation and was a 'dialectical process' (Jung 1935, para. 1). Analysis, Jung famously wrote, and, in so doing resembling today's 'relationals', is 'an encounter, a discussion between two psychic wholes in which knowledge is used only as a tool' (Jung 1939, para. 904).

Jung asserted that the analyst is a 'fellow participant in a process of individual development' (Jung 1935, para. 7). His focus was often on what has been called 'the real relationship', making his point in unmistakeable terms: 'In reality everything depends on the [person] and little or nothing on the method' (Jung 1957, para. 4). Relational psychoanalysts who haven't totally given up on Jung and the Jungians for reasons I will mention later really appreciate these ideas of Jung's.

One of the things that a Jungian approach brings to relational psychotherapy is the addition of the unconscious which, until very recently, was not quite acknowledged enough in relational thinking. Therapy was a bit flat, so to speak. Now, we can talk of the 'relational unconscious' and analyse dreams in a relational way. So this is a bonus supplied, to a great extent, by Jungian analysis.

The *second* strength on which I want to focus is the contemporary phenomenon known as 'trans', meaning everything to do with transgender. This is becoming a huge and complicated issue both clinically and culturally (and politically). I am thinking not only about the claim that gender can be chosen by an individual but also about the growing range of gendered behaviours open to females and males, and also thinking about the huge growth of sexual and relationship styles now available. I am also thinking about the intricate and multifarious exploration of trans in the consulting room.

However, we shouldn't forget that there are, in many countries, circumstances in which people are put at risk by being anything other than traditionally heteronormative.

My point for many years has been that the ideas of animus and anima can be understood as tending in a gender fluid direction. I wrote about this usefulness of animus and anima in a piece in *The Guardian* in 2012 titled *'This could be Carl Jung's century'*.

Not only is anatomy by no means destiny, but the primacy of fixed anatomy itself in identity is being increasingly challenged. All these developments are understood by many contemporary post-Jungian analysts as aspects of the soul, and not as signs of psychopathology.

Let's pull back a bit from the phenomenon of transgender. In more general terms, animus and anima, as concepts of something that is 'other' to what appears or is permitted to exist, massively extend gender roles.

For example, we live in an age that, in the West, celebrates women athletes, such as the amazing British Olympic boxing champion, Nicola Adams. And, again in the West, the *zeitgeist* for fathers is now that of nurture, care, and relatedness, not only discipline and protection (Samuels 2001, pp. 101–121). In that book, I wrote 'in praise of gender confusion'. Maybe now the simple term 'gender fluidity' is better.

Turning now to the *third* strength (polyamory), we begin by noting that, these days, in Western societies, we are witnessing an explosion in the range of intimate relationship styles. We may speak of varieties of relational experience. Here, too, Jung was a pioneer, especially of what is now called 'polyamory', meaning an agreement between members of a couple that one or both may have relationships, including sexual ones, with people outside the couple. I am thinking here of the polyamorous triangle between Jung, Emma Jung, and Toni Wolff.

When I compare Jung and Freud, I find Jung's unconventionality an appealing feature, and I expect I am not the only one. Of course, it is still a somewhat patriarchal polyamory, and I daresay jealousy was present, and to call it an 'agreement' might be naïve – but I don't think what Jung, Emma Jung, and Toni Wolff did deserves to be condemned as sexist or misogynistic or as injurious to Emma Jung. The three of them enjoyed regular Sunday lunches together. However, I learned recently that Toni Wolff grew angry at the gossip but did not deny what was happening.

The *fourth and last* strength of Jungian psychology stems from Jung the man. I have already opened up the theme of 'Jung the man' in connection with personal, intimate relationships. So I'll just add a few words about *The Red Book*. There was huge and unexpected international interest in *The Red Book* and its account of Jung's interior life. It highlighted the fact that people are struck, moved, and impressed by Jung's creativity and bohemianism.

To summarise, the strengths I have chosen and discussed here were *clinical, trans, polyamory*, and *Jung the man*.

Weaknesses

Now for some weaknesses. The ones I have selected are Jung's prejudices, the question of elitism and esotericism, and (again) Jung the man.

The *first* weakness concerns Jung's prejudices, how these are related to by Jungian analysts, and how they may undermine the standing of Jungian psychology in today's clinical and cultural milieux.

I had a wide range of prejudices to choose from. I could have referred to Jung's problematic ideas concerning women, or (again) to his many anti-Semitic comments (Samuels 1993, pp. 287–336). It can be confidently asserted that these have been very largely addressed. The reason why I am now going to focus on what Jung wrote about Africans, persons of African heritage (such as African Americans), and Indigenous peoples is because that is a hot topic today and has *not* been adequately addressed.

The international Jungian analytical community is divided over how (and whether) to respond to concern over Jung's writings in this area. The degree of disquiet may be indicated, as I said, by the fact that the most downloaded paper ever from the *British Journal of Psychotherapy* is in fact Farhad Dalal's 'Jung: a Racist' dating from 1988 (see also Dalal 2002).

Whatever concrete response emerges, if any, we have yet to see any significant public distancing of the international Jungian professional community from what Jung wrote about Africans and Indigenous people. This silence is a serious weakness. There may be many reasons for it. For example, the blunt suggestion in Dalal's title that Jung was a 'racist' is very problematic and has led to an understandable but regrettable defensiveness on our part. The main objection to the word 'racist' in relation to Jung is that, if Jung was a racist, then so were Freud and many others of that era. Why do we have to sort of *apologise* on behalf of Jung? He was just a 'man of his times'.

Succinctly, the question is not as clear and cut-and-dried as many of us have believed. One implication is that, though undeniably possessed of some validity, the 'man of his times' argument has some flaws in it).

I really and truly understand our knee-jerk defensive reaction to hearing Jung unfairly and unreasonably called a 'racist'. But the understandable protest against calling Jung a 'racist' is not a sound reason to postpone responding to the concerns I mentioned. Postponement will not satisfy our many articulate and influential critics. It doesn't satisfy me.

Returning to the present paper, let's consider a statement of Jung's like this one, originally written in *Psychological Types* in 1920 *and – significantly – still remaining uncorrected in the last edition of 1949:*

> An incident in the life of a bushman may illustrate what I mean. A bushman had a little son whom he loved with the tender monkey-love characteristic of primitives. Psychologically, this love is completely auto erotic that is to say the subject loves himself in the object. The object serves as a sort of erotic mirror. One day the bushman came home in a rage; he had been fishing as usual, and caught nothing. As usual the little fellow came to meet him, but his father seized hold of him and wrung his neck on the spot. Afterwards, of course, he mourned for the dead child with the same unthinking abandon that had brought about his death.
>
> (Jung 1920, para. 403)

The issue here is not whether this expressed a racist sentiment. *The issue is what today's Jungian analysts have to say about it.* Our silence underscores why these comments form part of the 'W' (weaknesses) part of the SWOT analysis.

Drawing these thoughts together, I believe that something needs to be done, not on Jung's behalf but on behalf of the international community of Jungian analysts who have let the issue fester for far too long. After all, it was back in 1987 that Polly Young-Eisendrath published her paper 'The absence of Black Americans as Jungian analysts'. Since then, there has been a steady flow of books and papers on the topic of Jung and 'Africans' – including, with no disrespect intended to those omitted, by Adams (1996, 2010), Brewster (2011, 2013, 2016), Helen Morgan (2003, 2008) and myself (1993, 2014). Ignorance is no excuse.

I believe that paying attention to these questions is important even if the community of analysts in certain countries – maybe like Japan – is not directly affected by them. I believe it matters if one belongs to a professional community that has not considered its collective, ethical responsibilities whether one is directly affected or not. But in Britain and in the United States, Brazil, South Africa, Australia, and other places, this is a direct problem.

Just to raise one last issue. In Britain, psychotherapy is a remarkably 'white' profession. This lack of diversity matters. But in our Jungian professional community, a small number of persons of colour, and specifically of African heritage, are significantly more marked. I have looked at statistics. *We are less diverse than other schools of therapy.*

Do we have to consider the possibility that what Jung wrote about 'Africans' is putting off more persons of colour from training as analysts or seeking analysis? There are not 'none'. But in the United States, where there are over 800 Jungians, only four are African Americans. Lest we forget, Young-Eisendrath's paper was written over 40 years ago.

Moving on, the *second* weakness in my little list concerns the élitism and esotericism of Jungian psychology. For many critics, Jung's recipe for individuation is fare only for an élite, even an elect: a sort of freemasonry. Of course, given the sheer quantity of his writings on this matter, Jung often contradicts himself and individuation, which is mostly portrayed as an internal process, is sometimes stated to include relationships and the social dimensions of life. But the impression still remains, despite international developments in China and Japan, that overall, individuation is for older European people who speak Latin and have a familiarity with the Jungian body of ideas. That was why it was so important for Adolf Guggenbühl-Craig to write *Eros on Crutches* (1980) which argued that even sociopaths or those with special educational needs could individuate. My teacher Fred Plaut made the same point when he wrote that individuation was not the same as 'mental health' or even 'maturity'. So the concern over élitism and esotericism is not new. These older generation Jungians had spotted the ongoing problem I am bringing up here.

Maybe these weaknesses could be countered by a kind of EXOtericism, meaning a conscious, collective reaching out to the seemingly unreachable. That is something to discuss.

The *third and last* weakness reprises the section on 'Jung the man' that appeared under 'strengths'. I think it is also a 'weakness'.

You know, whether we Jungians like it or not, the idea of 'The Jung cult', made famous in Richard Noll's 1994 book of that title, just won't disappear. And this is so despite Sonu Shamdasani's rebuttal in his *Cult Fictions* (1998).

I don't think either side in the Noll furore covered themselves in glory. It was very poor public relations by the Jung Estate to cause Routledge to pulp a collection of Jung's writings edited by Noll, for which they had given full permission, when they read the cult book. There was nothing wrong with the edited collection – except its editor, who had slipped from grace.

Yet it was equally poor judgement by Noll – truly disgusting if very effective – to write a supposedly thoughtful op-ed piece in the *New York Times* comparing Jung as a cult leader to Jimmy Jones, leader of the Jonestown group that went in for a mass suicide. At least the *Times* published my letter of outrage.

Just a quick final note on Jung the man as a weakness: The polyamorous relationships between Jung, Emma Jung, and Toni Wolff are seen by many as reprehensible and conducted entirely in Jung's favour. So, once again, a strength is also a weakness.

To summarise, the weaknesses I have chosen and discussed here were prejudice, élitism, esotericism, and Jung the man.

Opportunities

I want to devote my space to only one opportunity, which I call 'the political turn in analytical psychology'.

In 2004, in a keynote at the Barcelona Congress of the IAAP, I said that we had witnessed a 'political turn' in Jungian analysis. I believed Jung would have silently approved of this development which has greatly intensified in recent years, given what he wrote in 1946:

> We are living in times of great disruption: political passions are aflame, internal upheavals have brought nations to the brink of chaos. . . . The analyst feels the violence even in the quiet of his consulting room. The psychologist cannot avoid coming to grips with contemporary history. We need not mention duties as a citizen.
>
> (Jung 1946, p. 177)

Empirical evidence for 'the political turn' can be found in the book *Analysis and Activism: Social and Political Contributions of Jungian Psychology* (edited by Kiehl *et al.* 2016). Most of the chapters in this book were written by Jungian analysts who considered that they had additional roles as activists of one kind or another. For example, Kawai's chapter is titled 'Psychological relief work after the 11 March 2011 earthquake in Japan: Jungian perspectives and the shadow of activism'.

From a cultural perspective, Jung's ideas are, in the most general sense, expressive of a collective agonising over what is meant by 'the West'. What it means to be Western is a truly complicated topic. It is easy to define a rational, peace-loving, democratic version of the West against a concoction of Islam as nothing but fanatical and violent. This post-truth split – between the West and Islam – cries out for a Jungian input. Jung saw himself as a sort of therapist for Western culture and it is interesting that many of his profound criticisms of it resonate with critiques from commentators ranging from Judith Butler to Cornell West to Slavoj Žižek to Yanis Varoufakis to Naomi Klein – and with the messages from organisations like Muslims for Progressive Values.

What Jung saw in Western culture is indeed very familiar to what such contemporary critics perceive. He despaired of its over-rational one-sidedness and of the way it has become cut off from nature (Jung is the pioneer of what is now called ecopsychology). He hit out at the materialism and loss of individuality in our world, focused on the mind-body split, on mechanical approaches to sex, and the West's loss of a sense of existential and spiritual purpose and meaning. He even, in a characteristic moment of imaginative genius (1952), tried to be the therapist of the Judeo-Christian God in his iconoclastic book *Answer to Job*.

I realise there is more to be said about the political turn but, for the moment, that's enough on our opportunities. Now for threats.

Threats

I have had to be very selective in this brief concluding section of my SWOT analysis on threats because there seem to be so many!

I have often asked masters students in psychoanalytic studies and counselling psychology in several countries for their word associations to the word 'Jung'.

I now have over 1,000 responses. By far, the most common association is the word 'Freud'. I would like to discuss this but think I should, for reasons of transparency, swiftly tell you what the next associations were in order of frequency. The second association was: Anti-Semitism/Nazis/Germany/the War. Then came 'psychotic' and also 'mystical' but invariably also meaning 'psychotic'. Then, 'archetypes'.

So, I wonder what to make of the fact that when our name is introduced the name of our greatest rival comes up in people's minds. I think this is not only a problem with regard to psychoanalysis and depth psychology. It's across the board. As a Jungian, I feel I need to reflect deeply on this association.

When I spoke about this matter to my friend Tom Singer he commented that there is a cultural complex around 'Jung' that operates trans-generationally – these young students have kind of 'inherited' the denigration of Jung.

Moving on, the obsession with evidence-based therapies is another major threat, the second one I am mentioning. There is evidence that psychodynamic psychotherapy can be as 'effective' as CBT. But this has not dented the supremacy of the latter at all. This is because, as I have bored myself by saying so often, it was never about science or 'results' in the first place. It is about money, power and influence – and what fits best with the prevailing cultural and, above all, political ethos in society.

When I was the chair of the UKCP, I used to spend a lot of time trying to get NICE (the National Institute for Health and Care Excellence) to abandon their 'gold standard' of RCTs and look at other kinds of evidence. Finally, they agreed. But, after pressure from others, NICE went back on their word and refused to move from adherence to RCTs. As I have said, this is no longer about evidence at all, nor even about rational thought.

A threat that cannot be avoided is the clients' desire for a short-term and concrete result from their therapy. Actually, I have some sympathy with this. When people are distressed or in a suffering state the idea of open-ended three or more sessions per week analysis doesn't sound too hot, does it? Many clients in difficulties actually welcome a diagnosis, and sometimes ask the analyst for one. Asserting the value of 'depth' makes us feel good but is it effective or, indeed, always true?

Be that as it may, the growth of things like computer-based therapy, sometimes issued on CDs, is a real threat to all the relational depth therapies. And for those of you in private practice, do not be smug and complacent. What happens in the public sector, is stalking us right now. Maybe aged training analysts have full practices. But most other people do not.

Here's the by-now familiar summary. The threats mentioned were *Freud, evidence-based*, and *short-termism*.

Recommendations

In my playful and imaginary identity as an organisational consultant, I feel I have to end with just a couple of recommendations. These may seem rather provocative, for the two recommendations I offer are (1) that Jungian analysis becomes more promiscuous and (2) that we start to privilege doubt over certainty.

By 'promiscuity', I mean looking and moving outward, not sticking to what already exists, not worrying if it doesn't all conform to what we have been taught, or to what is expected of us. Let's link up with all manner of new bedfellows – and learn from them. The other therapists I mentioned earlier, academics, artists, activists, and persons of faith have much to teach us.

Maybe more than we have to teach them. Let's learn from them at home and abroad. This is the constructive way to manage the vestiges of colonialism and mission that I mentioned at the beginning of the paper. Colleagues working at the frontiers have ideas and practices that will benefit those of us in the heartlands of European Jungian psychology.

My second and final recommendation ('doubt') was inspired, not only by Jung but also by Lord Byron and Lao Tzu. I just want us to stop trying to be right all the time. It is so maddening! So I end with this from Byron, who famously wrote 'I deny nothing but doubt everything'. And this from Lao Tzu (not the famous quote from the end of *Memories, Dreams, Reflections*): 'Those who have knowledge don't predict. Those who predict, don't have knowledge' (Mitchell 1988).

The investment game revisited

At the lecture, before our discussion began, I asked the audience, as I am now asking my readers, *to go back in their minds to the beginning of the presentation/paper, and review their score on the scale of 1–10 about 'investing' in analytical psychology now and in the future. How has your score changed if at all?*

NOTE: For information: this chapter has been updated but I kept the older title. Later presentations used this title: The Balance Sheet: Positive and Negative Aspects of Jungian Analysis and Analytical Psychology.

References

Adams, M. V., (1996). *The multicultural imagination: 'Race', color and the unconscious.* New York: Routledge.

Adams, M. V., (2010). The sable Venus on the middle passage: Images of the transatlantic slave trade. *In*: G. Heuer, ed. *Sacral revolutions, reflecting on the work of Andrew Samuels: Cutting edges in psychoanalysis and Jungian analysis.* London and New York: Routledge.

Brewster, F., (2011). *The dreams of African American women: A heuristic study of dream imagery.* Ann Arbor, MI: Pro Quest UMI Dissertation Publishing.

Brewster, F., (2013). Wheel of fire: The African American dreamer and cultural consciousness. *Jung Journal: Culture and Psyche*, 7 (1), 70–87.

Brewster, F., (2016). *African Americans and Jungian psychology: Leaving the shadows.* London and New York: Routledge.

Dalal, F., (1988). Jung: A racist. *British Journal of Psychotherapy*, 4, 263–279.

Dalal, F., (2002). *Race, colour and the process of racialization: New perspectives from group analysis, psychoanalysis and sociology.* London and New York: Routledge.

Guggenbühl-Craig, A., (1980). *Eros on crutches: Reflections on psychopathy and amorality.* Dallas, TX: Spring.

Jung, C. G., (1920). Psychological types. *CW 6.*

Jung, C. G., (1935). Principles of practical psychotherapy. *CW 16*.

Jung, C. G., (1939). Foreword to Suzuki's introduction to Zen Buddhism. *CW 11*.

Jung, C. G., (1946). Preface to essays on contemporary events. *CW 10*.

Jung, C. G., (1957). Commentary on the secret of the golden flower. *CW 13*.

Mitchell, S., (1988). *Tao Te Ching: A new English version*. New York: Harper Collins.

Morgan, H., (2008). Issues of "race" in psychoanalytic psychotherapy: Whose problem is it anyway?' *British Journal of Psychotherapy*, 24 (1), 34–49.

Morgan, H. and Berg, A., (2003). Exploring racism. *In: Cambridge 2001. Proceedings of The Fifteenth International Congress for Analytical Psychology*. Einsiedeln: Daimon.

Noll, R., (1994). *The Jung Cult: Origins of a charismatic movement*. Princeton, NJ: Princeton University Press.

Samuels, A., (1993). *The political psyche*. London and New York: Routledge.

Samuels, A., (2014). 'Political and clinical developments in analytical psychology, 1972–2014: Subjectivity, equality and diversity – inside and outside the consulting room. *Journal of Analytical Psychology*, 59 (5), 641–660.

Shamdasani, S., (1998). *Cult fictions: C. G. Jung and the founding of analytical psychology*. London: Routledge.

Young-Eisendrath, P., (1987). The absence of Black Americans as Jungian analysts. *Quadrant*, 20 (2), 40–53.

Chapter 12

Jung and 'Africans'

A critical and contemporary review of some of the issues

Retrospective Introduction: One of the most significant developments in the troubled matter of what Jung wrote about 'Africans' was the creation of an Open Letter from a group of Jungians on the question of Jung's writings on theories about them. This may be found in Appendix 1, below. The Open Letter was not like a petition when numbers matter. People who signed were knowledgeable and concerned. Of course, lots of colleagues were upset by the Open Letter, which – to expressions of horror – was eventually published in ten journals in the psychoanalytic and Jungian fields. I continue to believe that this whole business is one of the things that Jungians cannot avoid engaging with. Aside from that, I will let the chapter, stemming from 2018, speak for itself.

Talking Points: The method in this chapter is to look at the objections that have been mounted to looking honestly into Jung and 'race'. A list of such objections is offered and respectfully challenged. This seems a better method than continuing to assert that Jung was racist (though he was). The fiction that Jung was 'just a man of his times' is shredded, though in a scholarly manner. The chapter also includes a series of quotes from Jung's work that are deeply problematic but are apparently unknown in many trainings in analytical psychology worldwide.

Introduction

Imagine an empty stage. The lighting design provides for one strong shaft of light to be directed diagonally across the stage. Whatever is in the line of light is sharply and clearly illuminated. But many areas of the stage to the sides of the arrow of light will also be lit up at varying degrees of intensity. So some things will be very clear, others clear enough and other parts of the *mise en scene* in total or near total darkness.

This chapter is like that! There is so much that can be said about the topic of Jung and 'Africans'. Indeed, much has been said and written about it, and by now there is an extensive literature. Hence, I have provided a 'selected bibliography' of works that I consulted – outside of the writings of Jung himself – which may be found in the end materials of this chapter.

I employed the image of the theatre because this matter has marked dramatic overtones and undertones. What Jung wrote about Africans has disturbed or

DOI: 10.4324/9781003598985-17

concerned many readers and commentators. For those who are unfamiliar with these concerns, here are a few instances. They are presented here, not to make a point or series of points, and in the fullest recognition that context is not provided – but because this author's experience is that many students and followers of Jung's do not know what the aforementioned concern is about. I suggest that those readers who are aware of what is being discussed skip the selection of extracts provided. Later in the chapter, I will discuss one such extract in detail. What follows is by way of being a general orientation:

> The expression of religious feeling, the revival meetings, the Holy Rollers, and other abnormalities [of American life and culture] are strongly influenced by the Negro, and the famous American *naivete*, in its charming as well as its more unpleasant form, invites comparison with the childlikeness of the Negro. (*CW*10, para 95, written in 1927a)

> The vivacity of the average American which shows itself . . . in his extraordinary love of talking – the ceaseless gabble of American papers is an eloquent example of this – is scarcely to be derived from his Germanic forefathers, but is far more like the chattering of a Negro village. (*CW*10, para 95, written in 1927a)

> He [the Black] reminds us – or not so much our conscious as our unconscious mind – not only of childhood but of our prehistory, which would take us back not more than twelve hundred years so far as the Germanic races are concerned. (*CW*10, para 962, written in 1930)

> The child is born with a definite brain, and the brain of an English child will not work like that of the Australian black fellow but in the way of the modern English person. (*CW*18, para 84, written in 1935)

> In the collective unconscious you are the same as a man of another race, you have the same archetypes, just as you have, like him, eyes, a heart, a liver, and so on. It does not matter that his skin is black. It matters to a certain extent, sure enough – he probably has a whole historical layer less than you. The different strata of the mind correspond to the history of the races. (*CW*18, para 93, written in 1935)

> I have not been led by any kind of wisdom; I have been led by dreams, like any primitive. I am ashamed to say so, but I am as primitive as any n*****, because I do not know! (*CW*18, para 674, written in 1939)

There is a footnote from the editors of the *Collected Works* appended to the 'n word ':

the offensive term was not invariably derogatory in earlier British and Continental usage, and definitely not in this case. (*CW*18, p. 286, Note 10)

The next two extracts are taken from *Memories, Dreams, Reflections* (Jung 1963):

All in all, Negroes proved to be excellent judges of character. One of their avenues to insight lay in their talent for mimicry. They could imitate with astounding accuracy the manner of expression, the gestures, the gaits of people, thus, to all intents and purposes, slipping into their skins. I found their understanding of the emotional nature of others altogether surprising. (p. 288)

General laughter arose; capering, they scattered in all directions and vanished into the night. For a long time we heard their jovial howls and drumming in the distance. (p. 301)

Aims and purposes of this paper

The present paper was first presented at the academic conference of the International Association for Jungian Studies in Cape Town in July 2017. The theme was 'The Spectre of "the Other"'. Such a decorous and serious venue is an advantage when it comes to consideration of an ethically, politically, and organisationally delicate and charged matter. Even so, I apologise in advance for presenting what follows in a somewhat dry and reserved manner.

I am referring, as my title suggests, to the rather intense discussion that has developed in the wider Jungian analytical and academic communities – as well as specifically within the IAAP – over Jung's writings about persons of colour (including those of African heritage) and Indigenous peoples. The 'statement of apology and acknowledgement' (hereafter, 'the statement') that the then Executive Committee of the IAAP presented to their Delegates' Meeting in Kyoto in 2016 was 'tabled', meaning no decision was taken about whether to issue such a public statement. Ongoing discussions that are both thoughtful and passionate have taken place. The IAAP is the international professional body that consists of over 30 national associations that regulate training and practice in Jungian analysis.

Here is the relevant timeline:

Polly Young-Eisendrath's paper 'The Absence of Black Americans as Jungian Analysts' appeared in 1987. Michael Vannoy Adams' *The Multicultural Imagination: 'Race', Color and the Unconscious* was published in 1996. More recently, Fanny Brewster's book *African Americans and Jungian Psychology: Leaving the Shadows* came out in 2016.

In terms of the IAAP, Andrew Samuels made the initial call for a public statement at the IAAP Congress in Cape Town in 2007. Because this was met with silence, Samuels advised the Jungian analyst Dr Gottfried Heuer not to repeat the call at the Analysis and Activism conference held with the support of the IAAP in Rome, 2015. However, Heuer went ahead, and it was more favourably received. Fanny Brewster, Heuer, and Samuels were asked by the then President of the IAAP, Dr Tom Kelly, to draft a statement. The result is shown at the end of the chapter.

In the chapter, I will not disguise my personal views. However, I used the moment and occasion of an academic conference (and now an academic paper) to review, in what I hope is an appropriate, responsible, related, and yet forensic manner, the many *objections* of some of my Jungian analytical colleagues to issuing a public statement. I am not, in this piece, going over the reasons in favour of issuing a public statement. That is to say, I am not presenting arguments supporting issuing a statement.

Instead, I shall merely be reviewing *the objections to issuing such a statement*. In this way, I believe that a level playing field is restored. We need this to work better together to bring a good conclusion to the business. Objections to the statement are herein being scrutinised just like the arguments in favour of a statement have been scrutinised. 'Doing something' has received stringent critique. Much of the critique has been thoughtful and interesting. Now is the time to critique the critique, if my readers see what I mean.

This *critique of the critique* is necessary because objections to making a statement have by now gone far beyond suggestions for editing the words of the various drafts so as to find a consensual mode of expressing things. There is a true difference of opinion or differences of opinions. Nevertheless, by constructing the paper in this way, I am trying to avoid the risk that this becomes an absolute and divisive matter.

What I am saying is that the objections now need to be as carefully considered as the statement itself has been.

So, this is not a presentation of the reasons why 'something should be done' (as the expression goes). It is an evaluation of those responses to the statement that have for the most part taken the form of objections. The etymology of 'objection' has proved interesting. It comes from the Latin *obicere* which means, among other things, 'to reproach'.

If this concise and targeted paper leads to further and deeper reflection, then so much the better.

The objections to the statement

I have collected a range of objections from a wide variety of sources. All of these objections were made in writing and can be studied. They are not attributed in this paper to any individual or organisation but all come from within the Jungian world. Making a list like this and discussing it critically is the best I can do to facilitate discussion.

I will show a general list of objections first and then go into detail afterwards. This is what has been communicated:

(1) The statement unreasonably and ahistorically castigates Jung who was just a 'man of his times'? What he wrote was typical for back then. Isn't it stupidly ahistorical to try to claim that Jung was a 'racist'?

(2) Will such a statement actually make any significant difference (positive or negative) to the reception of Jungian ideas and analytical psychology in the wider academic and clinical worlds? It may be asked, in addition, whether or not we Jungians are concerned about that? Isn't it a pointless exercise, to worry what people think?

(3) Existing and potential funders will be put off by making these matters public via such a statement.

(4) The project is too politically correct.

(5) To claim that Jung's writings are the reason for people of African heritage not entering the Jungian world is simplistic. There is a wide range of sociopolitical factors which have a greater influence on this than Jung's writings. The issues of discrimination and under-representation are problems not only for analytical psychology but also for many forms of psychoanalysis and psychotherapy. It is therefore important that this problem is not portrayed as a particularly Jungian one.

(6) From the perspective of an international organisation, the statement is written very much from a Western European/North American viewpoint and does not take into account the perspective of some of our Asian, South American and African members who also experience difficulties in the area of discrimination and under-representation but in very different ways.

(7) Some of our patients and candidates of African descent may find the statement condescending and infantilising. Rather than solving the problem, a simple acknowledgement statement may perpetuate and reinforce it by shaming or otherwise making it difficult for persons of colour already in our Jungian world.

So, drawing things together, we have a list of objections as follows, using shorthand tags: (1) man of his times, (2) pointless, (3) funding, (4) PC, (5) wider general issue, (6) Eurocentric, and (7) making things worse. As I said at the outset, I will now proceed to examine and evaluate each of these objections.

Man of his times

True enough, Freud referred to his patients as 'Negroes'. It was a joke about the lack of patients based on a cartoon: '12 o'clock and no Negroes'. He was the hungry lion lying in wait for them. Hence, it is argued, it is important not to apologise for Jung's racism as if he were working and writing today.

That said, it is by no means beyond scholarly debate that Jung was 'just' a man of his times. The racial hierarchy and the European cultural and civilisational superiority that appear in Jung's writings on 'Africans' were widespread but not universal.

Just to give one example: the esteemed anthropologist Paul Radin was very critical of what Jung wrote about Africans. As we know, Radin was a colleague of Jung's, taught at the Jung Institute, and invited Jung to write a response to his work on the Trickster. He was a Jungian, but he turned into a critical Jungian.

In 1927, Radin published a remarkable book *Primitive Man as Philosopher*. Synchronistically, it was re-published in the year of the conference. Although the use of the word 'primitive' has been thoroughly dissected in many places, I find it interesting in this context – as *philosopher*.

Radin zeroed in on the passage Jung wrote in *Psychological Types* about a bushman hunter. Forgive me for repeating this passage:

An incident in the life of a bushman may illustrate what I mean. A bushman had a little son whom he loved with the tender monkey-love characteristic of primitives. Psychologically, this love is completely auto erotic that is to say the subject loves himself in the object. The object serves as a sort of erotic mirror. One day the bushman came home in a rage; he had been fishing as usual, and caught nothing. As usual the little fellow came to meet him, but his father seized hold of him and wrung his neck on the spot. Afterwards, of course, he mourned for the dead child with the same unthinking abandon that had brought about his death.

(*CW*6, para 403)

This passage of Jung's was first published in 1921 and remained intact through many revised editions culminating in publication in the *Gesammelte Werke* in 1960. *I find myself wondering why nothing was done about it, as it was in other egregious cases.*

Radin writes (in 1927) of the passage concerning the Bushman hunter quoted above as follows:

No greater distortion of the facts could possibly be imagined. And yet Dr Jung obtained this example from what purported to be a first-hand account. . . . [It] illustrates the unconscious bias that lies at the bottom of our judgement of primitive mentality, the unconscious assumption of the lack of differentiation and integration to be found there. . . . That an example like the one used by Jung should in all good faith be given as representative of the normal or even the abnormal reaction of a primitive man to a given emotional situation, shows the depth of ignorance that still exists on this subject.

(Radin 1927/2017, pp. 39 and 63)

Back to Jung. Of course, he knew Radin and his work well, and it is probable that Jung was aware of Radin's criticism of his writing.

In addition to Paul Radin, one should also consider Jung's exposure to the anthropologist Franz Boas, whose distinction between race and culture was already well known before the First World War. Jung cites Boas in various writings.

In his paper at the Clark University conference of 1909, with both Jung and Freud in attendance, Boas made it clear that there was no 'justification for [racial] hierarchies'. He also spoke against the idea that European civilisation represented the peak towards which other races and cultures were developing (Shamdasani 2003, pp. 277–278).

Shamdasani (2003) takes us further in the same direction. He makes it clear that, prior to his trip to the United States where he 'analysed 15 Negroes', Jung had read the works of Marcel Mauss and Henri Hubert. They were followers of Emil Durkheim. Shamdasani writes that 'there was no reference in Hubert and Mauss to categories being inherited, and they strictly refrained from biological speculation, stressing the socio-genesis of concepts and customs' (p. 313).

Today, we should take a look at Africanist works like Achille Mbembe's book *Critique of African Reason* which develop and refine what Radin was saying.

On balance, though, I agree that merely calling Jung 'racist' and leaving it there is, indeed, too simple. But, equally, merely calling him a 'man of his times' suffers from a similar defect. What seems important is how these matters affect the Jungians today rather than Jung himself.

What I take from this objection in a positive way is that the issue of 'Jung and Africans' is now planted firmly in our court, in the Jungian analysts' court. *Our problem, not Jung's problem.* And, if this is generally accepted, then the question of why it has taken a long time for the matter to be discussed in the way it is now being discussed is of considerable interest. If there is an acknowledgement or apology to be made, it would not be by Jung or on Jung's behalf – *but by us for the delay.*

Pointless

We come now to the second objection, that to issue a statement is pointless. The idea here is that it is pointless to try to improve Jung's reputation in culture and academy because the prejudices are so entrenched. But if one thing is true of academic evaluation of thinkers of the past is that it changes and often quite dramatically. Yet, of course, such changes are often long-term matters. As to whether it matters what people think about Jungians, I think that, as we are really not a cult, it certainly ought to matter.

As noted in the previous chapter, It is always relevant to note that Farhad Dalal's 'Jung: a Racist' is the single most downloaded paper from the *British Journal of Psychotherapy*. This is of interest even if the paper is considered to be one-sided and in other ways tendentious. Be that as it may, to read passages from Jung asserting that Africans lack an entire layer of mind can be disconcerting.

Funding

The idea here is that people considering giving money to Jungian causes, or who have done so already, will demur or refuse or even take money back if they are confronted with assertions that his reputation is a bit disreputable. To be clear, I have no information about whether there have been threats of funding being withdrawn or not being forthcoming. Is the implication that those who have already funded Jungian projects are cancelling their plans for the future? It seems reasonable to ascertain whether or not this monetary anxiety is well founded. A counter-argument might be that either we'll get funding or we will not get funding – but this statement is not necessarily decisive in relation to that.

A sophisticated and more recent argument is that, if Jung is made a hate object or target of opprobrium, then people with funds who are solely 'into' Jung might demur. But if, as is intended, *the accent is on the Jungian professional and communities*, the danger of losing funding is, to say the least, diminished.

PC

Given the impact of the use of the term 'PC' on recent U.S. Presidential Elections, we should not treat this objection as a light matter. And the statement was indeed generated by 'the usual suspects', including myself. So it was indeed a politically motivated act. I confess it. But the accusation or reproach that the statement is PC is, I respectfully suggest, also politically motivated – and may have been very effective.

Wider general issue

This is a very serious point – that the absence of persons of colour and minorities in the Jungian field is not due primarily to what Jung wrote or said. Rather, the argument goes, there are wider economic and cultural issues to consider. Why, it is argued, would we feel impelled to say anything at all about the lack of diversity in the Jungian field when this is the case with all the schools of psychotherapy?

What follows in relation to this interesting viewpoint is a summary of naturalistic research that I have undertaken via e-mail questionnaire. It helps us to think about the merits of the objection that this is a wider problem.

The research thus far is limited to the United States, Britain, and Brazil. In all of these countries, in the broad psychotherapy field, persons of colour are under-represented. True. But it seems they are *even more substantially* under-represented in the Jungian professional community.

In Britain, across the two major therapy organisations, the average figure for therapists of colour is 5.5%. In the Jungian professional community, while no statistics are kept, the figure is very much lower, well below 1%. There are no Africanist Jungian analysts in Britain.

In the United States, there are, at present, only four African American Jungian analysts out of a total of over 800. This is a very low proportion. Though still below what would be representative of the population, the proportion is higher in the two American-based analytical organisations of which I am a member: the IARPP, and the Psychoanalysis Division of the American Psychological Association.

If the enquiry is limited only to 'Africanists', to use Dr Fanny Brewster's word, these gaps between Jungians and the rest when it comes to diversity are even more marked. In a nutshell, there may well be a problem here with regard to psychotherapy as a whole, but, in the Jungian professional world, the problem is that much bigger.

For these reasons, I consider it premature and not factually founded to close down debate about the impact of Jung's writings on people of colour seeking analytical training and Jungian analysis. *It is unlikely, surely, that what Jung wrote has had no impact whatsoever.*

I am grateful to Dr Alan Vaughan (personal communication 2017), one of the African American Jungian analysts, for informing me that it is common currency within the U.S. National Organisation of Black Psychologists that they should steer clear of things Jungian, including further training. The situation, particularly in San Francisco, may be moving in a more positive direction but Vaughan's account is significant.

I have heard something similar from a correspondent in the Jungian analytic field in Brazil who wishes to remain anonymous but wrote this to me via e-mail in July 2017:

I can tell you something about the Psychology Council, which contributes to the Public Policy Commission. In the Council, there is a group on race relations, with many black psychologists with African descent. This is a growing theme, enclosed with a document made by the Federal Psychology College, referring to a research with black psychologists.

There is a Black Movement formed by psychologists (those) that give visibility to this theme inside and outside the Counseling System of Psychology.

Statement from the Psychology Council: Psychology contributes to the dismantling of this modality of domination [i.e. racism]. It is up to the Council System, the unions of the category [of psychology], the universities of Psychology and the psychologists to help to think about it, to denounce it and to collaborate with the unveiling of social and subjective mechanisms that legitimize it, which requires action in Different scopes, all possible. They are practices to be carried out in the countryside and in the city, in the street and in the public services (legal, health, education, culture, work, etc.), private practice, research and alongside the Black Movement.

These Brazilian psychologists are not at all well disposed to Jungian psychology, as the side correspondences make plain.

Eurocentric

This is an ingenious objection because it is suggested that, in criticising analytical psychology for being Eurocentric, something Eurocentric has been done! Is this the case?

In March 2017, I gave the SAP Annual Lecture, which forms the basis of Chapter 11. The respondent was Professor Toshio Kawai, who went on to become President of IAAP. At a reception in his honour, Professor Kawai said that, as a Japanese man, in Britain he 'felt black'. And in his response (2017) to me, also in the *Journal of Analytical Psychology*, Kawai expressed the sentiment:

Being a non-European, I can be easily identified with the Africans and feel, to be honest, uneasy reading [what is described in] the statement or apology.

So, maybe this is not just an Anglo-American concern. Aside from what Professor Kawai wrote, the matter is palpably relevant in Latin America, Australasia, European countries like France. It goes without saying that the matter is relevant in South Africa, the host country for the IAJS conference.

A friend of mine commented that, even if this were agreed to be a 'Eurocentric' preoccupation, it should not then be assumed that the matter can therefore be 'tabled' forever. If we are as concerned about 'the Other' as it seems we are, then to drop things because the perspective is allegedly 'Eurocentric' is problematic.

Another (anonymous) correspondent from Brazil made a pertinent comment also in July 2017:

Racism is not a topic in the Jungian trainings. What Jung wrote about Blacks is not discussed. Normally, Jungians often pretend he didn't write such things. Maybe we are defensive against this historical wound. To sum up, we know Jungians don't want to talk about it in a deeper way.

At this point, it might be helpful to look into some of these issues in connection with psychoanalysis. In her book, *Aboriginal Populations in the Mind: Race and Primitivity in Psychoanalysis*, Brickman (2003) shows how even the most progressive clinical variants of psychoanalytic practice, such as the relational school, remain deeply characterised by the penumbra, or residue, of Freud's colonial prejudices. It has taken a good deal of work by writers like Kimberly Leary and Neil Atman to start to look at this legacy and how it has influenced who might develop an interest in psychoanalysis.

Much the same seems likely to be true of analytical psychology. Our work does not apparently radiate a racial hierarchy or a prejudice around the 'primitivity' of certain categories of clients. But it is there. Emergent Jungian writers, such as Fanny Brewster and Alan Vaughan, are engaging with these issues.

The celebrated British psychosocial theorist Stephen Frosh, reviewing Brickman, wrote:

> [P]sychoanalysis has tended to overlook the impact of ethnicity and culture in the clinical setting . . . to be overconfident about the generalizability of its theoretical claims to all cultures . . . [and] to be deficient in examining racist attitudes within its ranks . . . and in its theories.

This perspective on Freud also goes to the heart of the intellectual and political conundrums over Jung's writings on Africans, other persons of colour and Indigenous peoples. The focus is necessarily on *us*, the contemporary Jungian analysts, therapists, and academics, not on *Jung*. (Although I personally remain interested in the intricacies and subtleties of the 'just a man of his times' discourse.)

Making things worse

The argument in this objection seems to be that it will be upsetting 'infantilising and patronising' – to persons of colour training or in analysis for a statement to be issued. I suppose it means either (a) that such people will be made to feel misguided and foolish in their Jungian choices or (b) that they simply don't need the statement at all.

This objection puzzled me because, as far as I am concerned, it is from those actual sources – people in training and in analysis – that a good deal of the passion for some kind of action on behalf of the Jungian analytical organisations stems. What if it is doing nothing that will make things worse?

Alan Vaughan (personal communication 2017) has wondered if this objection to making a statement might not be tested empirically by asking persons of colour involved in Jungian clinical work, qualified or in training, what their view about it might be.

Conclusion

There are, quite deliberately, no conclusions here. My rather dry and limited stated academic goal was to stimulate discussion. I attempted this by developing a methodology in which the objections to the statement are themselves subjected to a critical and forensic evaluation. My evaluation of objections to the statement is similar to that made of the arguments in favour of the statement.

References

Adams, M., (1996). *The multicultural imagination: "Race", color and the unconscious*. New York: Routledge.

Brewster, F., (2016). *African Americans and Jungian psychology: Leaving the shadows*. London and New York: Routledge.

Brickman, C., (2003). *Aboriginal populations in the mind: Race and primitivity in psychoanalysis.* London and New York: Routledge.

Dalal, F., (1988). Jung: A racist. *British Journal of Psychotherapy*, 4, 263–279.

Jung, C. G., (1921). Psychological types. *In: The collected works of C. G. Jung.* Vol. 6. London and Princeton, NJ: Routledge and Kegan Paul/Princeton University Press.

Jung, C. G., (1927a). Mind and earth. *In: The collected works of C. G. Jung.* Vol. 10. London and Princeton, NJ: Routledge and Kegan Paul/Princeton University Press.

Jung, C. G., (1930). The complications of American psychology. *In: The collected works of C. G. Jung.* Vol. 10. London and Princeton, NJ: Routledge and Kegan Paul/Princeton University Press.

Jung, C. G., (1935). The Tavistock lectures: On the theory and practice of analytical psychology. *In: The collected works of C. G. Jung.* Vol. 18. London and Princeton, NJ: Routledge and Kegan Paul/Princeton University Press.

Jung, C. G., (1939). The symbolic life. *In: The collected works of C. G. Jung.* Vol. 18. London and Princeton, NJ: Routledge and Kegan Paul/Princeton University Press.

Jung, C. G., (1963). *Memories, dreams, reflections.* London: Collins.

Kawai, T., (2017). The historicity and potential of Jungian analysis: Another view of 'SWOT'. *Journal of Analytical Psychology*, 62 (5), 650–657.

Mbembe, A., (2017). *Critique of African reason.* Durham, NC: Duke University Press.

Radin, P., (1927/2017). *Primitive man as philosopher.* Reprinted by New York Review of Books.

Rank, O., (1910). Report on America. *In: The collected works of C. G. Jung.* Vol. 18. London and Princeton, NJ: Routledge and Kegan Paul/Princeton University Press.

Young-Eisendrath, P., (1987). The absence of black Americans as Jungian analysts. *Quadrant*, 20 (2), 40–53.

Select bibliography of works consulted excluding writings of C.G. Jung

Adams, M. V., (1996). *The multicultural imagination: "Race", color and the unconscious.* New York: Routledge.

Adams, M. V., (2010). The sable Venus on the middle passage: Images of the transatlantic slave trade. *In: G. Heuer, ed. Sacral revolutions, reflecting on the work of Andrew Samuels: Cutting edges in psychoanalysis and Jungian analysis.* London and New York: Routledge, 13–21.

Boechat, W. and Boechat, P. P., (2009). Race, racism and inter-racialism in Brazil: Clinical and cultural perspectives. *In: P. Bennet, ed. Cape Town 2007: Journeys, encounters: Clinical, communal, cultural.* Einsiedeln: Daimon, 100–114.

Brewster, F., (2011). *The dreams of African American Women: A heuristic study of dream imagery.* Ann Arbor, MI: Pro Quest UMI Dissertation Publishing.

Brewster, F., (2013). Wheel of fire: The African American dreamer and cultural consciousness. *Jung Journal*, 7 (1), 70–87.

Brewster, F., (2016). *African Americans and Jungian psychology: Leaving the shadows.* London and New York: Routledge.

Brickman, C., (2003). *Aboriginal populations in the mind: Race and primitivity in psychoanalysis.* London and New York: Routledge.

Burleson, B., (2005). *Jung in Africa.* London: Continuum.

Dalal, F., (1988). Jung: A racist. *British Journal of Psychotherapy*, 4, 263–279.

Dalal, F., (2002). *Race, colour and the process of racialization: New perspectives from group analysis, psychoanalysis and sociology.* London and New York: Routledge.

Gaillard, C., (1997). Les voyages de Jung en Afrique et leurs effets sur sa conception de la psychologie analytique. *In: H. Dahoui, ed. Ombres et Lumières. Le rêve tunisien de Carl Gustav Jung.* Hammanet: Centre Culturel International.

Gaillard, C., (2000). Otherness in the present. *Harvest: Journal for Jungian Studies*, 46 (2), 16–33.

Heyer, G., (2016). Race, religion and a cat in the clinical hour. *Journal of Analytical Psychology*, 61 (4), 434–449.

Hillman, J., (1986). Notes on white supremacy: Essaying an archetypal account of historical events. *Spring*, 46, 29–56.

Kaplinsky, C. and Singer, T., (2010). The cultural complex. *In:* M. Stein, ed. *Jungian psychoanalysis: Working in the spirit of Carl Jung*. London and New York: Routledge.

Kimbles, S. L., (2014). *Phantom narratives: The unseen contributions of culture to psyche*. London: Rowman & Littlefield.

Morgan, H., (2008). Issues of "race" in psychoanalytic psychotherapy: Whose problem is it anyway? *British Journal of Psychotherapy*, 24 (1), 34–49.

Morgan, H. and Berg, A., (2003). Exploring racism. *In: Cambridge 2001. Proceedings of the fifteenth international congress for analytical psychology*. Einsiedeln: Daimon, 417–432.

Ortiz Hill, M., (1997). C. G. Jung – in the heart of darkness. *Spring*, 61.

Papadoupolos, R., (1991). *Letter in newsletter of the International Association for Analytical Psychology*.

Ramos, D., (2012). Cultural complex and the elaboration of Trauma from slavery. *In:* P. Bennett, ed. *Montreal 2010. Facing multiplicity: Psyche, nature, culture. Proceedings of the XVIIIth congress of the International Association for Analytical Psychology*. Einsiedeln: Daimon, 51–67.

Samuels, A., (1993). *The political psyche*. London and New York: Routledge.

Samuels, A., (2014). Political and clinical developments in analytical psychology, 1972–2014: Subjectivity, equality and diversity-inside and outside the consulting room. *Journal of Analytical Psychology*, 59 (5), 641–660.

Segal, R., (2007). Jung and Lévy-Bruhl. *Journal of Analytical Psychology*, 52, 635–658.

Shamdasani, S., (2003). *Jung and the making of modern psychology: The dream of a science*. Cambridge: Cambridge University Press.

Singer, T., (2010). Playing the race card: A cultural complex in action. *In:* G. Heuer, ed. *Sacral revolutions: Reflecting on the work of Andrew Samuels – Cutting edges in psychoanalysis and Jungian analysis*. London and New York: Routledge, 252–260.

Singer, T., (2016). Snapshots of the Obamacare cultural complex. *In:* E. Kiehl, M. Saban and A. Samuels, eds. *Analysis and activism: Social and political contributions of Jungian psychology*. London and New York: Routledge, 147–156.

Young-Eisendrath, P., (1987). The absence of black Americans as Jungian analysts. *Quadrant*, 20 (2), 40–53.

Taken from *British Journal of Psychotherapy* 34, 4 (2018) 673–678

Open letter from a group of Jungians on the question of Jung's writings on and theories about 'Africans'

Dear Editor,

Thirty years ago, the *British Journal of Psychotherapy* published a paper by Dr Farhad Dalal entitled 'Jung: A racist' (Dalal, 1988). Regrettably, no adequate acknowledgement or apology for what Jung wrote, and Dalal critiqued, has been forthcoming from the field of analytical psychology and Jungian analysis.

We write now as a group of individuals – Jungian analysts, clinicians, and academics utilizing concepts from analytical psychology – to end the silence. We felt further encouraged to write to the *BJP* in particular because of the Journal's strapline making clear its interest in 'Jungian practice today'.

Via detailed scholarship, Dalal sets out what Jung wrote about persons of African and South Asian Indian heritage, as well as other populations of colour, and Indigenous peoples. Before and since the paper, Jung's views have caused considerable disquiet and often anger within the communities concerned. There has also been disquiet and anger about Jung's views in clinical, academic and cultural circles generally. Analytical psychologists and other Jungians have known about the implications of Jung's ideas for decades; there are signatories to this Letter who have campaigned for recognition of the problems. But there has been a failure to address them responsibly, seriously and in public.

We share the concern that Jung's colonial and racist ideas – sometimes explicit and sometimes implied – have led to inner harm (for example, internalized inferiority and self-abnegation) and outer harm (such as interpersonal and social consequences) for the groups, communities and individuals mentioned in the previous paragraph. Moreover, in the opinion of the signatories to this letter, these ideas have also led to aspects of *de facto* institutional and structural racism being present in Jungian organizations.

The intellectual and cultural environment of late nineteenth and early twentieth century psychology promoted many colonial and racist attitudes. Jung's largely uncritical embrace of these attitudes led him to conclude that he was justified in constructing a hierarchy in which people of African heritage were alleged to 'lack a layer' of 'mind' that white Europeans possessed, and thus were 'primitive' in their emotional and psychological functioning. In addition, he also failed to listen to warnings from within his circle that his views were problematic.

We doubt that any contemporary clinicians and academics in the Jungian and post-Jungian community would endorse these ideas now, but the absence of an open distancing from Jung on these questions has allowed for some implicit biases in use of skin colour as symbolic of both 'race' and certain psychological traits. Failure to acknowledge and apologize for these offensive attitudes, and their poten-tial harm and confusion, is also not in keeping with the spirit and ethos of people who, like us, currently participate in Jungian and post-Jungian communities that support and value diversity, gender equality, social justice, political activism, and respect for differences in populations, cultures, religions, and sexual orientations. Some of the publications in these areas are listed at the end of the Letter.

We want, moreover, to recruit more students, clinicians and scholars of colour to study, train, conduct research, and contribute to analytical psychology, developing and actualizing a more refined attitude towards human differences than the one we have inherited, or may now have.

And so, our statements here are not so much to chastise Jung as to take respon-sibility ourselves for the harm that has ensued in these 30 years in which little has been done to rectify Jung's errors.

We deeply regret our role in having taken so long to issue a statement like this. We realize that it has been extremely difficult for persons of African descent, and other populations that have been similarly maligned, to contemplate entering either Jungian training and treatment, or becoming a Jungian analyst. While it is true that people of colour are underrepresented in the psychotherapies generally, the social data suggest that, where comparisons can and have been made, the problem is even more marked within the Jungian clinical communities.

In light of this, we call on all involved in analytical psychology, including our-selves, to accept and insist on new obligations: to accept responsibility for correct-ing and changing theories that harm people of colour, to apologize for actual harm and discrimination, and to find new ways to keep analytical psychology engaged with communities and colleagues of colour. We call on all involved in Jungian training, treatment and scholarship, to increase attention in their programmes to in-depth study of clinical, social and cultural matters that relate to bias, prejudice, diversity, and transcultural or intercultural perspectives and knowledge.

We recognize that, collectively, to reach these goals will require engagement in dialogue, reflection, and change within our Jungian communities. We hope our col-leagues, throughout the Jungian world recognize and welcome our good intentions. We also seek conversations with individuals and institutions that are prepared to assist us in our efforts to make the changes that are now necessary.

DEIRDRE BAIR PhD. Independent scholar and writer. Author of Jung: A Biogra-
     phy (Gradiva Award for biography 2004). USA
JOHN BEEBE MD. C.G. Jung Institute of San Francisco. USA

FANNY BREWSTER PhD, MFA. Philadelphia Association of Jungian Analysts. Professor of Clinical Psychology, Pacifica Graduate Institute. USA

ROGER BROOKE PhD, ABPP. Professor of Psychology, Duquesne University. Affiliate Member, Inter-Regional Society for Jungian Analysts. Executive Committee International Association for Jungian Studies. USA/South Africa

STEFANO CARTA PhD. Associazione Italiana per lo Studio della Psicologia Analitica. Professor of Dynamic and Clinical Psychology, University of Cagliari. Italy

MOIRA DUCKWORTH BA, BEd. Association of Jungian Analysts. UK

BETTY S. FLOWERS PhD. Professor Emeritus, University of Texas at Austin. USA

HEATHER FORMAINI PhD. Australian and New Zealand Society of Jungian Analysts. Italy/Australia

LYNN ALICIA FRANCO, MA, MSW, LCSW. C.G. Jung Institute of San Francisco. USA/Colombia

CHRISTINE HEJINIAN PhD. C.G. Jung Institute of San Francisco. USA

BIRGIT HEUER PhD. British Jungian Analytic Association. UK

GOTTFRIED M. HEUER PhD. Association of Jungian Analysts. International Association for Otto Gross Studies. Independent Scholar. UK

BARBARA HOLIFIELD MSW, MFT. C.G. Jung Institute of San Francisco. Adjunct Professor, California Institute of Integral Studies. USA

ANTONIO KARIM LANFRANCHI MD. Analytical Psychologist. Italy/Egypt

SAM KIMBLES PhD. C.G. Jung Institute of San Francisco. USA

MONICA LUCI PhD. Associazione Italiana di Psicologia Analitica. Italy

BEGUM MAITRA MBBS, DPM, MD (Psychiatry), MRCPsych. Retired Child and Adolescent Psychiatrist. Association of Jungian Analysts. UK/India

JON MILLS PsyD, PhD, CPsych, ABPP. Professor of Psychology and Psychoanalysis, Adler Graduate Professional School, Toronto. Executive Committee International Association for Jungian Studies. Canada

HELEN MORGAN. British Jungian Analytic Association. UK

GORDON MURRAY MFT. C.G. Jung Institute of San Francisco. USA

KONOYU NAKAMURA PhD. Professor, Otemon Gakuin University. Executive Committee, International Association of Jungian Studies. Japan

EVA PATTIS PhD. Centro Italiano di Psicologica Analitica. Italy

DENISE G. RAMOS PhD. Brazilian Society for Analytical Psychology (SBrAP). Vice-President for Americas of the International Society of Sandplay Therapy. Full Professor at the Post Graduation Program in Clinical Psychology at Pontificia Universidade Católica de São Paulo. Brazil

SUSAN ROWLAND PhD. Professor of Jung and the Humanities, Pacifica Graduate Institute. USA/UK

ANDREW SAMUELS. Society of Analytical Psychology. Professor of Analytical Psychology, University of Essex. Past Chair, UK Council for Psychotherapy. UK

SULAGNA SENGUPTA MA. Former member, India Jung Centre. International Association for Jungian Studies. Author of Jung in India. India

THOMAS SINGER MD. C.G. Jung Institute of San Francisco. USA

KHENU SINGH MD. C.G. Jung Institute of San Francisco. Staff Psychiatrist, Adult Forensic Behavioral Health, Alameda County at Santa Rita Jail. USA

ANNA M. SPIELVOGEL MD, PhD. C.G. Jung Institute of San Francisco. Clinical Professor of Psychiatry, University of San Francisco. USA

MARTIN STONE BSc. Association of Jungian Analysts. UK

TRISTAN TROUDART MD. Israel Institute for Jungian Psychology. Israel

ALAN G. VAUGHAN, PhD, JD. C.G. Jung Institute of San Francisco. Core Psychology Faculty, College of Social Sciences, Saybrook University. Association of Black Psychologists. USA

RUTH WILLIAMS MA. Association of Jungian Analysts. UK

POLLY YOUNG-EISENDRATH PhD. Jungian Psychoanalytic Association. Clinical Associate

Professor of Psychiatry, University of Vermont. Past President Vermont Association for Psychoanalytic Studies, USA

LUIGI ZOJA PhD. Centro Italiano di Psicologica Analitica. Italy.

Selected bibliography of works consulted in preparing the open letter

Adams, M. V., (1996). *The multicultural imagination: 'Race', color and the unconscious*. New York: Routledge.

Adams, M. V., (2010). The Sable Venus on the middle passage: Images of the transatlantic slave trade. *In*: G. Heuer, ed. *Sacral revolutions, Reflecting on the work of Andrew Samuels: Cutting edges in psychoanalysis and Jungian analysis*. London and New York: Routledge, 13–21.

Bennett, P., ed., (2010). *Montreal 2010. Facing multiplicity: Psyche, nature, culture. Proceedings of the XVIIIth congress of the international association for analytical psychology*. Einsiedeln: Daimon, 51–67.

Boechat, W. and Pantoja Boechat, P., (2009). Race, racism and inter-racialism in Brazil: Clinical and cultural perspectives. *In*: P. Bennet, ed. *Cape Town 2007: Journeys, encounters: Clinical, communal, cultural*. Einsiedeln: Daimon, 100–114.

Brewster, F., (2011). *The dreams of African American women: A heuristic study of dream imagery*. Ann Arbor, MI: Pro Quest UMI Dissertation Publishing.

Brewster, F., (2013). Wheel of fire: The African American dreamer and cultural consciousness. *Jung Journal: Culture and Psyche*, 7 (1), 70–87.

Brewster, F., (2016). *African Americans and Jungian psychology: Leaving the shadows*. London and New York: Routledge.

Dalal, F., (2002). *Race, colour and the process of racialization: New perspectives from group analysis, psychoanalysis and sociology*. London and New York: Routledge.

Gaillard, C., (1997). Les voyages de Jung en Afrique et leurs effets sur sa conception de la psychologie analytique. *In*: H. Dahoui, ed. *Ombres et Lumiéres. Le rêve tunisien de Carl Gustav Jung*. Hammanet: Centre Culturel International.

Gaillard, C., (2000). Otherness in the present. *Harvest: Journal for Jungian Studies*, 46 (2).

Hillman, J., (1986). Notes on white supremacy: Essaying an archetypal account of historical events. *Spring*, 46, 29–56.

Heyer, G., (2016). Race religion and a cat in the clinical hour. *Journal of Analytical Psychology* 61 (4), 434–49.

Kaplinsky, C. and Singer, T., (2010). The cultural complex. *In*: M. Stein, ed. *Jungian Psychoanalysis: Working in the spirit of Carl Jung*. London and New York: Routledge.

Kimbles, S. L., (2009). 'Panacea and poison', presentation within panel on 'Poisons and panaceas in analytical training'. *In*: M. A. Mattoon, ed. *Florence 98: Destruction and creation – personal and cultural transformation: Proceedings of the fourteenth international congress for analytical psychology.* Einsiedeln: Daimon, 440–445.

Kimbles, S. L., (2014). *Phantom narratives: The unseen contributions of culture to psyche.* London: Rowman & Littlefield.

Morgan, H., (2002). Exploring racism. *Journal of Analytical Psychology,* 47 (4), 567–581.

Morgan, H., (2008). Issues of 'race' in psychoanalytic psychotherapy: Whose problem is it anyway? *British Journal of Psychotherapy,* 24 (1), 34–49.

Morgan, H., (2014). Between fear and blindness: The white therapist and the black patient. *In*: F. Lowe, ed. *Thinking space. Promoting thinking about race, culture and diversity in psychotherapy and beyond. Tavistock Clinic Series.* London: Karnac, 56–74. (Originally published in *Journal of the British Association of Psychotherapists,* 34 (3), 34–61, 1998).

Morgan, H. and Berg, A., (2003). Exploring racism. *In*: *Cambridge 2001. Proceedings of the fifteenth international congress for analytical psychology.* Einsiedeln: Daimon, 417–432.

Ortiz Hill, M., (1997). C. G. Jung – in the heart of darkness. *Spring,* 61.

Papadopoulos, R., (1991). *Letter in newsletter of the International Association for Analytical Psychology.*

Ramos, D., (2012). Cultural complex and the elaboration of trauma from slavery. *In*: P. Bennett, ed. *Montreal 2010. Facing multiplicity: Psyche, nature, culture. Proceedings of the XVIIIth congress of the international association for analytical psychology.* Einsiedeln: Daimon, 51–67.

Samuels, A., (1993). *The political psyche.* London and New York: Routledge.

Samuels, A., (2014). Political and clinical developments in analytical psychology, 1972–2014: Subjectivity, equality and diversity – inside and outside the consulting room. *Journal of Analytical Psychology,* 59 (5), 641–660.

Samuels, A., (2018). Jung and 'Africans': A critical and contemporary review of some of the issues. *International Journal of Jungian Studies,* 10 (4), 23–34.

Sengupta, S., (2013). *Jung in India.* New Orleans, LA: Spring Journal Books.

Singer, T., (2010). Playing the race card: A cultural complex in action. *In*: G. Heuer, ed. *Sacral revolutions: Reflecting on the work of Andrew Samuels – Cutting edges in psychoanalysis and Jungian analysis.* London and New York: Routledge, 252–260.

Singer, T., (2016). Snapshots of the Obamacare cultural complex. *In*: E. Kiehl, M. Saban and A. Samuels, eds. *Analysis and activism: Social and political contributions of Jungian psychology.* London and New York: Routledge, 147–156.

Singh, K., (2017). Can we have a conversation? Against totalization and toward a dialogical hermeneutics. *Jung Journal,* 11 (2), 20–34.

Vaughan, A. G., (2018). A conversation between Like Minded Colleagues and Friends: Alan Vaughan and Andrew Samuels. Questing for new Jungian paradigms on ethnicity, racism, and culture within the individuation of analytical psychology. *Jung Journal: Culture and Psyche,* 12 (2), 118–137.

Young-Eisendrath, P., (1987). The absence of black Americans as Jungian analysts. *Quadrant,* 20 (2), 40–53.

Draft of the IAAP statement as at March 2017 referred to above:

Statement by the International Association for Analytical Psychology (IAAP) concerning C.G. Jung's writings and his discussion of persons of African heritage, other persons of colour and indigenous populations:

(1) The IAAP is the international professional organisation responsible for the development and dissemination of approaches to analytical treatment and research that derive from the work of C.G. Jung (1875–1961). The IAAP has over 3000 member analysts and is active in more than 30 countries.

(2) Discussions among various members of the IAAP have, for many years, engaged the issues raised by Jung's writings concerning Africans and persons of African heritage, as well as other populations of colour including indigenous peoples. These aspects of Jung's work have caused significant disquiet, disappointment and often anger among the individuals and communities concerned, and in clinical, academic and cultural circles generally. Failure to address these issues directly influences the perception of analytical psychology and creates an environment that members of these populations may understandably consider hostile. These circumstances require both personal and institutional acknowledgment and the implementation of processes aimed at mitigating the negative impact of these aspects of the history of analytical psychology.

(3) We very much doubt that contemporary members of the IAAP share the language, imagery and evaluations of Africans, persons of African heritage and other populations of colour that one can find in Jung's works. We also take note of the Association's adoption of an encompassing statement of non-discrimination in its constitution, and the requirement for similar statements in the constitutions of all group members. By the same token, we view Jung's own relationship to these aspects of his life and writings as complex, culturally embedded in the world of late nineteenth and early twentieth century colonialism, and often balanced by expressions of deep admiration for the same groups. It is nevertheless the case that the problematic nature of these aspects of analytical psychology's heritage has never before been clearly acknowledged in a public forum.

(4) With this background in mind, the IAAP Executive Committee, with the endorsement of the Association's membership, wishes to state clearly that the IAAP deeply regrets the failure to acknowledge the impact of these elements of Jung's work and to take steps appropriate from an institutional standpoint to mitigate their impact on the effected populations as well as on the community of analytical psychologists generally. We realise that among other implications of these aspects of Jung's work it has often been difficult for persons who are African or of African or indigenous heritage to contemplate either entering Jungian analysis or training to become a Jungian analyst.

(5) By way of this public statement of the position of the IAAP, which has been discussed throughout the organisation, the IAAP calls on all involved in the dissemination of Jung's ideas, the training of Jungian analysts and other activities associated with analytical psychology to devote (or increase) attention in their programmes to the in-depth study of clinical and societal matters affecting all ethnic groups, incorporating transcultural and intercultural perspectives. Particular attention should be paid not only to Jung's often explicit comments on some populations but also to how language originally intended to communicate a symbolic sense of depth or hiddenness, such as 'primitive' or the 'darkness of the shadow', has led to a complex and often negative response to the theory and practice of analytical psychology. We emphasise that this is not a call for censorship of either Jung or the work of analytical psychologists, but rather for deeper reflection and consideration of the role that might still be played by these aspects of Jung's work in the ongoing development of analytical psychology in the twenty-first Century.

(6) We do not expect an immediate healing of wounds that may have been created in the past by failure to more publically acknowledge these matters. We realise that, collectively, we have a great deal of learning to do and reflection to undertake. Yet we hope that the constructive nature of our intentions is recognised. We seek dialogue with people and institutions who have been dismayed, not only at what they have read in Jung but also at the delay on the part of the international representatives of analytical psychology in making an adequate response. This call for action also reflects the conviction of members of the IAAP that analytical psychology holds much promise for informing and transforming many of the cultural and societal forces that lead to prejudice and conflict.

Chapter 13

Sinking like a stone

Activism, analysis, and the role
of the academy

*Retrospective Introduction and Talking Points: Somewhat biographical due to the
author's experiences living in Southern Africa (including a period in prison), the
chapter (whose title comes from the Dylan song 'The times they are a changin') proposes something called 'contemporary indigeneity'. This holds that what is happening
in non-Western locales is far from static and eternal. The chapter goes on to reprise
the author's career-long idea that the future of Jungian analysis and psychoanalysis
will depend on how it engages with the events of the day. The situation in the Middle
East would be one such issue. How we in the 'psy' field carry out political activism (assuming we want to) is a huge problem as we saw when events in Gaza utterly divided
and ravaged professional bodies, sundering colleagues from each other. To say this is
'parallel process' misses out on the huge problem of bringing therapy thinking to bear
on the public conversation. How can we marry up 'the spirit of the depths with the
'spirit of the times'? To paraphrase Freud, it is 'Impossible'. But it is not only impossible – it is also VERY DIFFICULT.*

My story

The organisers of the unique conference of the IAJS where this chapter began life
will remember how hard it was necessary to fight to make sure it took place in
South Africa, fighting in public and behind the scenes. There was opposition. The
reasons I personally was so committed were primarily autobiographical, and I want
briefly to share them with readers for the first time in public.

Starting in 1967, between school and university (in American terms, between
high school and college), I lived in Swaziland for over a year, about 60 years ago.
At that time, the small country, completely surrounded by South Africa, was a British Protectorate. I got a job with the British Colonial Office as a District Officer,
complete with ceremonial sword and solar topee (like you can see Jung wearing in
the photos of his African trip).

In short order, I was secretly recruited by the African National Congress, in part
because I had been involved with the Anti-Apartheid Movement in Britain. I performed certain tasks for the ANC that, as you'd expect, totally contradicted my task
as a District Officer. I comprehensively broke the Official Secrets Act. Eventually,
I was found out and fired. They threw me out of Swaziland and when I entered

DOI: 10.4324/9781003598985-18

South Africa I was arrested and flung into Pretoria Central Prison (of Steve Biko infamy). Of course, the British had betrayed me.

I stayed in jail for a few weeks, and it was not a pleasant experience. Still, attending a British public (i.e. private) boarding school prepares one for such ordeals as being kicked, hit, and shouted at.

What I am trying to convey is that this country was where I gained whatever understanding I have of the political process and of the necessity of struggle. Hence, I should like to honour my late friends and comrades Henry Malaza and Jerry Dlamini.

But it isn't just the politics that draws me back to South Africa. I still love Kwela and penny whistle music, drag on rough tobacco roll-ups, and even swig cane spirit. *Dagga* is smoked, if available (marijuana). But I also retain an aversion to wearing shorts which I still associate, not with an outdoors childhood but with the policemen in Pretoria.

This background led to numerous invitations to work in South Africa as a consultant. One memory worth recounting was meeting Nelson Mandela at a conference on nation building at Rhodes University in Grahamstown. (I wonder if the name of the institution will have to be changed in light of the 'Rhodes Must Fall' campaign?) I spoke on 'good-enough leadership' as the art of managing failure. He shook my hand afterwards and said with a twinkle in his eye, 'Well, I stayed awake during *your* talk!'

After this passage of personal confession (to use Jung's term), I want now to give a summary of the rest of this paper. There are three sections: (1) the political turn in Jungian psychology; (2) how the academy is the best critic of the clinic; and (3) clinical perspectives on academic research.

The political turn in Jungian psychology

In 2004, to repeat myself, at the Barcelona Congress of the IAAP, I said that we had witnessed a 'political turn' in Jungian analysis and psychology. I believed Jung would have silently approved of this development which has greatly intensified in recent years, given what he wrote in 1946 of 'the analyst's duties as a citizen'.

In the political turn, which has intensified over time, people seek to see how (and if) depth psychology and Jungian analysis can provide understandings of the political events of the day, coupling the spirit of the depths to the spirit of the times. My own contributions may be found in Samuels (1993, 2001, 2015) and also in Kiehl *et al.* (2016).

In practical terms, a series of conferences have been held with the support of the IAAP called 'Analysis and Activism'. The first two were in London (2014) and Rome (2015), the third was in Prague (2017), the fourth was pandemically on line but based in San Francisco in 2020, while the fifth was in Ljubljana in 2023. Readers may note that, in the title of this brief paper, I have reversed the terms so as to write of 'Activism and Analysis'. This is because I have become suspicious and impatient of incessant depth reflection on the social and political crises of our times that analysts go in for.

Analysts and psychotherapists shy away from action, which all too often is castigated as 'acting out'. Of course, thinking is fine and necessary; I am not in favour of mindlessness. But sometimes we need to recall what Hamlet said in a notable piece of self-criticism:

> Thus conscience does make cowards of us all,
> And thus the native hue of resolution
> Is sicklied o'er with the pale cast of thought,
> And enterprises of great pith and moment
> With this regard their currents turn awry,
> And lose the name of action.

Marx was there too, with these words on his monument in Highgate Cemetery in London: 'Philosophers have up to now only interpreted the world, the point though is to change it.'

The academy is the best critic of the clinic

I want to propose that field of Jungian and post-Jungian studies can contribute to the political turn so decisively entered into by our clinical brethren. As I said at the first IAJS conference at Essex in 2002, the academy can often function as the best (and friendly) critic of the clinic. So, I've tried to take from Western academic discourses three ideas that might of benefit to the clinic as it struggles to make its contribution on the social level as well as to the alleviation of individual distress.

The ideas are (1) multidisciplinarity (including intersectionality), (2) *contemporary* indigeneity, and (3) paying attention to issues of diversity and equality.

Multidisciplinarity

In today's Western universities, the talk is constantly of interdisciplinarity, multi-disciplinarity, and trans-disciplinarity. In the human and social sciences, solo performances are increasingly regarded with suspicion. They do not cut the mustard. There are numerous implications of this. One is the development of intersectionality, in which we do not split race from gender from socio-economic class (but without lumping everything together).

Here's a cautionary note, though, with intersectionality in mind. Jungian psychology on its own – or any kind of therapy thinking on its own – is useless when facing the crises our world is faced with these days. The task is to find people, meaning organisations and movements, with whom to ally ourselves. As I said, let's have an analyst or therapist on every policy committee, but, not a committee of analysts!

Ideally, these partners will be progressive movements and campaigns. They will be interested in social justice, racial, gender and economic equality, and climate change. Specific groups might welcome an alliance: for example, refugees, migrants, and asylum seekers – or veterans' groups. Or those working with and behalf of what we in Britain call 'ethnic minorities'.

Multidisciplinarity and intersectionality are problems for a clinical discipline like Jungian analysis that is for the most part esoteric, elitist, and proudly indifferent to criticism from within or without (see Samuels 2017). Individuation is a kind of 'fuck off' to critics who are, allegedly, 'not psychologically minded'. So becoming EXOteric is a tough call for many Jungian analysts. I believe the academy can provide support and sustenance in a renunciation by the analysts of the top table, of their conscious and maybe unconscious focus on the individuation of the 1%.

Instead, academic perspectives suggest to the clinic that it is worth standing up with the materially disadvantaged and the socially frightened, especially Indigenous people. This is different from sitting down with educated and adequately funded analysands. In our field, one notable pioneer is Eva Pattis Zoja with her sand play work in crisis situations.

Clinicians across the board may have to question the milieux in which many of them work, for private practice with a privileged clientele is not politically neutral – which, let me hasten to say, does not make it insignificant. Indeed, therapy may be a politicising experience for some.

Be that as it may, in overall terms, the private practice mode of working has affected depth psychological clinical thinking. Context has driven ideas. Clinicians suggests that this academic perspective may have to explore why it has taken so long for challenges to be mounted to their automatic preference for the inner world and the tendency to make 'inner' and 'outer' or 'private and 'public' into polar opposites.

Here I turn to Achille Mbembe, and his book *Critique of Black Reason* (2017). I read Mbembe as issuing a clarion call to the Western clinic, and the Jungian variant of it in particular. He writes, 'The path is clear: on the basis of a critique of the past, we must create a future that is inseparable from the notions of justice, dignity and the *in-common*' (p. 74).

The implication of this is that analysts and therapists need to think more intersectionally about those for whom the right to have rights is refused, those who are told not to move and those who are turned away, deported, expelled. That is to say, the new wretched of the earth. Those that Hillary Clinton called 'the deplorables' and we call 'the Others' (see Chapter 1).

Contemporary Indigeneity

The second academic perspective concerns a rather different from the usual revaluing of Indigenous wisdom, especially when it comes to therapeutic work. The paradox of '*contemporary* Indigeneity' is purposeful, with the emphasis on the word 'contemporary'. I am suggesting that it isn't necessary to look only into Ubuntu, or at Xhosa healers, or Australian Aboriginal healers, or Shamans. Sometimes, new ideas crop up in the most unlikely contemporary settings. In today's Africa, there are all kinds of innovative and creative hybrids from which to learn. *Africans are doing their contemporary thing in an African way.*

Here's an example. This is from the mental health field, and it is the 'friendship bench' scheme in Zimbabwe. Therapy on a bench not a couch!

(There is a video about the friendship bench scheme here: https://www.the guardian.com/global-development/video/2017/apr/14/therapy-on-a-bench-grandmas-mental-illness-in-harare-zimbabwe-video)

One in four Zimbabweans suffers from some form of mental illness, but there are only 13 psychiatrists in a country of 16,000,000. A solution had to be found, and it came in the way of a bench and the tradition of respect for African matriarchs. The therapy room is a patch of waste ground, and the therapist's couch a wooden bench under a tree. The therapist is an elderly Zimbabwean woman, in a long brown dress and headscarf. Her patients call her 'Grandmother' when they come along to sit on her bench and discuss their feelings, their depression or other mental health issues. Outside the clinic in Highfield, a poor suburb just south of Zimbabwe's capital Harare, there are lots of grandmothers – trained but unqualified health workers – who take turns on the park bench to hear stories. They listen to the battered wife who has attempted suicide twice, the man who hates women after he became infected with HIV, the unemployed single mother driven to despair by the driven to despair by the struggle of raising four children.

The benches are a safe place for people struggling with depression, which in the Shona language is called *kufungisisa*, 'thinking too much'. The grandmothers, all of whom are trained to improve a patient's ability to cope with mental stress, listen and nod, offering only an occasional word of encouragement.

The scheme has been researched and outcome studies performed, and the evidence base is that this works.

I see this project as an illustration of what Frantz Fanon called 'situated thinking'. It arises from a lived experience that was always in motion and in progress. Yes, such a scheme is unstable and changing but, understood a certain way, such praxis smashes, punctures, and transforms the legacies of colonialism and racism. It can be 'our' guide received from 'them' through the devastation of our Western present with its global crisis in mental health.

I should like to expand this section on the 'contemporary Indigenous' to say a few words about the global devastation, the impending apocalypse, the environmental crisis, climate change, sustainability, and so on. Here, as members of the responsible party, whether they try to deny it or not, ecologically minded Westerners need to pause for a moment. It goes almost without saying that the richer countries ('the North') will be less affected than the poorer countries ('the South'). But the poorer part of even one quite small district in a city like London will also suffer disproportionately, as we saw in the Grenfell Tower fire.

Alongside this, it is also useful to reflect on the ways in which poverty and inequality (global, regional, national, and local) inflect and problematise our thinking about Earth. I am far from the first to raise the question of how it can be ethical to insist that people and groups that have never enjoyed the ill-gotten gains of Western capitalism must eschew them in advance. Are they supposed to leapfrog capitalism to enter a new state of political togetherness?

I have to ask this next question, disturbing and challenging though it may be: Are Indigenous peoples simply to be required by us liberal Westerners to revert to or remain in traditional ways, whether this is what they want or not. Achille Mbembe is but one key writer on the avoidance of a sentimental return to the past. Following Edward Said (1978) in *Orientalism*, he stresses the patronising and dominating shadow of what looks like admiration for the Other and research into non-Western cultures.

For sure, we need to speak *to* the Other. But do we need to speak quite so much *about* the Other? And maybe we should be ultra-careful when speaking *for* the other? And let's not forget the Other within the other. I mean the poor within the poor, the dispossessed among the dispossessed – such as the Black poor and working class in relation to the Black monied middle and upper classes worldwide. It is interesting that so many undeveloped countries have agreed to take on their share of what is required by the Paris accords? Good news. Or is it? Won't the ruling classes of undeveloped countries escape? For there is a privileged 'Northern' element in 'Southern' countries like South Africa? Just as there is, for sure, a 'Southern' element in 'Northern' countries like the United States or UK.

For there are two sides to the coin of this 'Other'. The first is that we in the North and West are definitely engaged in overdue reparation for colonial, heteronormative, and neoliberal oppression. This includes the role of the psychological professions in both perpetration and repair.

But the second is that just at the very moment we enter or encounter the world of the Other, we often use the moment to conceal a failure to challenge the power relations, barbarism, and inequality of our own Western world.

The third academic perspective concerns the lack of diversity in the professions of psychotherapy and analysis. What can the academy offer in this context?

The question of a lack of diversity on Jungian analysis is a bigger problem than the admittedly significant problem of such a lack in all schools of psychotherapy (see Samuels 2018). Can anything be done about it? Here are some relevant questions. Where is the evidence that affirmative action or positive discrimination would lower clinical standards? Does reducing or sometimes abandoning the demands for paper qualifications necessarily lead to a lowering of such standards?

The problem is that *high standards contribute to patterns of exclusion and inclusion*. Universities know about it, and worry about it. I am not convinced that the therapy world has fully caught up with the extent of self-created discrimination and prejudice, which, all too often, is based on 'race', ethnicity, and culture – as well as money and class.

Clinical perspectives on academic research

As promised, the final section of this talk turns the spotlight back onto the academy, and I want to explore questions of mission and motivation in academic research. After having performed an academic act on the clinic, here's a clinical act performed on the academy.

I always ask my PhD candidates to explain what they see as the social utility of their research. What is it for? What is its meaning? I ask these questions even when the work is, for example, in the arts or religion or clinical process. What is the mission? And then, a further enquiry, what is your motivation for doing this research? I am, of course, thinking of the 'wounded researcher' made famous by Romanyshyn (2013) – but with an added systematic stress on ordinary psychody-namic, developmental self-analysis.

To give a personal example, I have written and researched a lot on the father, with a focus on the benevolent aspects of the father's body for his relationship with his chil-dren of all sexes. The problem I was depicting I called 'the dry father', a nice guy, not abusive – but lacking in energy, passion, and animation. Why did I develop these ideas?

Well, my father of blessed memory was a good example of the dry father. He was a gentleman in every way. But whatever was missing for me led me to create the notion of the 'dry father' and use it in clinical work. So many patients, male and female, yearned for more paternal passion.

I could go on and give other examples, but I think this way of thinking, looking for causes, explanations, and hints, is typical in the clinic, but not all that prominent in the academy. Maybe that is in the process of changing but I do not know for sure.

A concluding thought

The chapter title is drawn from the famous Bob Dylan protest song of the 1960s 'The times they are a –changin'. Hence, this is a 'protest chapter', full of anger about the state of play in two disciplines that I that I also love. I think we will sink like a stone if we don't pay attention. I don't claim this is the only way to think about our future. My chapter suffers from an inflated, prophetic tone and I apolo-gise for it. It has a history in having been invited to give the closing keynote in Cape Town. I wrote it especially for that IAJS conference because it is time for us, whether in academy or clinic, or in both, to change.

(For those readers who would like to copy what the conference audi-ence did and sing along with Bob, here is the link: https://www.youtube.com/watch?v=JxvVk-r9ut8)

References

Kiehl, E., Saban, M. and Samuels, A., (2016). *Analysis and activism: Social and political contributions of Jungian psychology*. London and New York: Routledge.

Mbembe, A., (2017). *Critique of African reason*. Durham, NC: Duke University Press.

Romanyshyn, R., (2013). *The wounded researcher: Research with soul in mind*. London and New York: Routledge.

Said, E., (1978). *Orientalism*. New York: Pantheon Books.

Samuels, A., (1993). *The political psyche*. London and New York: Routledge.

Samuels, A., (2001). *Politics on the couch: Citizenship and the internal life*. London and New York: Karnac.

Samuels, A., (2015). *A new therapy for politic?* London and New York: Karm.

Samuels, A., (2017). The future of Jungian analysis: Strengths, weaknesses, opportunities, threats ('SWOT'). *Journal of Analytical Psychology*, 62 (5), 636–649.

Samuels, A., (2018). Jung and 'Africans': A critical and contemporary review of some of the issues. *International Journal of Jungian Studies*, 11 (2), 23–34.

Part V

Clinic

Chapter 14

From sexual misconduct to social justice

Retrospective Introduction: I was undecided whether to include this from 1996 in the book even though I was and am proud of it. I am glad I did because it weaves together many of my evolving ideas about clinical practice, the public domain, and the problematic of the father. In subsequent work on the topic of sexual misconduct and boundary violations, I stress even more that this is an issue of and for men. For the avoidance of doubt, my impression is that in the intervening 30 years or so since first publication, the prevalence of sexual misconduct by male analysts and psychotherapists has not diminished. Although I take a different path, there is by now a huge amount of impressive work, particularly on the psychopathology of perpetrators, and the word 'abuse' is used much more frequently.

Introduction

Sexual misconduct by analysts and psychotherapists is a topic that causes great public concern. The profession should certainly respond to this concern. But the problem of sexual misconduct also provides a stimulus to new theorising leading to an engagement with issues of social justice. I argue that there are three contentious issues: First, I criticise the growing practice of 'safe' analysis, seen as a misplaced response to the problem of sexual misconduct. Second, I urge a fresh look at the theme of incestuous sexual fantasy in family process. This would provide a broader theoretical base for the exploration of sexual desire in analysis. Third, I seek to retheorise the father in general and paternal sexuality in particular. New thinking about paternal erotics turns out to have many sociopolitical implications.

Psychoanalysis is a field that is divided about almost every thing. We analysts just do not get along, whether in clinic, professional organisation, or academy. But one theoretical, practical, and moral thing on which we all seem to agree is that sexual activity taking place in analysis and therapy is a profound abuse of power, hence wrong, and therefore liable for punishment when discovered. It is one of the supreme values of psychotherapy. Another is that we should try to understand a problem, not merely seek to suppress or eliminate it.

What we know from the psychological study of incest is that when one meets a universal moral taboo with which everyone in a culture seems to agree, one is probably also in the presence of a universal impulse. No need for taboo without impulse.

DOI: 10.4324/9781003598985-20

Therefore, the common view, that sexual behaviour in analysis and therapy is damaging to the patient or client – with which I am in total agreement – stems in part from a universal impulse and desire in therapists and analysts to engage in sexual behaviour in the session (Stein 1974).

On this issue, the public is right! The public is right to focus on sexual misconduct by practitioners of analysis and psychotherapy. As our social critic – perhaps even the term analyst would be fitting – the public is having an empathically attuned response (which we could even call a countertransference) to our difficulties when it, the public, focuses on the question of sexual misconduct by practitioners. Of course, one could at this point cite the statistics and refer to the empirical research into sexual misconduct. But this is not the path taken by this chapter. It is by now common ground that a significant amount of sexual and other misconduct by practitioners (mostly but not all male) is going on. The point I want to make is that we should not dismiss the public's concern as misinformed or as energised by its supposed unconscious conflicts or complexes. Outrageous as it sounds to say it, the public is a better analyst than that.

The public has understood very well that intimacy between practitioner and patient or client may be the most important part of the process of analysis and psychotherapy. Maybe the public has grasped, if not yet articulated, the necessity of there being a sexual tone to analysis.

Can psychoanalysis respond to the concerns being expressed by its analyst, the public? I want to discuss certain issues that, in my view, will determine whether or not psychoanalysis will respond positively and constructively. Taken together, these contentious issues enable us to make a move from the problem of sexual misconduct to matters of social justice. For I see public concern over sexual misconduct as providing a stimulus and an opportunity, not only to address the problem itself but also, on the basis of an engagement with sexual misconduct, for analysts to go on to make a contribution to several key issues of social justice.

Social justice

Social justice is, of course, a familiar term from politics and social science. As used here, the reference is not only to a set of abstract principles that might govern the formation of a good or just society. Following current usage in the UK, the idea of social justice also encompasses the organisational and cultural changes necessary to fashion such a society. Thus discussions about measures to alleviate poverty increasingly are not divorced from questions of constitutional change – for example, to a less rigid electoral and parliamentary system incorporating proportional representation, devolved government, and a bill of rights. The Labour Party once set up a Commission on Social Justice to explore these issues and publish a report on them, so this kind of thinking is by no means a fringe phenomenon.

Gender issues are prominent when social justice is under consideration, and that is one reason why what might be thought of as the microcosmic phenomenon of sexual misconduct by analysts and other professionals is useful as both a symbolic and an intellectual entrée to social and political concerns. But there is also a wider background to my introduction of politics at this point.

In my book *The Political Psyche* (1993a), I suggest that politics in the West is experiencing a paradigm shift in which old definitions, assumptions, and values are being transformed. Whereas politics will always be about struggles for power and the control of resources, a new understanding of all that is political has evolved since feminism introduced the phrase 'the personal is political'. This new kind of politics is often a feeling-level politics, or a politics of subjectivity, that encompasses a key interplay between the public and private dimensions of power. For political power is also manifested in family organisation, gender and race relations, connections between wealth and health, control of information, and in religion and art. Hence, together with abstract principles of social justice and the organisational changes that are inspired by such principles, we can add a frank recognition of psychology's role in political analysis – an awareness that there is something like a 'political psyche' to factor into political discourse.

It is the tragicomic crisis of our *fin de siècle* civilisation that incites analysts to challenge some boundaries at the same moment that they reinforce others. Conventional boundaries that might be challenged include those between the public and the private, the political and the personal, the external world and the internal world, life and reflection, being and doing, extraversion and introversion, politics and psychology, between the fantasies of the political world and the politics of the fantasy world. If we mount this challenge, then it is easier to accept that subjectivity and intersubjectivity have political roots. Constructed as they are, subjectivity and intersubjectivity are not nearly as private as they seem.

Psychology and the therapies can fill crucial roles in this late modern world we have made. Not only in the rich countries of the West but also in the former Soviet Union, Eastern Europe, and the developing countries, politics and questions of psychological identity are linked as never before. This is because of myriad other minglings: ethnic, national, socio-economic, and ideological. The whole mongrel picture is made more intricate by the exciting and rapid course of events in the coruscating realms of sexuality and gender.

Gender is the gateway or threshold between the public and the private dimensions of experience. Gender is an exceedingly private story we tell ourselves about ourselves; gender is also a set of socio-economic and cultural realities. I carried out an international survey into what therapists and analysts do when their clients bring overtly political material to the clinical setting (Samuels 1993a). Among the questions asked were some designed to find out which political issues or themes were most commonly introduced by clients. This survey went to 2,000 practitioners from 14 organisations of differing theoretical orientation in seven countries. Nearly 700 replied. In a worldwide table of issues, 'gender issues for women' came out highest for every group except German Jungian analysts. For their clients, the number one issue was the environment and gender issues for women came second. 'Gender issues for men' came fourth worldwide.

The American groups that I surveyed – two well-established psychoanalytic organisations and three Jungian analytic societies – produced results broadly along these lines. The point here is not that these findings are surprising – they are not, given the liminality of gender referred to above. What is highlighted is that gender issues – which must include desire itself – and sociopolitical issues have become completely intertwined.

Taken overall, the responses to the survey suggest that the clinical office can be a bridge between the inner world and the political world as well as being the source of a divorce of the two worlds. This is why I do not support calls for the ending of the project of therapy and analysis. Clinical practice has been accused of being a bastion of possessive individualism and narcissistic introspection for 100 years; it is not a new criticism. And it is right to criticise greedy and myopic clinicians who cannot perceive that their work has a political and cultural location and implication. But it is not right to indulge in simplistic, populist rhetoric that would do away with the entire clinical project. Without their connection to a clinical core, why should anyone in the world of politics listen to therapists and analysts at all?

The huff-and-puff rejection of the clinical forecloses what is, for me, a central issue: the relations between the private and the public realms of life. The funny thing about this foreclosure is that it mimics the attitude of the most conservative, dyed-in-the-wool clinicians and mental health professionals – the keep-politics-out-of-the-office types. As I see it, the high-profile apostates and renegades of therapy and analysis are as terrified and perhaps as incapable of exploring the relations between the personal and the political as are the fanatical adherents of therapy and analysis.

Outline of the chapter

First, I discuss the growing practice of what I call 'safe analysis', meaning a style of analysis in which the exploration of sexual desire is repressed by the institutions of analysis themselves. It is a misplaced response to the problem of sexual misconduct which brings a whole new set of power problems with it.

Second, I try to show that a fresh look at the theme of incestuous sexual fantasy in family process is urgently needed. This would provide a broader theoretical base for the exploration of sexual desire in analysis.

Third, I attempt a retheorising of the father in general and paternal sexuality in particular. The father is important here because more subtle understandings of his sexuality will benefit male and female individual practitioners when they become the father in the erotic transference-countertransference. Such understandings will also help our thinking and training about what Rutter (1989) calls 'forbidden zone relationships'. Moreover, new psychological thinking about fathers and the sexuality of men will have many sociopolitical implications (as I shall show later).

Safe analysis

There is a consensus among practitioners that sexual desire in analysis is not what it seems. Sexual desire in analysis may be interpreted as transference, a defence, an infantile wish, a replication or recapitulation of a real event in the patient's past life, a zonal displacement (what is sought is not genital but oral or anal gratification), or there may be a narcissistic problem in the analyst. Relationship not orgasm is the secret goal of the sexually aroused patient. Power not orgasm is the secret goal of the sexually active male analyst as he replicates the power relations between men and women in our culture.

All of us who have practised or been in analysis know about the deliteralisation of sexual desire by interpretation of it. In fact, without interpretation couched in the metaphorical language of deliteralisation of desire, one might even ask if the work is psychological at all. But this leads us to a formidable problem. How are analysts to make interpretations about the metaphorical and symbolic dimensions of sexual desire in the analysis, how are they to explore sexual imagery and sexualised emotions, how can the myriad styles of object relating be revealed within monolithic sexual excitement, without there being something literal, actual, concrete, corporeal, real, experiential in either or both of the participants in the first place? But a reluctance to stay on or with this level, a reluctance presented now as a feature of much contemporary analysis, later as something to explore in family process, is a background part of the problem of sexual misconduct by practitioners. An analyst cannot make a symbolic interpretation of nothing without identifying that nothing; cannot say much about the significance of a desire that is not, or not yet, embodied without apprehending that desire; cannot respond to, say, the homosexuality within the relationship of a non-homosexual analysing couple without its being experienced in soma as well as in psyche. An analyst can certainly interpret the patient's reluctance to enter into the sexual material, but analysis of what is apparently absent or unthought is a different line of exploration altogether, depending even more than usual on a set of expectations about what should be there to be analysed. As my first training patient put it, when referring to her reluctance to meet the expectations of her analyst: 'An orgasm a day keeps the analyst at bay'.

The problem of safe analysis cannot be solved merely by noting the emergence of sexual arousal in the analytical relationship, for that state brings with it its own conundrum: How, when it's all so real, so infused with physical reality, are the analysing couple going to reach the very symbols and metaphors they are hoping to work with?

I do not think we can solve the problem by opting for certitudes: this sexuality is literal, this sexuality is metaphorical, and this sexuality is both literal and metaphorical. The matter may be undecidable and resist foreclosure. A comparison may be drawn with the difficulty in maintaining a hard and fast line between images of literal and images of metaphorical parents in analytic material: that father literal, that father metaphorical. In and out of analysis, I have come to see that a new category is needed, hard to name and anxiety-provoking to contemplate – a take on sexuality that is neither literal, and hence prone to being acted upon, nor meta-phorical, and hence prone to abstraction and denial, or both, which is the easy way out. Neither literal nor metaphorical, as well as either literal or metaphorical, that is the new category.

The problem of safe analysis stems from and is exacerbated by the evolution of a style of analysis mainly based on object relations theory but practised by many analysts using a variety of appellations designed to distinguish the practitioner from adherents of the drive/structure models of classical psychoanalysis. It is analysis that has become dominated by the numinous power of the very mother-and-baby imagery it often sets out to explicate. Analysis that gets into a panic over incestuous sexuality and flees into a milky *Weltanschauung* or perspective. No ethics problem there. Now I do not expect any reader readily to own this style of analysis as his or hers, and I am sure my racy depiction truly is, to some extent, a distortion, for some distortion of the views of others is inevitable in psychological dispute (see Samuels 1989, 1993b). But that does not mean that what I am saying is a lie as well! The style of analysis to which I am referring (which is increasingly influential worldwide) makes entry into the metaphorical and symbolic aspects of the sexual virtually impossible. In safe analysis, there is no sexual *prima materia* for the nec-essary symbolic work of the analytical opus. (See Samuels 1989, pp. 175–193 for a fuller discussion of the use of the alchemical metaphor in relation to these matters.)

Incestuous fantasy in family process

In examining the role of incestuous fantasy in family process, I think it is worth looking at a slightly different set of questions than are usually asked by psychoana-lysts concerning sexuality in general and incestuous sexuality in particular. Differ-ent, I mean, from the questions on a Freudian agenda, crucial though that listing has been. Maybe, following Jung's example, we should begin to explore once more the why and the whither of sexuality, as well as the what and the whence of it (Jung 1912). We might even overcome intellectual embarrassment to ask what is the psychological 'function' of incestuous sexual fantasy, what is it for beyond reproduction, why do we suffer and enjoy it, why is it as universal as the universal taboos suggest it is? What is the telos, the goal, the aim, the magnet, the aspiration, the prospect, the dream of human incestuous sexual fantasy? Where does human incestuous sexual fantasy lead – and do we need human incestuous sexual fantasy to get us there? Why is human incestuous sexual fantasy constructed by culture in the way it is? Let us make judicious use of teleology, of final causes. Maybe Jung's teleology and phenomenology's stress on affective embodiment and lived experi-ence will turn out to be compatible.

I want now to write directly about incestuous sexuality in the family – and I will try to do it without idealising either incestuous sexuality or the family.

The central question, it seems to me, is, how do we grow? Or, put differently, how do personality structures become or seem to become more extended and encompassing over time?

We may reply to the question, how do we grow? by saying that it is all the outcome of psychological, biological, and cultural interactions, or something anodyne like that. But the elephant's child continues to ask, exactly how does it happen, how does it work? One often-invoked answer focuses on relationships in general and relationships with parents in particular. We can unpack certain implications of this. Getting really close to someone who is more developed than you are psychologically (whatever that 'more developed' might mean) leads to some kind of enhancement or enrichment or expansion of the personality by virtue of the extreme closeness. The idea that a person grows inside by relating to people outside who have qualities that he or she has not yet manifested is at the heart of all the depth psychologies.

We have to ask, then, what in our general human make-up enables us to get that close in the first place? If you're a parent and I'm your child, and I need to be close to you to grow, close enough to internalise you, something other than my mere dependence on you is needed to make it happen. We cannot do it by willpower. It happens – and this is my point – by way of a variety of psychological processes, such as the build-up of trust, the vicissitudes of ambivalence, and mutual recognition; and these are, to a degree, held together and organised by ordinary human sexuality. The psychological function of fantasies of incestuous sexuality is to inspire and facilitate that multilayered closeness we call love. This means that incestuous sexuality and the social bond are also interrelated just as pleasure and power are interrelated. Experientially, as parents know, sexual desire between parent and child means that neither of them can ignore the other. Is not that what adult sexual experience also suggests? When one is aroused, it has to be that individual, that precise one – a permitted, humane fetishism. Desire in a relationship guarantees the importance of that relationship, guarantees the regenerative importance of that relationship to both participants. It can and does go horribly wrong. It can and does get enacted and embodied. It can and does possess generation after generation. But incestuous sexual desire also has the function, the goal, the telos of providing the fuel for the means by which we get close to other people and hence grow. Then we can get into the early object relations algebra of projection, introjection, identification, internalisation.

Physical incest results from incest fantasies that have, for whatever reasons, become enacted. We know that a child's fantasies cannot be adequately understood as the child wishing for intercourse with the parent. A response on that level is totally inappropriate. Adults who take their own incestuous fantasies or what are deemed or theorised to be those of children as such are mistaken and destructive.

But I think that alongside a stress on the many adults who deliver excesses of sexual communication and attention to children, we should also try to explore the less apparent forms of abuse and deprivation in what could be called sexual deficit. Quite understandable and necessary concentration on sexual excess has made it very hard to speak of sexual deficit without being misunderstood as advocating incest or being indifferent to it.

At the height of the 'Cleveland crisis' (a child sexual abuse episode in Great Britain in 1987, one of the first to receive attention), my then next-door neighbour, a man I do not like, confessed to me that he was frightened to cuddle his two-year-old daughter in public. Media discussion of child sexual abuse was rein-forcing difficulties that many fathers (in particular) have over physical aspects of their relationship with their children (not just with daughters, though we see it more clearly with daughters). Years later, when some daughters enter analysis, past inhibitions about bodily contact and apparent failure to establish a warm, shared physical rapport with the father turn out to have been very wounding. In a sense, these wounds are at the opposite extreme from the wounds caused by actual incest, but they generate their own brand of profound psychic pain. The understandable, appropriate, and vital stress on the avoidance and detection of actual incest can mask this other problem.

I hope it is clear that I see similarities between this problem of sexual deficit in the family and the problem of safe analysis. Let us now consider the problem in terms of a retheorisation of the father.

Retheorising the father

Before developing my argument in detail, I want to mention a few important themes that I have omitted from this essay for reasons of space.

The father is not the only parent implicated in sexual deficit, any more than he is the only parent implicated in sexual excess; maternal sexuality has its own vicis-situdes. Nor is some temporary and much-needed concentration on the psychology of the father relation an ignoring or depreciation of the mother. Nor are daughters the only victims. Mine is not a heterosexist text. Nor do single-parent families suf-fer in any inevitable and predictable way in regard to sexual deficit. On the basis of 20 years' research work with single parents, I say that the main deficit single-parent families suffer from is a deficit of money. The more work you do on the father, the more qualified your enthusiasm for him becomes – hence my coining of the term 'the father of whatever sex' (Samuels 1993a, pp. 125–135). Nor is there any reason why two homosexual women or two homosexual men bringing up children together would be more likely inevitably to get it 'wrong' than so-called ordinary families. And this may be the moment to say in print once again that no analytical or psychotherapeutic training programme that bars persons of homosexual sexual orientation can ever be considered a good training, no matter how prestigious and productive the training appears to be. (See Samuels 1993b, for a fuller account.)

Finally, in this list of necessary omissions, let me say that I do not deny the existence of different clinical dynamics according to the sexual combina-tion and sexual orientation combination of the analysing couple. A great many papers claim to know the specific features of each combination (see Schave-rien 1995). But let us be careful before indulging too freely in specificity here lest it lead to an omniscient efflorescence of new essentialisms: For example, the sexual transference-countertransference of female analyst and female patient is such-and-such; the sexual transference-countertransference of female ana-lyst and male patient is such-and-such; homosexual sexual orientation on the part of one or both participants in analysis does such-and-such to the sexual transference-countertransference. These differences need for the moment to be spoken with more diffidence, and it may be better to say 'we don't really know'. One thing we do not really know much about yet – not even what the terms of reference might be – is sexual misconduct by female practitioners. Female practitioners may sleep with their patients and they certainly experience sexual fantasies about patients of both sexes in the countertransference. But there may also be a kind of misconduct that we have not yet learned to recognise as such. This would be a sort of maternal abuse, taking the form of overinvolvement with the patient and resulting in gratification of power urges in the analyst. Indeed, maybe male analysts could also be guilty of such maternal abuse. These thoughts raise all kinds of questions about the relations between gender and power – which are surely a key element in any discussion about sexual misconduct.

One thing that does seem clear about sexual misconduct on the part of female practitioners is that people are quite shocked and outraged to hear of it. This point emerges clearly in Eileen McNamara's (1994) account of the celebrated case in which the suicide of her patient led to charges of sexual misconduct being brought against a psychoanalyst.

In 1995, I conducted a small-scale informal research project in which, having elicited the sexual fantasies in relation to their clients of analysts of both sexes, the material is presented to a panel of experienced clinicians for review. The object of the exercise is to see whether or not there are specific styles of countertransferential sexual fantasy according to the practitioner's sex. A second panel examines the same material, but this time the material is doctored to remove indications as to the practitioner's sex. Both panels reach a broadly similar and unexpected conclusion, namely, that it is extremely difficult to put into words what, if anything, divides the male and female fantasies. The problem seems insuperable when the doctored version is under consideration. At the moment, the data are insufficient to permit more than anecdotal reportage, but it strikes me as an extremely interesting phenomenon.

Now back to the father. When Winnicott coined the phrase 'the good-enough mother, he had a number of aims in mind. Undoubtedly, he wanted to highlight the undesirability of either idealising or denigrating the mother. He wanted to make sure that his ideas about mother-baby relating did not become some sort of persecuting ideal for mothers. He also sought to introduce the notion that a kind of graduated failure of mothering, leading to the possibility of there being hating feelings between mother and baby, was a good thing. Mutual hate was a vital step on the road to achieving what Winnicott called 'unit status'. To be good enough, a mother had to be able to fail, to become a very bad mother indeed, and to hate her baby as much and as thoroughly as her baby fantasised she did.

The good-enough father has not been written about very much. Why not? Why do we prefer either to idealise or to denigrate the father? What would graduated failure of fathering look like? What can psychology say about the nature and quality of the relationships in which the good-enough father participates? He only exists in relationship, after all.

Retheorising the father is necessary for psychoanalysis in particular because it is becoming clearer that psychoanalysis has introjected an image of the father that is politically biased, reflecting a specific historical and social moment in Western culture. When Winnicott (1968) disputes the seriousness for a small baby of having a psychotic father (as opposed to a psychotic mother) or when he speaks of the father showing his gun to the children as a way of explaining what the outer world is like in 1944, it reeks of cultural and historical contingency. Yet psychoanalysis worldwide continues to offer what I call the 'insertion metaphor' as the penetrative unwavering root image of the father's psychological role in early life. The preoedipal father is supposed to insert himself, like a giant depriving and separating penis, between mother and baby who would otherwise stay locked in a psychosis inducing and phase-inappropriate symbiosis. In fact, the distinction between oedipal and preoedipal begins to look increasingly artificial and defensive. In Margaret Mahler's amazing language, the father awakens a two-year-old from sleep and turns that child towards the (or is it his?) world (Mahler 1971). This comforting but reactionary story about fathers – *father holding mother who holds baby* – with its third-term denial of the detail of a more direct relationship with children, is one that urgently requires critique, not least because of the appalling insult to mothers and to babies contained in the notion that they have no commitment and no capacities in themselves to becoming separate. Do mothers and babies really want to be psychotic? Moreover, what's so wonderful about the rapture of psychoanalytic separateness, rapture over the strong ego, a question well posed by feminist theorists (e.g. Jordan *et al.* 1991) on both sides of the Atlantic?

And what if Lacan's father turned out to be – well, Lacan's father, Lacan's dad, Lacan's old man, Lacan's pater, a French pre-First World War bourgeois father, and not a metaphor at all. It would be ironic if the 'third-termism' of Lacanian psychoanalysis itself turned out to be a culturally and historically contingent production, a highly conventional developmental psychology. Unlike some, I do not look to France for a solution of what is often presented as an Anglo-American problem over the father (see Samuels 1993a, pp. 138–142 for a fuller discussion).

Retheorising the father will have profound sociopolitical implications in the long term. But there are also some shorter term gains to be made. We can achieve a more subtle understanding of paternal erotics and even of male sexuality, understanding these as historical constructs, hence relative and mutable. Such understandings would dispute Klein's locus for the father's penis, moving it from inside the mother's body and reattaching it to the father's body.

What of Jung? readers will ask. Because of the absence of a coherent developmental psychology in Jung's own writings, the post-Jungians have had to be in close attendance on psychoanalysis here (see Samuels 1985, pp. 133–172). And, as we have seen, today's psychoanalysis is mother centred. Crucially, Jung overlooks the way in which father–child relationships are built up as he seeks to identify the essential and invariant features of such relationships. But if we do explore the father–child relation, we see that, in most cultures, it is made up out of the interaction of two other relationships – between mother and child, and then between woman and man. A man does not become a father in any formal sense unless something happens between these two other relationships. What that 'something' is and what the father does varies from culture to culture and across time. Nevertheless, to be a father in a full emotional sense, a man needs to have a connection to the woman and for her to have a connection to the child. It is still a direct, primary relationship, still passionate and intense – but it is a constructed, discovered relationship. Actually that makes the father–child relationship no different from the mother-child relationship, which, as many writers have shown, is not as natural, biological, innate, and given as we used to think. Motherhood has a history; it changes over time (see Badinger 1981).

Realising that the father himself is a culturally constructed creature of relationship leads to all kinds of rather exciting possibilities. If the father relation is always a product of two other relationships, and hence of culture, then it cannot be approached via absolute definition; it is a situational and relative matter. If we can face this, then we will sense that a new judgement is required on our part towards what seem like hopelessly idealistic and utopian attempts to change the norms of father's role. The father's role can change because written into father's role is the refusal of an absolute definition of it. This refusal is made possible, not to put too fine a point on it, because of male power and because of the historical and cultural mutability of the father relation that I have just described. Hence, in one sense of the word, the only 'archetypal' element in connection with the father is that there is no archetypal element in connection with the father. In full paradoxical form: The archetypal thing about the father is that he is culturally constructed.

Let me ground this outrage at once with something from empirical research. It has been generally agreed that fathers and mothers play very differently with their children and that these differences can be clearly seen on videos. Fathers are more physical, outgoing, and so forth. Mothers are quieter and encourage more reflective play. The picture seems logical and eternal. But if we observe videos of the play of fathers who, for whatever reason, are the sole or primary caretakers of the children, their play resembles that of mothers (see Leff 1991, pp. 372, 533). Fathers can change. Maybe men can change. Moreover, the lesson we learn from multicultural experience, that differing cultures do the family thing differently, not always along nuclear lines, reinforces this challenge to the conservative deployment of archetypal theory.

If fathers can change in principle, and if there is no father archetype of the kind that would hold us back here, then what can we do to help the process along? For bringing the good-enough father into existence would truly mean the dismantling of the patriarchy we all say we want. We can learn a good deal from cross-cultural studies of fathering patterns and practices that make it difficult to hold to 'archetypal' certitudes.

It is not enough to set up a nostalgia game in which the traditional family is portrayed as that which can salve all, but especially male, wounds. Anyway, what was this traditional family? It is becoming ever more apparent that the so-called traditional family, the one politicians and some leaders of the men's movement encourage and exhort us to get back to, with its clear demarcation of roles on the basis of gender, is not really the 'traditional' family at all (Seccombe 1993). The stable family unit in the Western countries between 1850 and 1950 was only one step in the ever-changing trajectory of the family in our culture. If we glance back to 1780, in the early days of industrialisation in Europe, we find a very different kind of 'traditional' family. For one thing, it was positively crawling with children, all of whom would be in work, whether at home or in a factory, from the earliest age. Married women, too, were working women in this traditional family. As the social historian Roy Porter points out, the move from the disorderly working family of the late eighteenth century to the sober, respectable unit that we see between 1850 and 1950 was mainly a response to economic change (Porter 1993). The family has always mutated in a duet with economic and industrial organisation. That is one reason why it is so important not to fall for the temptations of underclass theory (see e.g. Murray 1990) and pillory today's lone parents and their families. It is supine, ridiculous, and nasty for analysts to fall in with the dominant ideology that yearns with scarcely disguised racism for yesterday's model family in today's marketplace. (I wrote this last sentence well before the publication of Charles Murray's latest offering on race and intelligence – Herrnstein and Murray 1994.)

Researching the depth of psychological literature, it is still hard to find texts of paternal sexuality that depict its benevolent aspects as opposed to seizing on its undeniably malevolent aspects. To the contrary, in my vision of it, the father's body may turn out to resist censure and to contain a hidden sanctioning of the cultural diversity and political emancipation of others, particularly his children. It has become common to note the mobility, enfranchisement, and emancipation of men in contrast to the oppression and subordination of women. But very little has been said about the father's potential to carry a positive attitude towards the mobility, enfranchisement, and emancipation of others. Maybe some will feel that there isn't anything to say about it! It is certainly not something we can exhort or force fathers to do. Nevertheless, I suggest that images and experiences of paternal sexuality often carry a secret symbolism for social and political change. Regeneration and renewal stand alongside the far better-known symbolism of an oppressive, repressive, and static political order. This would be a far more radical argument than seeing the penis merely as a useful weapon for beating the mother back (a point Jessica Benjamin makes independently of my work in one of the very few psychoanalytic books to address any of these issues – Benjamin 1988).

But we cannot make use of a text or testimony that tells of the father's progressive reinforcement of political and social change until we acknowledge the potential existence of such a text, protect it from the vicissitudes of sexual deficit, try to avoid idealisation, and then raise it to a level of consciousness that allows for entry into cultural discourse. The fact is, we still do not really know what fathers do or could do. If we did, then we could get on with the business of finding out how much or how little of fathering has to do with maleness.

The father and social justice

To put my various suggestions in a necessarily abbreviated form, mutual sexual communication that is not acted out – what I have called 'erotic playback' – between father and daughter cannot be understood primarily as freeing the daughter from symbiosis with her mother (see Samuels 1989, pp. 77–91 and 1993a, pp. 125–175 for fuller versions of these ideas). Rather, what flows from erotic playback is the daughter's own recognition of her erotic viability; an inner as well as an outer recognition. This helps to shatter the equation in her mind that woman equals nothing but mother. That, in turn, opens up the possibility of a simultaneous exploration and filling-out of psychosocial pathways in addition to motherhood: a spiritual path, a work path, a path that integrates her aggressive side, a path of sexual expression, maybe a path of celibacy. Crucially, there also have to be paths that are not man-oriented, that involve movement away from the father – for example, a path of solidarity and community with other women. Here, the mother's conscious and unconscious attitudes to the psychosocial tensions within her own self come into the picture, but the present cultural reality is that there are limits to a mother's capacity to point to other ways of being a woman as alternatives to the singularity of motherhood.

Most fathers and most daughters know already that some kind of mutual renunciation of the hell of actual incest is going to have to happen. Provide we scan it with a politicised eye, such renunciation may be read as a negotiation by both daughter and father of what Butler (1990) calls the 'heterosexual matrix' itself. And both (not just the daughter) benefit from this partnership. Safe analysis, no; safe incest, yes (to use Emmanuel Ghent's epigram, personal communication, 1995).

My point is not that the father simply liberates the daughter or permits her to take up different psychosocial roles, including maternity if she desires it. No, the father-daughter relationship has something to do with the special contemporary problem of plurality of differing psychosocial roles – the ways in which all those paths I mentioned do or do not shake down for women into a workable inner and outer blend of oneness and manyness. Who can doubt that this will be one of the key sociopolitical issues of the next century? This psychological pluralism facilitates the daughter when she says to us 'Don't ask me to stay the same' and when she says to herself 'I'm me'. Nowadays, men are starting to speak in the same way.

For the son, erotic playback from the good-enough father helps to lead to the growth of what, I want to call 'homosociality'. (I am grateful to Sonu Shamdasani for pointing out this term to me; see also Sedgwick 1985.) It means a recognition that community-mindedness and non-hierarchical relating between males can exist alongside the pecking order and the rat race. Men can learn from other men and homosociality is illustrated by the ways in which the gay community responded to AIDS, particularly at the time when AIDS was thought to be a problem only for homosexuals. Here we have practical and inspiring models for different variants of masculinity: love between men, as between father and son, as a kind of political praxis. Notice the paradox: Many among the group of men regarded by Western culture as the least manly have become the pioneers, the frontiersmen, the leaders in forging a fraternal way through a huge and hostile territory. What is pointed up here, of course, is the enormous diversity within the term men' and what is emerging from gay life and endeavour today may be reframed as the political telos or goal or end product of erotic playback between the good-enough father and his son. In saying this, I have not forgotten that the category of homosexual is of relatively recent origin (Weeks 1985) and, as time passes, has less and less of a precise meaning. The category of homosexual should really be abandoned. And I certainly have not forgotten what we learned from Foucault (1979–1988) and others about homosexuality as the means by which our culture has sought to regulate everyone's sexual and social behaviour.

Specifically, dominant heterosexual culture has employed a fear and loathing of homosexuality to frighten men so that a man will be tied into the role of provider in the family, the one who must remain emotionally distant. The payoff for men has been access to economic and political power – though gay men, or groups of men living in poverty and homelessness, or physically challenged men, or African American men, or men in countries that have been invaded would certainly dispute that they possess effective political or economic power. We do have to take care when generalising about men (see Dollimore 1991). In my thinking about the good-enough father, I have come to see that a tremendous fear that the ordinary, devoted, good-enough father will somehow be effeminate (which means homosexual) is perhaps the most difficult obstacle to overcome.

Father-son homosociality is a striking illustration of the upside-downness of 'sexual dissidence' (Dollimore 1991). For daughters and for sons, the relationship they have with the body of their good-enough father has implications far beyond the individual and private spheres. There is also the part such relationships play in the formation of social organisations in the public sphere. Erotic playback – not sex itself – can inspire cooperative activity in the political world. Is not desire also a social phenomenon? There are special bonds shared by those who share the same bondage (again, the use of this imagery evolved independently of Benjamin's pathbreaking work). For sexual desire is primarily constructed. There is no unsocialised and ahistorical essential sexuality, no 'archetypal' sexuality that is innocent and individual prior to its acceptance of the role of serving society's economic, political, and reproductive needs. In my view, sexuality is itself manipulated by gender, class, ethnicity, and history. Heterosexual relationships are themselves rarely if ever relationships of mutuality and equality to the extent claimed (or promised). Many homosexual relationships, despite being marginalised and condemned, have this secret, dissident, queer power to destabilise and interrogate the so-called normal at the centre.

The good-enough father of whatever sex

When the father's body, and the penis, are the foci of attention, the question of literalism cannot be avoided. Is the penis an anatomic organ in this context? Or a metaphor, a signifier of difference, a phallus? Or a bit of both? Or, as I hinted earlier, something in another category altogether? I want to turn to the social realm for a possible elucidation of this seemingly psychoanalytic problem (a nice reversal of so much depth psychological critique of culture, my own included).

Scanning the huge and passionate debate about lone parenthood in most Western countries leads to the suggestion that there is both more and less to fathers than the moral panic of such debate suggests that there is. In many Western countries, as I pointed out earlier, we are witnessing a damaging and misleading idealisation of fathers and the roles men play in families. It would be folly to base policy on this idealisation. But the fact that there is an idealisation is giving today's political debate about lone parenthood a marked psychological character. The politics are psychological and the psychology is highly political.

At the same time, we are witnessing the emergence of many new ideas about fatherhood that depict and sometimes advocate father's active, direct emotional involvement with his children from the earliest age. The new models of fatherhood support an egalitarian, cooperative, non-hierarchical family, rather than just seeking a pointless restoration of father and his authority as the (flawed) source of rules and regulations – not to mention his role as the source of sexual and physical abuse of women and children. As I see it, there are two crucial psychocultural implications of these new approaches to fathering. The first has to do with the debate that rages over the consequences (or lack of them) of lone parenthood for child development, especially or even exclusively when the lone parent is a woman. We could call this for convenience the lone mother question. The second implication has to do with the equally tempestuous debate over what fathering is these days, even when it is done by men. We could call this the crisis in fatherhood question.

The insight I want to share is that these two apparently different questions – the lone mother question and the crisis in fatherhood question – lead us in a surprisingly similar direction. Addressing one question helps us in engaging with the other. Both questions stimulate responses based on the same search, which is to find out what fathers do, or can do, that is life-affirming and related, beyond being at best a sort of 'moral presence' in the family (to use a phrase from the London Times of November 19, 1993).

If we do this, then I think we can begin to create and assemble a sort of psychological information pool or resource both for women bringing up children either on their own or together with other women, and for men contemplating or engaged in fathering. Such women are truly fathers of whatever sex when the father is re-visioned as being able to be less like a patriarch. In saying this, we immediately undermine everything that our society assigns or wishes to assign to men. Anatomy would cease to determine parental destiny and the lone mother question would be thereby completely reframed.

There is a crucial sequence in which this project has to be carried out. Initially, we have to find out more about fathers, then move on to see if we can depict the father in a less hypermasculine way, and then finally address women. To women: Can you do these things that male fathers do? Do you want to do them? The invitation is for women to assert their capacities to be fathers of whatever sex, which would make them good-enough fathers, rather than setting them up to fail as phony ideal fathers. Men fail to be ideal fathers, too.

I am not anticipating that women would choose to perform all of our list of fatherly functions, nor would they necessarily perform these functions (including erotic playback) in precisely the same way that men might perform them. But would that matter? Some may say that might be a pretty good thing! Difference does not mean deficit. Gathering enough information about the father might enable women to decide how much of it they could do themselves. This is why I give twists to the usual formulations and propose that we perceive women who parent alone as good-enough fathers. I am sure that many women who parent alone or parent together with other women are doing a lot of being a good-enough father of whatever sex without naming it as such. This group of women represents an incalculably valuable resource. We need educational campaigns fuelled by some of these thoughts about gender politics and organised in some way around the images of the good-enough father and the father of whatever sex. This could herald a whole new approach to parenting that taps into the fluidity in gender roles that has evolved since the Second World War and that is not going to be wished or legislated away by governments. You cannot pass acts of parliament that control what people feel and experience. That is what the collapsed totalitarian regimes in the East learned the hard way.

To those who have a negative gut reaction to the idea that women can be good-enough fathers and play the father's role, I say: Men, too, only play the father's role. Fathering does not come 'naturally' to men, along with penises and stubble – it has to be learned, and every new father finds there are rules in our society about how to do it; there is a masquerade of manliness, a male masquerade (Rivière 1929). Women who father as good-enough fathers of whatever sex may teach a thing or two to men who father – who knows? I remember my daughter setting up a game with me by saying 'You be the daddy, Daddy' – and then, at some point in our family play, announcing 'Now I'll be the daddy, Daddy'.

This is the fundamental lived-experience point arising from all the academic work on the cultural construction of gender and its roles (see e.g. Foucault 1979–1880; Weeks 1985). Men already play the role of fathers as much as women will come to play the role of fathers. It is surely significant how much we all use this word 'role'. So, for the sake of completeness, I want to reverse what I have been saying. Men who look after very small children are not playing at being mothers one jot or tittle more than women who mother play the role of mother. Motherhood, too, is not as 'natural' as some people continue delusively to think it is. Maternity and paternity have evolving histories.

What of the question of the crisis in fatherhood, what fatherhood is and means for men? Let's see what happens if we make use of the same words and images but this time with a focus on fatherhood and men. We certainly need to make the role of the male parent more interesting and meaningful for our younger men who have, quite rightly in my view, started to reject a dictatorial, Jurassic style of fathering – even if their female partners were prepared for them to be like that, which, thank God, they mostly are not. This refusal of male dominance by women, coupled with men's beginning search for inspiring ideas about manhood and fatherhood, are crucial social and psychological changes on which the debate about fathers should be focusing. There is scarcely a social critic (feminist or non-feminist) who has not explored the question of what would happen if fathers were to become more active parents of very small children.

Men are being scrutinised nowadays in ways that hitherto they have scrutinised everyone and everything else. 'Men' has become a category, one of many, and not some sort of privileged vantage point. This huge change in Western consciousness concerning men does not mean that men and women now have identical agendas; I have become suspicious of simplistic calls for partnership between the sexes. Men will not give up their power that easily, and there is a lot of making up to be done. But the notion of partnership between the sexes in pursuit of social justice remains as an ideal to aim at.

Lone-parent families need more resources, support, and approval from the community and not less. In addition, we need to work out strategies for making sure that lone parents and their children are not simply seen as victims, deserving of the ministrations of well-meaning folk like me. Writing as a man, a father, an analyst, and one who has researched into lone parenthood and fathering for decades, I have come to see that, strange as it may seem, it is not the actual maleness of the person from whom we obtain fathering that is the key issue. Saying this does not mean I deny difference between the sexes when it comes to parenting; I have already said that women and men might not do it in precisely the same way but that this might not matter very much. The main thing is that what happens in the relationship between the father of whatever sex and her or his children be good enough.

In this chapter, I have been trying to sketch out some of my ideas about what fathers do, or can do, that go beyond discipline, order, morality, and so forth. The essay is supposed to work on two levels, both derived from the focus on sexual misconduct: as a resource for women who parent alone, and as an agenda for contemporary men who want to father in a new way that is psychologically realistic.

If some readers cannot agree with me, if the idea of a father of whatever sex being good enough just goes against everything they believe in, I would ask merely that they note that it is possible to say it, it is possible to depict the father of whatever sex as a good-enough father, it is possible to challenge the assumption that only a male can do some of these things. I would urge such readers not to forget how many men do not or cannot do them before it is regarded as impossible for a women to do them.

One way in which men in general are changing is that they are becoming more aware of a deal that they have made with our society. In this deal, the male child, at around 4 or 5 years old, agrees to repudiate all that is soft, vulnerable, playful, maternal, 'feminine' by hardening himself against these traits. In return, he gets special access to all the desire-fulfilling goodies that Western capitalism seems able to provide. Increasingly, and especially in midlife, men (including analysts and therapists) are becoming aware that the deal was not altogether a good one from their point of view. Among many experiences that are denied them by the deal, the experience of being a hands-on, actively involved father of very small children is the one that is relevant for us.

I have always urged caution in relation to men changing! The parallel some men's movement leaders make with feminism and the women's movement is a fallacious one because of male possession of power and resources. (Also, to refer to the sobbing little boy inside every powerful man as 'feminine' is highly sexist.) We should certainly listen to what the empirical social scientists tell us about the unchanging picture in most households with men not looking after children, not doing their share of the chores, and being responsible for most of the sexual and physical abuse that is perpetrated.

But something is changing – what I have called the 'aspirational atmosphere' is changing. This is very hard to measure empirically, and the intuition of a depth psychologist sometimes does not pass muster when compared with 'real' social science. What we can say is that if men are changing, if we are about to see good-enough fathers in larger numbers, then the very existence of male power takes on a new significance. The existence of male power means that if changes are taking place in the world of men and fathers, there will be immense political and social effects in the not too distant future. This is almost the key background political issue of our times. It is certainly something mainstream politicians should pay attention to. I was in the United States in 1991 at the time of the Anita Hill-Clarence Thomas congressional hearings (on the question of his sexual harassment of her and its impact on his nomination to the Supreme Court), and the implications of those events changed the American political scene. I think the attack on lone-parent families and its aftermath is having a similar effect on politics in several Western countries. As Bill Clinton found in his 1992 election campaign, there are profound electoral spin-offs from paying heed to identity politics (see Butler 1990). The backlash of the 1994 midterm elections further illustrates the point. As I mentioned earlier, gender issues are especially important because gender is something that sits midway between the outer world and the inner world. Our subjective and public lives are riddled with gender issues. Indeed, one way of understanding the never-ending sex scandals in British and American politics is to see them as highlighting how shaky and shifting are our present images of masculinity and how problematic we are finding it to work out what are and are not acceptable modes of behaviour for men.

From sexual misconduct to social justice

This is a list of the sociopolitical themes to which our exploration of sexual misconduct has led us:

1. changing the pattern in which only women look after small babies;
2. fostering a culture in which parenthood and work may coexist;
3. working towards more cooperative and less hierarchical forms of social organisation;

4. getting a clearer understanding of male sexuality in general and paternal sexuality in particular so as to work better with the problem of child sexual abuse;
5. changing how we define and what we expect from good-enough families to include lone-parent families and other transgressive modes of family life.

A sixth theme affects analysts and their clients. When supervising, I have found these ideas to be helpful in expanding the clinical repertoire of analysts as fathers in the transference, especially female analysts.

To conclude: In spite of having written a good deal on many of these topics, I felt more anxious about submitting this for publication than I can recall feeling before. I think this is because raising the issues involved in the problem of sexual misconduct is rather confidence-sapping. I do not want to be heard as saying that psychic pain is caused (in a positivistic sense) exclusively by sexual deficits in inner world, family, or society. Nor do I want to be understood as saying that the mere overcoming of such deficit in analysis would be some kind of personal or social panacea, or would stop sexual misconduct by practitioners.

The difficult thing to do is to move from a consensus about ethical ideals to a consensus about ethical practices when sexual (or other) misconduct takes place. From a British perspective, it long ago became clear that the private psychotherapy organisations (including the psychoanalytical ones) are not adequate for the self-policing of the professional practitioners they have produced. Other European countries report the same difficulty, as meetings of the European Association for Psychotherapy have demonstrated. The cross-profession organisations that have emerged in many countries must take on a role in this area. It follows that any cross-profession organisation worth its salt should equip itself with powers to intervene or function as a court of appeal in relation to complaints. What this would mean for the United States is a national psychotherapy umbrella organisation covering all the therapies, not just psychoanalysis. Such a body might itself have to be organised along federal lines, with each professional orientation having some (but not unlimited) 'state's rights', and the federal part having equally limited and clearly defined powers.

We need to talk more about the nuts and bolts of worst case scenarios. For example, what kind of procedures will be needed if an analyst and client decide that they want to convert their relationship into a nonprofessional relationship – get married, say? What do we think about cooling-off periods? Or should there be an absolute ban as there is now in California? And how much (if any) of this should apply to supervisor and supervisee? Another crucial question concerns what to do about perpetrators. Can they ever be rehabilitated? Under what conditions? Can treatment of the perpetrator ever be true analytic psychotherapy given its manifest agenda of rehabilitation?

The way I see it, the development of new and better theory – what I have been trying to achieve in this essay – is a central and pressing requirement. New theory inspires and is inspired by new moral and ethical attitudes leading to changes in practice. We can, however, reframe this question of theory by saying that in the public expressions of concern over sexual misconduct by analysts and therapists (concern, that is, over sexuality in analysis), collective awareness has provided all of us in depth psychology – clinicians, patients, academics – with a marvellous stimulus. Responding to the stimulus is more than having to put our house in order. It is more than an exercise in discipline and regulation, absolutely vital though that is. It is more than an attempt to refresh our theories and ideas about sexuality. It is more than a matter of trying to heal, or at least to ease, the crisis of our incurably wounded profession – because some sexual misconduct is always going to occur. Above all, responding to the stimulus provided by the public in its role of analyst of the analysts might give us a slightly better basis from which to make a contribution on the levels of social and political justice.

References

Badinger, E., (1981). *The myth of motherhood*. London: Souvenir.
Benjamin, J., (1988). *The bonds of love*. London: Virago.
Butler, J., (1990). *Gender trouble*. London and New York: Routledge.
Dollimore, J., (1991). *Sexual dissidence*. Oxford: Oxford University Press.
Foucault, M., (1979–1988). *The history of sexuality*. London: Allen Lane.
Herrnstein, R. and Murray, C., (1994). *The bell curve*. New York: Free Press.
Jordan, J. *et al.*, (1991). *Women's growth in connection*. New York: Guilford.
Jung, C. G., (1912). Symbols of transformation. *CW5*.
Mahler, M., (1971). A study of the separation-individuation process: And its possible application to borderline phenomena in the psychoanalytic situation. *The Psychoanalytic Study of the Child*, 26, 403–427.
McNamara, E., (1994). *Breakdown*. New York: Simon & Schuster.
Murray, C., (1990). Underclass. *In*: D. Anderson and G. Dawson, eds. *Family portraits*. London: Social Affairs Unit, 2–29.
Porter, R., (1993). Review of weathering the storm by W. Seccombe. *London Sunday Times*, 8 August.
Raphael Leff, J., (1991). *Psychological processes of childbearing*. London: Chapman & Hall.
Rivière, J., (1929). Womanliness as a masquerade. *International Journal of Psychoanalysis*, 10, 303–313.
Rutter, M. P., (1989/1990). *Sex in the forbidden zone*. London: Mandala.
Samuels, A., (1985). *Jung and the post-Jungians*. London and Boston, MA: Routledge & Kegan Paul.
Samuels, A., (1989). *The plural psyche: Personality, morality and the father*. London and New York: Routledge.
Samuels, A., (1993a). *The political psyche*. London and New York: Routledge.
Samuels, A., (1993b). What is a good training? *British Journal of Psychotherapy*, 9, 317–323.
Schaverien, J., (1995). *Desire and the female therapist*. London and New York: Routledge.
Seccombe, W., (1993). *Weathering the Storm: The history of working class families*. London: Verso.
Sedgwick, E., (1985/1992). *Between men: English literature and male homosocial desire*. New York: Columbia University Press.
Stein, R., (1974). *Incest and human love*. New York: Penguin.
Weeks, J., (1985). *Sexuality and its discontents*. London: Routledge & Kegan Paul.
Winnicott, D. W., (1944). What about father? *In: Getting to know your baby*. London: Heinemann, 160–174.
Winnicott, D. W., (1968). The effect of psychotic parents on the emotional development of the child. *In: The family and individual development*. London: Tavistock, 125–142, 321.

Chapter 15

The 'activist client'

Social responsibility, the political self, and clinical practice in psychotherapy and psychoanalysis

Retrospective Introduction: I'd like to underscore what I say in the chapter: reference to an 'activist' client is both literal and metaphorical. The chapter caused ructions when it was originally published in 2017 though gradually people seemed to see what I was getting at. I think that Jungian and psychoanalytic circles were alarmed that I was placing faith or trust in theory from person-centred psychotherapy. The chapter brings together many core themes in my work. I deleted the passages referring to political art (much discussed in Chapter 4) to avoid more repetition. There are repetitions in this book, for which I apologise.

Talking Points: When first published in the relational journal Psychoanalytic Dialogues, a great deal of the issue was given over to discussion of these ideas. The client in the psychotherapies is too often seen as passive and dependent and in need of safety, holding and containment. Is this the only way to approach your clients. There are numerous clinical vignettes in the chapter. One explores the political development of a male patient and another attempts to illustrate how putting empathy judiciously to one side is sometimes necessary, adopting a problem-solving ethos.

Introduction

My main aim is to fly the idea of the 'activist client'. The paper is focused and somewhat exaggerated, to make a point. It may seem cheeky or wrong-headed to some, or as having only niche utility due to its militancy. Yet a strong single beam of light is shone across a stage, brightly illumining what is in its direct path, hence also revealing something on either glimmering side of the beam. So the paper is not only about clients who are already activists, though it is clearly relevant to them. Other clients with other therapists may also come into the picture – for all clients and all therapists are citizens with the rights, responsibilities, burdens, hopes, and despair of citizens. I hope what I am suggesting will resonate with a wider range of clients and therapists than might seem apparently to be the case, if not with every single client at all times. With this wider applicability in mind, I suggest that the 'activist client' is to be taken metaphorically as much as literally. In many ways, the linkage I am making is between two kinds of client activism – *the mobilisation*

DOI: 10.4324/9781003598985-21

of political activism in society and *the discovery of a kind of clinical activism in session.*

In general terms, the paper is intended to contribute to the emergence of a critical psychotherapy (see Chapter 9 in this book; Lowenthal 2015) in which psychotherapy and psychoanalysis reflect on and problematise their own practices. On an anodyne level, that is why I call citizens who want therapy clients rather than patients. And their paid professional would then be a 'therapist'. Throughout, I have been careful with my use of the terms therapy, psychotherapy, and psychoanalysis.

More specifically, the ideas in the paper stem from the long-standing project of bringing therapy thinking to bear on politics, and political thinking to bear on therapy (Samuels 1993, 2001, 2002, 2015b). I felt it was necessary to explore some key themes stemming from this project before introducing the activist client in a more direct manner. In the background lies our ever-deeper understanding that the self is a political self, that one form of psychic energy is political energy, that people have a line of political development and experience that can be elucidated and even theorised, that the unconscious is 'normative' to use Layton's term (e.g. 2004). Psychoanalysis and psychotherapy generally are professional acts that cause us to discover (or maybe to rediscover) that they are by nature political. In and out of session, we are often dealing with what I call 'the inner politician'. Isn't the task of the therapy to facilitate people in stopping thinking like the state wants them to think, just as we try to facilitate judicious freedom from persecutory, authoritarian, and judgemental parental introjects?

Social responsibility and social spirituality

A political or social focus does not remove clinical work from the psychological field. Social responsibility, freely and fully entered into, contributes to individual psychological vitality, not only in Daniel Stern's sense of 'vitality affects' (e.g. 2010) but also in terms of life itself, of the principle of life itself. This piece of therapy thinking could contribute to a revitalisation of our democracy: increased liveliness, energy, spirit, dynamism, passion, fire, vigour, élan, vivacity, exuberance, bounce, verve, vim, pep, brio, fizz. (These words are just a few of the synonyms one finds for 'vitality'.)

I think there is a variant of social vitality, which I call 'social spirituality', to consider. Some clients (and probably some therapists) have never or rarely experienced this, and I think the absence is as much of a psychic problem as its opposite: an manic overinvolvement with or fetishisation of politics. In social spirituality, people come together to take action in the social sphere, doing this in concert with other people. When this happens, something spiritual comes into being. Being actively engaged in a social, political, cultural, or ethical issue, together with other activists, initiates the spiritual. This is a very different perspective from one that would see social spirituality as being something done in the social domain by spiritual people. On the contrary, there is a kind of spiritual rain that can descend onto ordinary people who get involved with others in political and social issues (see Samuels 1989, 2001). For example, the Occupy movement or the protests against global capitalism and planetary despoliation come to mind – and, sadly but inevitably, do less salubrious movements of the right – racist, xenophobic, populist, and demagogic. Spirit has no politics as such; God has a right hand and a left hand after all!

What people are doing when they get involved in the anti-capitalist movements and the environmental and ecological movements is to participate in a general 'resacralisation of culture' (Samuels 1993). To play on the word 'politicised', many activists also become 'spiritualised' via their involvements and engagements. When one gets involved in idealistic politics, sometimes, not always, one gets spiritualised, and so something like the anti-capitalist movement is creating its own spirituality and, in turn, is being reflexively informed by the spirituality that it creates. Political action leads to spirituality of some kind and spirituality informs political action. Of course, eventually it may all fall to pieces; either the police wreck it or people (allegedly) 'grow up', but there is a basic resacralising tendency worth recognising. Now the clinical point concerns the people I mentioned who have never experienced this.

When meeting a prospective client, or interviewing a prospective candidate, shouldn't we ask them about their political histories – nonjudgementally, accepting that some will not have always been on a progressive, 'lefty' path? As I said, spirit is not always 'good', whether we like that or not, and experiences of social spirituality are available to fascists, rednecks, and homophobes. So, too, are the services of therapists, and that is as it should be.

Nevertheless, whatever the politics of the therapist or the politics of the client, shouldn't we explore why, if there has been little engagement with public issues on the part of an individual, this has been the case? Not 'Why have you been so manically political?' but 'Why haven't you been involved in politics at all?'. It's important to do this in the knowledge that there are no correct answers, for many reasons quiescence might exist, such as reacting to experience in a hyperpolitical family in which individual feeling was an apolitical luxury. But the point is that not to go into these areas is a truncation of what is possible in therapy.

Political material in the therapy session

Yet I believe we continue to struggle to find ethical ways of working *directly*, as opposed to making symbolic interpretations, with political, social, and cultural material as it arises in the clinical encounter. Many of us seek to fully meet such material, in a responsible and relational manner. However, we still experience the psychoanalytic dead hand, the penumbra of criticism that this *Weltanschauung* or perspective is non-analytical and that the analyst will simply foist his or her political views on the patient. When we add a 'political turn' to the relational turn, it may be asserted that we are acting *ultra vires*, beyond our authority or responsibility as analysts. It is a serious and important critique that can only partially be rebutted by saying – as I and others do – that yesterday's bad or impossible practice may be the cutting edge for today's clinicians. The purposes of this chapter include (a) the development of an adequate theoretical model to use as a basis for responsible handling of political material in the clinical session and (b) discussion of how a supportive context for such work might be created.

Let's recognise that psychoanalysis and the psychotherapies are not alone in making a discovery or rediscovery of a latent political mission. For example, as is discussed later, liberation theology sets out to engage with societies experienced as unjust and destructive despite criticisms from the Church establishment. So, too, have practitioners and theorists in the arts, despite criticisms from critics who regard the results as 'boring' and a betrayal, nothing to do with 'real' art (see Chapter 4).

Empirical research via international and multimodality questionnaires (Samuels 2006) shows that, in many countries, clients bring political, social, and cultural material to therapy much more than they did (and, I would add, they will bring even more when they know it is 'permitted' to do so, that the rules of the game allow it). Therapy becomes a place where, in dialogue, client and therapist can work out their political attitudes and engagements. This can be as psychologically transformative for each as a purely personal alchemy – and may be done even when one of them finds the political positions of the other to be horrid or reprehensible. It remains necessary to acknowledge professional fears of exerting too much influence and of 'foisting' one's political views on the client. But, apparently, the risk of foisting strikes some commentators as being greater when the context and material are political than when they are sexual, aggressive, spiritual, or developmental. I am not sure this is so. The risk is there, and we should respect the history of our clinical theory about boundaries, suggestion, and neutrality. But I am not sure there truly is a special problem when it comes to politics – or, if there is, whether that should give us cause to retreat immediately into neutrality and the eschewing of the political dimensions of life.

Emergence of an activist client

Here is a brief example of how a client got in touch with his inner politician. An Italian man, who came to therapy because, he said, of an intense depression, dreamt of *a beautiful lake with clear deep water*. He said this represented his soul and then immediately associated with *the high level of pollution on the Italian Adriatic coast*. The image of the lake, and the association to coastal pollution, suggested, in the form of one symbol, the client's unconscious capacity for depth and his present state, of which he was all too conscious – a state of being clogged up by 'algae', like the coastal waters of the Adriatic.

The client gradually became aware of the tension between the individual and the political presences of the imagery. What, the client and I asked together, is the role of pollution in the soul, or even in the world? What is the role of pollution in the achievement of psychological depth? Can the soul remain deep and clear while there is pollution in the world, in one's home waters? Did the lake, with intimations of mystery and isolation, clash with the popular, extroverted tourism of the Adriatic? Eventually, the client's concern moved to the social level: Who owned this lake? Who should have access to such a scarce resource? Who would protect the lake from pollution? These were his associations. From wholly personal issues, such as the way his problems interfered with the flowering of his potential, we moved to political issues, such as the pollution of natural beauty, not only by industry but also by the tourism. And we also moved back again from the political level to the personal level, including transference analysis. I do not mean to foreclose on other interpretations, but rather to add in a more 'political' one so that the client's unconscious political commitments can become clearer.

He subsequently made a choice to return to Italy and, in his words, to 'get more involved', perhaps in environmental politics. Therapy supported what was there in him, rather than encouraging his activism. But without therapy, would this particular individuation have taken place? I remain open-minded about this question – for spontaneous remission is not a notion to be dismissed lightly.

For Samuels, politics plays an almost ontological role (Mitchell 2000, p. 506)

Continuing to look at clinical phenomena, we come to this rather strange section heading. But the section illustrates, I believe, that the introduction of political language and dynamics into the session requires both an adequate supportive theoretical model and also a context in which there is support for the act itself. In this section, the accent is on the context; later, in a section on a Brechtian take on therapy, I work up the theoretical aspect.

Back in 2000, the journal *Psychoanalytic Dialogues* produced a 'Jungian issue' (Vol. 10, No. 3), for which I acted as the liaison person. Seven Jungian analysts set out their stalls as clinicians and then commented on an extract from Stephen Mitchell's (1997) book *Influence and Autonomy in Psychoanalysis* (pp. 155–164). This extract concerned a piece of work with his patient, given the disguised name of 'Andrew'. (*En passant*, I would add that this was a marvellous project and is still the single best way to discover the range of what contemporary Jungian analysts from across the world actually do.)

The interaction and dialogue between Mitchell and me, characterised by a high degree of agreement, may bring out many of the topics and issues covered in the present paper more convincingly than an assertive solo piece of my own could. I'd like to add as a personal note that I was working on this paper and had a dream of a political scenario in which Stephen Mitchell played a part and in a political context. This gave me the idea to present the fragment of dialogue as part of my paper.

In the extract, Mitchell described his work with Andrew, who had made a switch from being a music composer to being a businessman. He brought to analysis his profound sense of meaningless and of having no personal value. Andrew's father was 'economically marginal'. Work with Andrew led Mitchell to remember and reflect on certain experiences of his own and to evince concern that he was getting too muddled up with this patient and/or using too much suggestion.

In the book extract we were given, Mitchell was clarifying his views as opposed to those of other leading contemporary psychoanalysts. Believing the context of intellectual work to be significant and polemic to be at the heart of advances in any field, I wondered if Mitchell was perhaps a bit too worried about getting professionally smeared for showing that relational analysts get too mixed up with their patients, work only in the positive areas, and disclose their autobiography, including their political histories – blah, blah, blah. (In fact, if I had a criticism at all, it was that Mitchell was too cautious in his evaluation of the marked Trickster elements in the clinical narrative.)

Whatever, the relevance of this illuminating dialogue to the current chapter are illustrated in this comment I made on some dream imagery that Mitchell (1997) reported: *a prestidigitator (sleight-of-hand artist) was doing tricks with coins and there is a ring made of gold:*

> The clinical material is full of economic and related imagery. The prestidigitator uses coins, the ring is of gold. Mitchell tells us that the father was economically marginal. Andrew's job in a corporation is reported as lacking meaning and value. Although the principal association on the part of the analyst was not economic, it was markedly political, and in any society the economic and political reams are connected – not only in terms of results and bottom lines but also in terms of meaning and values. Hence, the economic is psychological.
>
> (p. 421)

I think that one way into Andrew's pain would have been through a psycho-economic exploration of what his job actually was and what it meant to him. Early on, I found myself wondering why the move had to be so huge, from composer to executive. It is an example of what Heraclitus called *enantiodromia*, the swing of one extreme into its opposite: the artist, all pure and high-minded, into the venal (though comfortable off) businessman.

I would have engaged Andrew in what I now openly call a discussion of some of these economic and political themes. Maybe (in my fantasy) it would lead him to find a job somewhere between the two extremes.

I think I would also have explored as much as possible what the relations were between his father's economic situation and his own. To what extent is he still terrified of poverty? To what extent engaged in oedipal rivalry via his economic success? If there is a rivalrous element here, then could it not be the case that, at an unconscious level, Andrew actually strives to be less successful than his father? Obviously, one cannot say what the outcome of any particular line of exploration would be but this is what occurred to me.

I got the impression that what Andrew lacked was connection to any sense that involved *communitas*, a sense of emotional investment in his own society. I see this missing connection as imaged in the dream by the filaments that link the moving coins. Andrew has yet to realise that the work he has chosen could be work that has contributed to there being no filaments in existence between him and other parts of the world (Samuels 2000, pp. 421–422).

Mitchell (2000) replied:

Samuels raises fascinating questions about my concerns about influence. He wonders about the intrusions of conventional morality, my fears of being smeared by my colleagues, and possible regrets about my own life choices and defenses against unconscious analytic sadism. Politics and economics play a fundamental, almost ontological role in Samuels's sense of life, so he would want to use the dream to open up questions in these areas.

(p. 506)

Class and the inner world

Mitchell's account of the work with Andrew, and the psycho-economic aspects of his relationship with his father, serves as an introduction to a brief consideration of class issues in therapy work. As Corpt (2013) wrote, in an incisive and moving account of social class in the context of psychoanalysis:

When client, analyst, and the very profession of psychoanalysis disavow the psychological complexities of social class, important conflicts and injuries are inevitably over-looked and therefore are unavailable for analytic understanding.

(p. 65)

The topic of economic inequality is discussed everywhere these days (e.g. Piketty 2014), though little is done to challenge the fundamental sadism of the financial arrangements in Western polities. Thinking about inequality for a moment, it is clear that a relationship exists between *class* and the individual's *inner world*. Many people have achieved a higher socio-economic status than their parents. Yet, in their inner worlds, encountered in therapy, in dreams perhaps, the social class they grew up in is still the social class they are in in terms of psychic reality and narrative truth.

A client who worked as a banker dreamed frequently of the coal mine where his father had worked. The (male) solidarity of the miners – for example, when there was a disaster underground – struck him as different from the atmosphere and ethos of his large Wall Street investment bank. We did of course play a little with what we were 'mining' in the analysis, but the main thrust of our dialogue about these dreams was in terms of a thorough, many-layered, compassionate, and healing *comparison* of his entire situation with that of his father's. Not competition with the father. There's more to intergenerational male relating than Oedipus – and the Oedipus complex is not a politically neutral idea.

The typical move – or at least it used to be typical, it may not be nowadays – is from working class to middle class. To the extent that a passion for social and economic justice exists (for good reasons) in the working class, you can see how destabilising and ego-dystonic their ruthless rise to the top is for some people. I have had several clients like that. This specific point about class and

the inner world applies with particular force when the client is a member of a minority ethnic community. What can't be avoided is that we may be up against a psychodynamic barrier to social mobility and economic equality. The good news is that I think, clinically and culturally, we can do something about it. (I develop these points at length in Samuels 2014a.)

Political roots of depression

This section probes the political phenomenology of clinical work in the therapy field. It was observation and conversation with colleagues that led me to suggest that some, maybe many, clients suffer from a kind of repression of their political selves. They are cut off from the vitality of social spirituality. They are struggling to get in touch with their inner politician. Other clients have intense political engagements – but doubt that, as an individual, they can make a difference. Hence, their idealism goes underground and may be sometimes understood, incorrectly in my view, as political apathy or even political despair. But is it? What looks like apathy is actually a pervasive sense of powerlessness, often coupled with intensely guilty self-criticism. Sometimes apathy follows on from what is believed by the subject to be failed activism. It is a special kind of depression, with political roots.

What does it mean when people use a psychological word – depression – about a political or social issue? About a general election? If you say you feel depressed or guilty about the election, the environment, climate change, or species depletion – what are you saying? Many psychotherapists understand depression as resulting from feeling angry and destructive towards someone you basically love and need. The classic example is at a time of bereavement. The mourner may feel at some level that their bad feelings towards the dead person somehow caused the death. Or they may be angry at having been left. In either case, there is a feeling of being responsible that leads to guilt, self-reproach (often of delusional proportions), and very low spirits with a lack of emotional, cognitive, and physical energy. The capacity to act is vitiated. That feeling of guilty responsibility interests psychotherapists who want to bring 'therapy thinking' to bear on political problems. In terms of climate change, for example, we can see similar dynamics (though it's important to be careful in mapping off from individual psychology to collective psychology). We love the earth yet we can see how destructive we can be towards it. Our guilt then paralyses us and we enter a political depression that we struggle to overcome. In order to avoid the depression, some may even deny that climate change is taking place. Hence it is reasonable to suggest that depression has social and political roots beyond revulsion at mainstream politics – and does not only have to do with parents, partners, relationships, and all the usual therapy lines. Paradoxically, political depression also has to do with commitment and activism themselves.

The question of anger comes up in therapy in relation to almost any political theme: economics, multiculturalism, war, leadership. It doesn't matter which side of a debate you are on to feel angry. In addition, you do not have to be directly affected to feel angry, though excluded and disadvantaged people are, of course, more likely to feel it. The point is that when you have political anger in a form that cannot be managed or resolved, you will find some kind of depression and guilt, and as mentioned, this works against a sense of political agency and possibility.

I recall this vividly from work with a client, called, for the purposes of this paper, Lorraine. She was a very active feminist, undertaking spectacular public events that found their way into the media. As time passed, she began to feel it was all a waste of time and futile. She became depressed, a burned-out activist by the age of 25. I am not going to narrate that therapeutic exploration rekindled her political ardour to its former intensity and efficacy, but it did enable her to see how it was her very passion and anger, not their shameful dribbling away, that led to her intensely painful depression. She was angry with herself, her 'sisters', her parents, men, the patriarchy, the corporations, and me. She had begun to feel destructive in the political sphere, and this was implicated in her depression. Gradually, Lorraine came closer to accepting that political perfection is unattainable. She discovered that if she asked of herself only that she be a good-enough citizen, she might be less mired in her sense of depressive despair. Then a small degree of political hope might reawaken, as it did in her case.

Focusing on the client

The preceding sections of the paper offer an essential backdrop and introduction to a consideration of the politics of being a client. What we are currently seeing in the literature, and hence we may assume is taking place in practice, is the emergence of a rather new conception of the client, a perspective that sees *the client as the motor of therapy*. This client is a heroic client, a client who knows what she needs, a client who can manage her own distress. Some clients engage less in a process of healing or cure and more in a process of ongoing personal and political enquiry. This multifaceted new client is potentially a healer of others, especially the therapist, and, in a sense, of the world.

Summarising a mass of research findings, Norcross (2011) forced us to consider whether it truly is the therapy relationship that does the business. Is the private and highly personal therapy relationship the main thing that makes therapy work? Not really. In common with other leading researchers, such as Lambert and Wampold, Norcross summarises that 'unexplained and extra-therapeutic factors' amount to 40% of efficacy, the client accounts for 30%, the therapy relationship 12%, the actual 'therapist' 8%, the 'school or tradition or modality' of the therapist 7%.

More recent thinking about the client has moved in this general direction of envisaging the client as 'active'. From the person-centred approach, we find Bohart and Tallman (1999) referring to the 'active client'. This is an important corrective to the psychoanalytic expectation that the role of the 'patient' is to provide unconscious material via free association. While often very important, it is not hard to see how this perspective may reduce the value given to the client's active involvement in the work.

Rogers (1951), in the era when the discourse was of 'client-centred' therapy, makes it clear that the client knows for herself what is needed, where she wants to go. Jung (1946) wrote of entropy in the client, an innate process of self-regulation. From relational psychoanalysis, we read that Hoffman (2006) regards the client as having responsibilities to the analyst and the analysis, more than just for the co-creation of the therapy relationship.

So the therapist is, in a way, adjunct to the therapy process. But they are also a contingent figure, product of a particular social circumstance. Frank (1961) suggested that what makes the therapist is not only training, techniques, and wounds but also having been socially sanctioned as a therapist, a sort of overarching placebo effect. The therapist is socially sanctioned, granted permission to be a therapist – by society, *and, I must add, by the client*. Hence, it behoves us to have in mind that all the analytic creativity and innovation that we rightly applaud is an epiphenomenon of the client's having sanctioned the therapist to be so safe, smart, and related in the first place. As Paul Atkinson (personal communication 2015) put it, 'The client's gift to the therapist – firstly appearing at their door and then constantly activating the work – is the most energetic factor in therapy'. This is, I think, even now a rather new version of a client: a person who does not want the therapist to be the one who knows, or even the one who is supposed to know.

This chapter began life as part of a project for a more critical psychotherapy and has the frank aim of valorising the client's contribution. But, in true critical fashion, one needs to remain aware that active clients have the potential to ruin as well as to fashion the work. Co-creation cuts both ways, destructive and positive, hard as that is to take in sometimes.

Be that as it may, let's see what happens if we revision the therapy relationship with all of these thoughts about the client in mind. It has gradually dawned on me that clients sometimes do not dare to deploy their tacit knowledge and emotional literacy. We therapists are fine with this because it leaves us free to do our work. But that could, and, from critical and political perspectives, maybe should change.

The activist client

These observations on the politics of the therapy relationship lead me to suggest that the new model client, the client as the motor of therapy, is increasingly a politically aware client at some level. But not all politically aware people are activists, nor are all clients. Yet the argument of the paper is that how deeply 'activist' a client maybe remains something to be curious about and explicate in therapeutic dialogue. One possible outcrop of therapy might be that, during the work, the client may develop her capacity for alterity, meaning, among other things, an empathic concern for the other. Yes, this does mean other people – but there is a more-than-personal version of alterity to consider. For example, for a client living in a multicultural world, meeting his or her inner psychological diversity in a new and positive spirit could lead to developing an analogously positive attitude to outer diversity in society, one that had not been there before. This, in turn, might lead to active support for those discovered by the client as hitherto subject to social exclusion. The move would be from self-acceptance of previously disowned or marginalised elements in the personality to political acceptance of similar elements in culture. In general, therapy work often leads to a sharpening or awakening of various latent political 'commitments' possibly entered into without full buy-in from the conscious ego.

To the idea that a client is an active client, we could now add that activist clients have the potential to be citizen-therapists for the wider world with its environmental problems, economic injustice, and ubiquitous violence. The therapy client, revisioned as a sociopolitical healer, may now be understood to be a socially responsible agent of *Tikkun Olam*, the drive to repair and restore the world.

Back in 1975, Searles published his paper 'The client as therapist of his analyst'. In summary, if part of 'mental health' is to want and be able to help and heal others, then isn't this something to work on in analysis? If so, said Searles, then isn't the analyst the obvious person for the patient to practise being a healer on? In a sense, I am extending Searles's vision. His arc was the move from healing the analyst to healing other people. I extend it to embrace healing beyond specific human others, to reach out to the social and political crises of our times. This, I am saying, is good for the soul. *Activism is good for the soul.* Mostly. I enter this caveat because it has to be admitted, as I have done on previous occasions (e.g. Samuels 2001, pp. 124–125), that you can't guarantee that the activism in question is one of which you approve. Sometimes what unfolds is of a prejudiced or extreme right-wing nature. Sometimes it may strike the therapist as extreme from a left-wing perspective. Whatever the therapist thinks about this, she must stay true to her task of facilitating the client in whatever direction the client has chosen to go.

But the therapist, too, may have to change direction, eschewing, possibly temporarily, what she has typically thought and done in the session. Such a change of direction in theorising practice is the focus of the next section.

Beyond empathy – a Brechtian angle on the therapy encounter

In Chapter 4 on political art, I discussed Bertolt Brecht's much-studied attempts *to avoid empathic identification by the audience with the characters in a drama.* This seems at first sight to be utterly foreign to the values and practices of all the therapies, including psychoanalysis. Empathy is our stock in trade, isn't it? Can you imagine relationality without empathy and a degree of identification with your client? Surely 'analytical distanciation' would just be a return to the bad old days of neutrality and abstinence? Let's suspend quick reactions and discuss these points for a while. I hope to persuade readers that Brecht's take on human and social dramas can be perceived as coming to the aid of the practitioner who seeks to work with the political dimensions of social experience in therapy – but may feel that there is little extant theory to act as a heuristic guide.

What does this mean for clinical work? Earlier I was discussing the problematic of working with openly expressed political material. Now, as I suggested earlier, this is still a minefield, though it is clear that many of us want to pick our way through such dangers, sensing there is gold dust to be found.

I am proposing that Brecht's theories of theatre practice are challenging and inspiring in this context. If therapist and client think together, argue together (whether it is with one another or as political allies in relation to some opponent or crisis), then it still stays in the affective realm, still contributes to vitality.

Connection and distanciation function as two poles of the therapy project

The suggestion I am making is that clients, and their relationally involved thera-pists, start to practise 'exvolvement', a neologism that implies standing outside the play of images, affects, and bodily processes that constitute the therapeutic (or any other) relationship. So the analysing couple might, in some circumstances (not all the time), reverse the poles of what they ordinarily do and distance themselves from emotion. It is pretty extreme, actually, this suggestion of a deprivileging and radical reframing of the personal level. Affect, emotion, even intimacy itself – all become things to interrogate.

As far as the client is concerned, for me these lessons from Brecht chime with what was referred to above, coming out of person-centred humanistic psychother-apy, as the active client. I've added, with a little help from Brecht, the notion of what the role of a more active or even activist therapist might be.

Here is a very brief clinical vignette of exvolvement in the clinic. Yasmine is, let's say, Egyptian and a TV reporter on politics. I've disguised her identity. She came to analysis hoping that something might be done about her virginity at the age of almost 40. She was feeling an intense sense of failure as a woman both in terms of her background in an Arab culture and in her lived experience in a Western country. She could not comprehend how this double blow had come to pass.

Yasmine chose a Jewish male therapist on purpose. I had decidedly mixed feel-ings about being informed that Jewish 'doctors' were legendarily smart and that the Indian general practitioner she had consulted was 'useless' on account of her South Asian origins. The idealisation of my Jewish background was, of course, both defensive and reactive. When the conversation turned to the Palestine–Israel situation, she was not slow to link Israel's 'sadism' (her word) with the Shoah experiences of Jewish people.

It became clear that Yasmine had never really explained her sexual symptoma-tology to a health professional. With the general practitioner, she had ducked the issue out of shame and embarrassment. It took a long time for her to be able to trust me with a description of her sexual experiences, and what she told me reminded me of what a girlfriend of mine had gone through

Over 50 years ago. I invited Yasmine to the side of the room where the com-puter was located and together we Googled 'hymenitis'. On subsequent medical examination by an 'English' gynaecologist, it turned out that there was a physical problem and the next step was to consider surgery.

All of this needs to be understood as going on against a backdrop of Yasmine's belief that, despite no actual memories, she had been sexually abused by someone in the family. There were dream images and narratives that she felt supported this hypothesis, and I considered that it was likely to have been the case. This mixture of material involved some psychological and cultural issues of great profundity and delicacy concerning femininity and the female ideal at work in Yasmine's consciousness and unconscious.

I do not think I could have worked with her through the emotional densities attached to all the apparently outer world themes if I had not practised a kind of exvolvement. The Brechtian place was one that provided a foundation for a series of 'arguments' about ethnicity, geopolitical conflict, fertility, and sexuality, with a two-way didactic flow. Maybe neither of us used placards, but we came very close to it. To be clear, I am not saying that a therapist without the Brechtian bee in his bonnet could never have achieved a rather positive outcome. But the vignette does show, I contend, that without some kind of theory upon which to base interventions into the 'real', there is a greater risk of it going wrong.

Drawing back the camera a bit, the question I am introducing based on this brief clinical summary concerns the potential deceptiveness of the personal dimension. We know this often hides and leads to a wider issue. Brecht's ideas are useful for providing a backup for the temporary avoidance of the personal and the highlighting of the political. He says to the clinician (and also to the supervisor, I think) 'Follow the story, follow the argument – don't only get caught up in the human drama'. Brecht might well say that empathy is itself often achieved by a suspiciously heroic effort and therapists and analysts need to see through that and question whether, in empathy, they have found their gold standard.

A note on some conservative aspects of relational psychoanalysis

I think there may be some institutional or even ideological obstacles to what I am putting forward, and I would like to anticipate and explore them. (A fuller account of the ideas contained in this section of the paper may be found in Samuels 2014b).

Have psychoanalysis and psychotherapy overdone the stress on providing a secure container within which a therapy relationship can thrive? Safety and security will always be needed at some time or other – but all the time? There may be a risk of a tilt in the direction of behavioural conformism and a corresponding moralism. This isn't going to help the activist client.

What are the disadvantages of the current stress on the frame, on boundaries, and on the container? Doesn't this lose the element of surprise, the risk inherent to psychotherapy, the exposure to danger that is involved in any radical or revolutionary process of self-understanding and/or growth? Are we witnessing the deformation of psychotherapy in the relational mode into nothing more than an attuned offer of nurture, safety, and a secure parental base. Is this not therapist as parent – or, more often, therapist as mother? Could it be that when we valorise attachment and intimacy we are not aware of the political and cultural structures we have created and instead put our own conceptual needs first?

Democracy

I want to push this critique of relational work, including my own, a little further to consider whether we have created an elitist or at least nondemocratic ethos in psychotherapy and psychoanalysis. I need to pull the camera back a little to look at how an orthodox doctrine with elitist tendencies and a top-down history was tweaked so as to develop its emancipatory and inclusive potential. I am saying the same can be done with psychoanalysis.

Liberation theologians, mainly in Latin America between 1950 and 1990, reoriented the Roman Catholic Christian project in their countries. As Seligman (personal communication 2016) put it, 'They added Christian universalized charity-love to Marxism in a political activist direction'. To achieve this, liberation theologians took issue with Marx. Marx considered that the lowest of the low, the lumpenproletariat, were incapable of making a revolution. Liberation theologians, such as Leonardo Boff, challenged this Marxian elitism. For Boff, it is the poorest, most downtrodden, most out-of-it, most derided and excluded who will make the revolution. Was Boff thinking of the Psalmist's image (118:22, New American Standard Bible) that 'the stone which the builders rejected has become the chief corner stone [of the Temple]'. Another critic of Marx's elitism, George Orwell (1949/2013), got there too: 'If there is hope, it lies in the proles', thinks Winston Smith in *1984* (p. 78). Orwell wasn't concerned with Marxist theory, so by proles he means those of whom Boff was writing – people not considered fit to make revolutionary changes.

These thoughts about liberation theology male me wonder what a more 'democratic' and inclusive therapy might look like. One that extends beyond the conventional clinical office with the usual range of clients, and one that is truly open to all, including those clients, many them male, who are 'hard to reach'.

I am not referring, on this occasion, to the power dynamics of the therapeutic relationship and process, or to its micro-politics. Nor to analysis and therapy as social institutions with a precise places in culture, one that varies from locale to locale, era to era. Nor do I have time and space in this chapter to join in the recuperation of how it was in the past – the Polyclinics, Marx–Freud projects, red therapy, and so on. All these are tremendously important topics that many colleagues have worked on. But my focus right now is a little different.

I sometimes imagine this:

I am the initiated analyst, ready (trained) to enter into an intense, mutual, empathic relationship and therapeutic alliance with you that, though it will benefit us both, is at your disposal, whether for relief of your symptoms, or for growth, or simply for exploration.

But the client all too often replies, in effect:

Fuck off, you narcissist, you are so self-centred and self-important. You have put yourself up on a pedestal and you reach down to me with an outstretched hand to haul me up to your level. Big deal. Are you really and truly so much above me to start with? How can we have an 'alliance' if we come from such different starting points?

It is something I have heard from the mouths of clients who are not white, not middle class, and not straight. But I have also heard it from the mainstream as well, and particularly from men. My imagined protest speech could be what a lot of male clients want to say and, even if I am only partially correct in this, we should be very cautious at dismissing those male traits that have been researched: the reluctance to admit that something is wrong (and this pertains to physical illness as well as psychological distress); the emphasis on quick solutions; the lack of emotional expressiveness and communicativeness. My experience, and that of others who work with men with whom I am in contact, is leading me to wonder if we have maybe underestimated men as a group when it comes to analysis and psychotherapy. Hence, holding working with men in mind, there may be a need to consider breathing life into the hope for a democratic therapy.

References

Bohart, A. and Tallman, K., (1999). Empathy and the active client: An integrative, cognitive-experiential approach. *In:* A. Bohart and L. Greenberg, eds. *Empathy reconsidered: New directions in psychotherapy*. Washington, DC: American Psychological Association, 393–415.

Corpt, E., (2013). Peasant in the analyst's chair: Reflections, personal and otherwise, on class and the forming of an analytic identity. *International Journal of Psychoanalytic Self Psychology*, 8 (1), 52–69.

Frank, J., (1961). *Persuasion and healing*. New York: Basic Books.

Hoffman, I., (2006). The myths of free association and the potentials of the analytical relationship. *International Journal of Psychoanalysis*, 87, 43–61.

Jung, C. G., (1946). The psychology of the transference. *CW16*.

Layton, L., (2004). A fork in the royal road: On defining the unconscious and its stakes for social theory. *Psychoanalysis, Class and Society*, 9 (1), 33–51.

Lowenthal, D., ed., (2015). *Critical psychotherapy, psychoanalysis and counselling: Implications for practice*. London: Palgrave Macmillan.

Mitchell, S., (1997). *Influence and autonomy in psychoanalysis*. Hillsdale, NJ: The Analytic Press.

Mitchell, S., (2000). Response to commentaries. *Psychoanalytic Dialogues*, 10, 505–507.

Norcross, J., (2011). *Psychotherapy relationships that work*. Oxford: Oxford University Press.

Orwell, G., (1949/2013). *1984*. Harmondsworth: Penguin.

Piketty, T., (2014). *Capital in the twenty-first century*. Cambridge, MA: Belknap Press.

Rogers, C., (1951). *Client-centered therapy*. Cambridge, MA: Riverside.

Samuels, A., (1989). *The plural psyche: Personality, morality and the father*. London: Routledge.

Samuels, A., (1993). *The political psyche*. London: Routledge.

Samuels, A., (2000). Post-Jungian dialogues. *Psychoanalytic Dialogues*, 10, 403–426.

Samuels, A., (2001). *Politics on the couch: Citizenship and the internal life*. London: Karnac.

Samuels, A., (2002). The hidden politics of healing: Foreign dimensions of domestic practice. *American Imago: Studies in Psychoanalysis and Culture*, 59, 459–482.

Samuels, A., (2006). Working directly with political, social and cultural material in the therapy session. *In*: L. Layton, N. C. Hollander and S. Gutwill, eds. *Psychoanalysis, class and politics: Encounters in the clinical setting*. London: Routledge, 11–28.

Samuels, A., (2014a). Economics, psychotherapy, politics. *International Review of Sociology*, 24 (1), 77–90.

Samuels, A., (2014b). Shadows of the therapy relationship. *In*: D. Lowenthal and A. Samuels, eds. *Relational psychotherapy, psychoanalysis and counselling*. London: Routledge, 184–192.

Samuels, A., (2015b). *A new therapy for politics?* London: Karnac.

Searles, H., (1975). The patient as therapist to his analyst. *In*: P. Giovacchini, ed. *Tactics and techniques in psychoanalytic therapy*. Vol. II. New York: Aronson, 95–151.

Stern, D., (2010). *Forms of vitality*. Oxford: Oxford University Press.

Willett, J., (1959/1964). *The theatre of Bertolt Brecht*. London: Shenval Press.

Chapter 16

The transcendent function and politics

No!

Retrospective Introduction: In the Critical Dictionary of Jungian Analysis (Samuels et al. 1986, p. 150), we defined the transcendent function as 'the function which mediates opposites . . . the transcendent function enables thesis and antithesis to confront each other on equal terms'.

I have put this chapter in the section called 'clinic', though it could as easily gone under 'politics' or 'Jungian'. The reason is that the chapter shows how difficult it is to juggle the practice of therapy and its associated ideas with the practice of politics and its associated ideas.

I was at a Jungian meeting in California in 2007 during the Presidential election campaign that Obama won. Someone said that he exemplified the transcendent function because he had a white mother and a Black father. The vast majority of those present agreed. Over the years, I had noticed that Jungians who commented on politics did so from the vantage point of the transcendent function, meaning a great desire to avoid polarisation and 'one-sided' thinking about politics. I reacted badly to this. However, it is not just the Jungians who misuse depth psychological theory. Kleinians look at this through the prism of the depressive position. All of us want to bend the real world to a shape that will fit our own theories. And that brings in a problem I have constantly written about: If you want to be depth psychological about politics, you will find that it is really extremely hard to be wrong!

Talking Points: This chapter is a polemic, for sure. Succinctly, if you use Jung's idea of the transcendent function in relation to political conflict, then you stand outside and above the conflict, taking the role of mediator or omniscient observer. You are 'mediating the opposites'. But are the political opposites just like psychological opposites within an individual? Isn't there an inbuilt playing field that is not a level one? This use of the transcendent function won't do, if therapists really want to make a difference at the political level. The chapter contains a list of the ideas and concepts the author has himself found useful when engaging in therapy thinking with politics. He is also careful to acknowledge that he can make the errors of which he accuses others.

DOI: 10.4324/9781003598985-22

Introduction

No school of psychotherapy is making a greater contribution to the alleviation of the suffering of the world than Jungian analysis and analytical psychology. How wonderful to be able to say such a thing, with hand on heart! Jungian analysts, supposedly the most unworldly, introverted, even mystically inclined group of therapists on the planet, are getting passionately involved in a huge range of cultural, social, and political problems. They have become part of the attempt to recover the political from the swamps into which it has sunk in many countries. This turnaround probably derives its energy from a sense that the change of direction was urgently needed, perhaps as reparation for past misjudgements, mainly in the 1930s. Anyway, the job is well started and is carried out these days by so many of us that I don't think I can produce a list of names. Many have sensed the danger of losing the revolutionary idealism of Jung's pioneering work if we stand still and rest on our laurels. Many of us know that our common interests will collapse if we only pursue our common interests, if we only invest in what advantages us.

I believe we are now in the middle of developing Jung's radical intuition, floated in the 1930s, of the need to create a culturally sensitive psychology. A culturally sensitive psychology does not level out all differences in the psyche that stem from politics, ethnicity, religion, nation, social class, gender, and sexual orientation. Jung was against the universal imposition of a single system of psychology. Inevitably, so-called universal psychologies (like Freud's) are in fact context-bound, limited, personal confessions. So Jung was perhaps the first to anticipate the ethical and political disaster of a one-size-fits-all colonial psychology. Hence he is one of the founding fathers of transcultural and intercultural psychotherapy. He was also one of the first to understand that we cannot insulate clinical practice from contemporary political history, saying that the analyst 'feels the violence of its impact even in the quiet of his consulting room' (1946, pp. 177–178). And he goes on in the same passage (which is from the Preface to *Essays on Contemporary Events*) to make a suggestive and evocative reference to the analyst's having 'duties as a citizen'.

Politics in many countries is broken and in a mess; we urgently need new ideas and approaches. Jungian analysts, working alongside other psychotherapists, economists, social scientists, religious people, environmentalists, and others, can contribute to a general transformation of politics and, step by stumbling step over many years, to an alleviation of the suffering of the world.

The actions of today's mainstream politicians leave many people in agony, with a sense of deep despair and disgust. The politicians themselves seem to lack integrity, imagination, and new ideas. Across the globe, and in response to the challenge, a search is on to remodel politics. Jungian analysts can contribute to this search by opening up a two-way street between inner realities and the political world. So we need to balance attempts to understand the secret politics of the inner world of emotional, personal, and family experiences with the secret psychology of pressing outer world matters such as leadership, the economy, environmentalism, nationalism, and war.

Here are some things I think most of us interested in this work are agreed on. We sense possibilities for deeper understandings of social and political processes, and possible healing of difficult conflicts, on this occasion via the usage of Jung's seminal idea of the transcendent function. We agree that there is a psychological dimension to politics but also that it is very important not to reduce everything in the social world to psychology. We agree that we would not want to foist ideas developed for use in individual analysis and personal growth onto the body politic without testing that out thoroughly. I think we all agree that just bringing depth psychology and politics into one frame does not in it self constellate the transcendent function and up to now, has generated as much heat as light.

Less certain is whether we agree on the necessary humility of interdisciplinary work when it comes to politics? By all means, let's have an analyst on every committee – but please God not a committee of analysts! If we are to organise more conferences on political themes, let's involve people from the political world, mainstream big names if we can get them, but also activists and political visionaries.

Do we also agree that our track record in the political arena is not that good? I am referring, of course, to Jung's anti-Semitism and attitudes in the 1930s and also to a certain kind of casual elitism or aristocratic approach with regard to issues of gender, class, and ethnicity. Moreover, the history of psychoanalysis in general with regard to homosexuality has been unedifying. And the professional politics of our field are a notorious mess. So we don't really start from a particularly credible base as political commentators.

An action ethos

To make it worse, I have become increasingly dismayed over two features that are typically seen when analysts engage with the political. I call these 'triangulation' and 'hyper-reflection'. In triangulation, the analyst takes themselves outside of the dispute and struggles to see the arguments on both sides from a detached, Olympian standpoint. The analyst is never *in* the dispute, only in the role of a kind of mediator or arbitrator. There is a sort of attempt to personify the transcendent function going on as opposites interact or combine, or maybe an identification with the position of the 'third element'. Triangulation is usually intended to show the mature wisdom of the analyst, resulting from deep inner work done on herself, when it comes to the hurly burly of the political street. In my view, what this really shows is supercilious detachment, bogus maturity, and a corralling of moral and judgemental power. Middlebrow psychology. It's like the old joke in the bars of Liverpool where I grew up: 'Let's you and him fight'.

So what I often see in conferences and on listservs is the Jungian analyst stepping up to the plate to mediate (invited or not), to clarify (but exclusively in psychological terms), and to solve (at least on paper) some of the most violent and divisive issues of our times. I *hate* this, in part because it is undermining the much more productive yet less magical efforts to work at the interface of politics and analysis. And I hate it because, sometimes, I slip into it myself and do the triangulation from on high as well. Yet my overall point remains: we should not unquestioningly condemn adversarialism – or unquestioningly praise a politician (e.g. Obama) who says they are against it.

What drives triangulation, is hyper-reflection. This is more of a phobia with regard to action. All action is taken to be mindless action. Sometimes, action is regarded as masculine and reflection as feminine (which insults both sexes, in my view). But there is a general valorisation of sitting still and thinking deeply, as if 'being' is deeper than actually *doing* something. It has even been claimed as the key political virtue of the psychotherapy perspective on politics. Not that thinking and reflecting deeply is a pathological thing to do – I have been known to indulge – but if it is always done at the expense of spontaneous and passionate action then it can certainly become very pathological.

A further problem with hyper-reflection is that the opinions it generates are often stated to be 'realistic'. Let me address this via an anecdote. When I was working in a psychiatric hospital, the medical director always used to issue the most pessimistic prognoses. Once, I asked him why. He explained that if the patient got well, this would be regarded as due to his treatment. But if the patent did not get well, he had displayed his clinical acumen by predicting it all along.

Let me reframe the problems I am depicting in a less polarised way. The really important and interesting thing is to try and hold that reflective space while also becoming engaged in action. There will be a tension between what one discovers via reflection and the pragmatic exigencies of action, bearing in mind that when we act there is always an opponent acting too, often against ourselves. When we reflect, we may reflect all we like upon our opponent's existence and opinions, but no one is actually opposed to our reflections (except maybe our noisy household or demanding job).

My proposal is that we think in terms of an 'action ethos'. This would be an explicit recognition of the following: (1) action and reflection are different and neither is better than the other; (2) action inspired or backed up by reflection is our goal; (3) we do not invariably condemn action that is not backed up by reflection; and (4) after the action is done, we insist on reflection about it.

The tools for the job

I have been attempting to bring the insights and practices of analysis (what I call 'therapy thinking') into the political world since the early 1980s. One thing that I have learned is that it's necessary to find and choose the right tool for the job. This should be driven by the nature of the problem under consideration as well as by one's preferences and knowledge. What it does not mean is using one huge concept, such as the paranoid-schizoid position or the cultural complex as if this could settle everything. Psychological analysis of political problematics needs to be a bit more detailed and fragmented. It needs to accept that such analysis might be wrong or fail. Saying there is a cultural complex at work or that the paranoid-schizoid position is in the field are statements that will never be wrong. I try not to go for the temptation of a massive single explanation, seeking instead to be a *bricoleur*, promiscuous in owing loyalty to no one specific concept or one particular school of psychology.

Here, again, are some illustrative examples from my work:

(1) In terms of leadership, I have found (Samuels 2001) Winnicott's notion of 'good enough' very useful – the good-enough leader for whom the binary divide success/failure is less rigid than is usually considered to be the case. Additionally, thinking derived from contemporary revisions of the father's role has been illuminating as regards leadership (see below).

(2) In terms of the economy, I turn to Freud's account of sadism as a backdrop to the state we are in and to relational psychoanalytic ideas as the (admittedly Utopic) way ahead (Samuels 2001).

(3) Nationhood and national character may be understood more deeply by Jung's writings in the 1930s on national psychology – the valuable (and overlooked) part of his work on cultural psychology during that period (see Samuels 1993).

(4) When we consider foreign policy, all that has been written on empathy and the obstacles to empathy is relevant, plus up to the moment ideas like the notion of the moral third in geopolitics.

(5) Finally, when it comes to vision in politics, what could be more apt than the Trickster, who models the denial of the realities of time, space, and place just as any revolutionary or social reformer has to defy the social and cultural realities of her or his present moment.

Returning to the action ethos, the trick is to behave as if analysts actually matter! Then we will. Analysts don't matter much in all the obvious ways. In fact, people usually find analytical takes on politics to be too extreme and exaggerated – or too theory-driven (psychobabble). James Hillman claimed that we've had 100 years of psychotherapy and that the world is getting worse so we should shutter up the consulting rooms. But, as I've shown, this claim was ahistorical and ill-informed (Samuels 1993). Totton (2000) has also shown that we've had much more than 100 years of all the schools of psychotherapy trying to change the world – but, sadly perhaps, the world has stayed pretty much the same. The world didn't turn up for its first session with us. As these writings detail, all the pioneers of psychoanalysis (and humanistic psychology as well) were deeply committed to improving the world. *Pace* Hillman, it is by no means a new thing.

Aggression and violence in political transformations

In his 1916 essay on the transcendent function, referring to the relations between the conscious and unconscious minds, Jung states (CW 10, para 186):

[I]t is exactly as if a dialogue were taking place between two human beings with equal rights, each of whom gives the other credit for a valid argument and considers it worthwhile to modify the conflicting standpoints by means of thorough comparison and discussion.

This is a beautiful sentiment, but, aside from the political referent – 'rights' – what might this have to do with politics as we know it? Is Jung so bewitched by Swiss national pride over its federal politics that he can seriously claim that citizens have equal rights in anything other than a strictly formal or legal sense? Rather, don't we know, and maybe to our cost, that when it comes to politics, the warring opposites very rarely engage in political activity possessed of equal rights – or equal power, resources, information, military might, and so on. That's what social class is all about, and economically deprived ethnic minorities, and military dictatorships. These all show the problem with utmost clarity. Perhaps Jung realised he had been too anodyne when he added that 'the present day [1916] shows with appalling clarity how little able people are to let the other man's argument count'.

For politics is, quintessentially, a process in which *unequals* dispute and contest control of power resources and information. They do this primarily by means of engaging in conflict and struggle, including armed struggle. Persuasion, polemic, and rhetoric serve this struggle. But the struggle does not take place on a level laying field and, as I am arguing in this short piece, most attempts to deploy the transcendent function in political analysis, as a means of reconciling or even establishing dialogue between opposites, forget that. (See Singer, 2006.)

There is also a spoken and unspoken hope that, via the healing properties of the transcendent function, whatever changes there may be in a society or in the world will be achieved non-violently. I think this involves the most profound dissociation and denial of the valuable role historically played by armed struggle – for example, in wars of national liberation. One might think of both the American War of the Independence and the Civil War in this regard. (Chapter 5 reviewed the rationality of political violence.)

From the perspective of the political psyche, I think we need to seriously re-value the presence of aggression in the pursuit of social justice. My long study of South African politics suggests that without the forceful military contributions of *Umkhonto we Sizwe* (*Spear of the Nation, the military wing of the African National Congress and led for a while by Nelson Mandela*), plus the South African Communist Party, and the mainly Black Cuban troops in Angola, the new South Africa would never have come into being: No Mandela, no Truth and Reconciliation Commission, no books on restorative justice. And, to complicate it even more, all of the liberation struggle was financed and supported by the Soviet Union.

Let me widen this, to take in less conventional and broader definitions of politics. From the point of view of gender politics, aggression and especially aggressive fantasy can be an individuation path, especially for women: an imaginal way to be thrusting, penetrative, and seminal, to break out of the coils of Eros where the woman is only responsive to the needs of others in a reproduction of mothering. But are women really less aggressive than men?

From the point of view of political morality, there is a critical *telos* (goal, point, aim) for political aggression. How can you develop concern for an Other if there is no reason to do so? Aggression just has to be in the picture or there is no reason why concern for the Other should flower at all.

From the point of view of metapsychology, aggression is part of ego-consciousness – the way we become conscious by breaking wholes into parts. The very etymology of 'analysis' is aggressive – Erich Neumann said that symbols of consciousness involved the teeth and biting.

Returning to a more conventional definition of politics, we can also see an immense cultural and ethical relativism with regard to political aggression. I will give a complicated and controversial example. As one who has been deeply immersed in the politics of the Middle East, I have been struck by the way the inter-relation of Jews and aggression seems very problematic for all parties. We can note this as originating in Western and Arab responses to the birth of modern Zionism and the establishment of the pre-Second World War settler-colonial communities in Palestine, and subsequently moving on to intense soul-searching about the Holocaust. For example, the debates on alleged Jewish 'passivity' on the one hand and the valorous resistance of the Warsaw Ghetto on the other. And then to the policies of the State of Israel. Whatever one's position on Israel/Palestine, it is possible to agree, I think, that thoughtful discussion is interfered with by ethnically based assumptions and generalisations about political aggression.

I would like now to delve more deeply into my ungrateful argument that the transcendent function is actually a rather poor explanatory tool when it comes to political conflict. Although reference is made to the 'ceaseless' interplay of opposites, and the idea is thereby rescued from being excessively static, there is no doubt in my mind that some sort of harmonious resolution lies behind the idea of the transcendent function. This idealism is part of its importance for individuals but may be the very problem the notion suffers from when it comes to politics.

Let's take as an example, a conflict between a racist and a non-racist, or between a racist group and a non-racist group. What does it mean in such a situation to look for and find the middle position? Are we looking for the establishment of a semi-racist group? A racist-enough group? Surely, in situations like these, it is a question of each side struggling for dominance over the other. For me, and for many reading this, we would hope that the non-racist group will prevail. But it may not. If the conflict is played out along the dialectical lines of the transcendent function, which comes first, racism or non-racism? Then, the other group becomes the antithesis. But, as I say, there just isn't any synthesis here, nor were the two groups equal to start with. No, it doesn't work.

Leadership and the transcendent function

Applying the transcendent function to leadership, I'd like to point out the dangers in seeing the leader and the led as 'opposites' because this would make the leader all conscious (I suppose) and the led all unconscious. The fascist potential in such a perspective is clear. Yet, in some of his remarks in the famous interview with Dr Weiszacker on Radio Berlin in 1938, that is what Jung is close to saying: 'As Hitler said recently, the leader [*Fuhrer*] must be able to be alone and have the courage to go his own way. But if he doesn't know himself, how is he to lead others?' (Jung

1938, pp. 773–779). Here, we find the idea of the leader as a sort of individuated being who can contain all the glorious diversity of the nation.

Sound familiar? I believe that some (not all) of the chorus of praise for President Obama (this was first published in 2010) has this kind of danger buried in it. Can a leader who wins a democratically contested election ever create an undivided country? Of course not. But what is so wrong with a divided country, with accepting pluralistic adversarialism as I mentioned earlier? (See Samuels 1989, for an account of the role of aggression in pluralistic discourse.) There are battles to be won and lost and there will be opponents to engage with. This is politics, and leadership involves knowing how far to go before the opposition goes ballistic. While there is assuredly a psychology of leadership, being a leader is not *a priori* about individuation or some version of the 'balance' or absence of one-sided development which may be necessary for an individual in analysis. Churchill, Mandela, and even Blair – they have all known how to fight. Of course, a leader can work against too great a degree of destructive polarisation in the country and can point out how something – say, racism – puts unmanageable stresses on the system as a whole. But there were 47% against Obama at his election so it is just pie-in-the-sky to see him as a unifying figure and even more remote an idea to see him as unifying opposites via his inter-racial background. If whites and blacks in America were or are 'opposites', they are not now nor have they ever been in an equal fight; that is my point. Rather, Obama may be for the moment the least polarising figure in American politics as a result of his victory – but even that is in doubt.

Leaders have to lead struggles – for economic justice, for an empathic foreign policy, and so on. Sadly, we may find that they also struggle for lower taxes, reduced services, military aggression abroad, and the preservation of elite privileges. Then 'we' have to fight back. This is politics. It is depressing, I know, but I feel I have to write this to stem the tide of unruly optimism that a wave of transcendent function is sweeping across post-Obama America and that this will reach to the corners of the globe.

We certainly wish for unifying leaders, individuated leaders. This desire is a very important thing. And what some people wish for is, in some Western countries, slowly starting to happen. The internet generation (and others) are less impressed by heroic, macho leaders, recognising the troubles they have visited on the planet. We are still more infatuated with such leaders than we realise, perhaps. But what we understand by 'father of the nation' is changing. Maybe what is understood by 'nation' doesn't change that much, but the father is a personage undergoing rapid and positive change in the West. The interplay between new fathers and new leaders is extremely interesting.

To change our perceptions of what being the father of the nation means, we need a positive account of the father that does not stupidly build him up to an unrealistic degree. An account that makes it much more difficult for our old-style political leaders to masquerade as the only kind of fathers that there could be. An account that does not dwell on the malevolent power of the father but on his affirming warmth. Not on his holding the mother who holds the children but on his holding of the children himself. The stay at home father. The sensitive and affirming father, the playful father, the wounded and unhappy father, not the punitive, stern self-contained father. *Not the commander-in-chief father.* We need a story of the father in which emotional security is as important as physical security. That would be a useful beginning to an equally new and analogous story about political leadership whether conducted by men or by women – for female leaders are sometimes also caught up in the hero thing.

Conclusion

To conclude: at this point in the evolution of my ideas, I am more impressed by the healing political power of some simple behavioural changes in the family, such as the rise of the more nurturing father, than I am by metapsychological abstractions such as the transcendent function, no matter how useful and deep, and tried and tested in the arenas of personal growth and individuation they may be.

References

Jung, C. G., (1916). *The transcendent function. Collected Works 8.*
Jung, C. G., (1938/1978). *C. G. Jung Speaking.* W. McGuire, ed. London: Thames and Hudson.
Jung, C. G., (1946). Preface to essays on contemporary events. *CW10.*
Samuels, A., Shorter, B. and Plaut A., (1986). *A critical dictionary of Jungian analysis.* London and New York: Routledge and Kegan Paul.
Samuels, A., (1989). *The plural psyche: Personality, morality and the father.* London and New York: Routledge.
Samuels, A., (1993). *The political psyche.* London and New York: Routledge.
Samuels, A., (2001). *Politics on the couch: Citizenship and the internal life.* London and New York: Karnac.
Singer, T., (2006). Unconscious forces shaping international conflicts: Archetypal defenses of the group spirit from revolutionary America to confrontation in the Middle East. *The San Francisco Jung Institute Library Journal,* 25 (4), 6–28.
Totton, N., (2000). *Psychotherapy and politics.* London and Thousand Oaks, CA: SAGE.

Index

Note: Page numbers in bold indicate a table on the corresponding page.

For Product Safety Concerns and Information please contact our EU
representative GPSR@taylorandfrancis.com
Taylor & Francis Verlag GmbH, Kaufingerstraße 24, 80331 München, Germany

www.ingramcontent.com/pod-product-compliance
Lightning Source LLC
Chambersburg PA
CBHW050351270326
41926CB00016B/3696